PENGUIN BOOKS

DEATH'S MEN

D0552341

DEATH'S MEN
SOLDIERS OF THE GREAT WAR
DENIS WINTER

PENGUIN BOOKS

PENGUIN BOOKS

Published by the Penguin Group
Penguin Books Ltd, 80 Strand, London WC2R 0RL, England
Penguin Group (USA) Inc., 375 Hudson Street, New York, New York 10014, USA
Penguin Group (Canada), 90 Eglinton Avenue East, Suite 700, Toronto, Ontario, Canada M4P 2Y3
(a division of Pearson Penguin Canada Inc.)
Penguin Ireland, 25 St Stephen's Green, Dublin 2, Ireland (a division of Penguin Books Ltd)
Penguin Group (Australia), 707 Collins Street, Melbourne, Victoria 3008, Australia
(a division of Pearson Australia Group Pty Ltd)
Penguin Books India Pvt Ltd, 11 Community Centre, Panchsheel Park, New Delhi – 110 017, India
Penguin Group (NZ), 67 Apollo Drive, Rosedale, Auckland 0632, New Zealand
(a division of Pearson New Zealand Ltd)
Penguin Books (South Africa) (Pty) Ltd, Block D, Rosebank Office Park,
181 Jan Smuts Avenue, Parktown North, Gauteng 2193, South Africa

Penguin Books Ltd, Registered Offices: 80 Strand, London WC2R 0RL, England

www.penguin.com

First published by Allen Lane 1978
Published in Penguin Books 1979
Reissued in this edition 2014
001

Copyright © Denis Winter, 1978
All rights reserved

The moral right of the author has been asserted

Printed in Great Britain by Clays Ltd, St Ives plc

ISBN: 978-0-241-96915-1

www.greenpenguin.co.uk

CONTENTS

List of illustrations   7
Acknowledgements   9
Map   11

Introduction   15
1. The Kitchener armies form   23
2. The training of 'Other Ranks'   37
3. Coming to terms with the army   50
4. Training the officers   63
5. Over to France   70
6. Trench life   80
7. The weapons of trench warfare   107
8. The strain of trench warfare   129
9. Into rest   141
10. Home leave   162
11. Battle   170
12. After battle   186
13. Attitudes to the Germans   209
14. Attitudes to the war as a whole   223
15. After the war   235

Notes   267
References   269
Index   275

LIST OF ILLUSTRATIONS

1. The recruits are kitted out
2. Platoon training in the harsh atmosphere of a 'bull ring' in France
3. Marching men in column of fours
4. The ten-minute rest after fifty minutes' marching
5. A study in headgear
6. A road near the front line
7. Trenches in a back area
8. A typical dugout in the support trench line
9. A 9.2 in. howitzer
10. A shellstore in Britain
11. Communion before the battle
12. A stretcher-bearer carries a wounded man to the rear during the Somme battle
13. A shell victim
14. Men just back from the line
15. The Maxim machine-gun
16. Men in a back area watch an 8-inch gun being towed by its tractor
17. Battle fatigue
18. A rest camp improvised in the devastated war zone
19. A flimsy structure of wire-netting and timber packs as many resting men into a barn as possible
20. Battalion sports
21. Cooks with their field kitchen and mascots
22. The field kitchens in use
23. Fatigue for the RGA as resting men are brought in to move shells by light railway to the dump
24. A digging fatigue for the sappers
25. The trophies of 'Wild Eye', the Australian souvenir king
26. Graves dug before the battle
27. Probably the luckiest men after the battle were the prisoners
28. The wounded are gathered from the battle area, helped by German prisoners
29. Men temporarily blinded by mustard gas wait for treatment
30. A magnet is used to extract shell fragments from the eye
31. Men wait for their new limbs to be adjusted
32. A soldier with extensive plastic surgery to his face exercises a mutilated hand

The author and publishers are grateful to the Imperial War Museum for permission to use the photographs.

ACKNOWLEDGEMENTS

No book on war can be written without accumulating many debts. My deepest gratitude is to those hundreds of writers, dead for the most part, whose works are the basis of the book. I was often moved by their memories, while the vigour and immediacy of the battle scenes disturbed my sleep over several years. This book, however unworthy, is their memorial. Most of my published material was digested, a suitcase a week, from the basement shelves of West Hill Library, Putney. Without the free run of their shelves the book could not have been written. I am also grateful to the following for permission to quote material: Anthony Shiel Associates for extracts from P. Maze, *A Frenchman in Khaki*; Newnes-Butterworths for extracts from E. Swinton, *Twenty Years After*. 'The Lament of the Demobilized' by Vera Brittain is included with the permission of Sir George Catlin and her literary executors. The majority of the unpublished material used was from the Imperial War Museum. Mr Suddaby and his staff made their resources freely available to an irritable inquirer with odd working habits. Valuable material came from the libraries of Eton College and Cambridge University. The courtesy and helpfulness of both libraries went even beyond what I came to expect from library staff. It is a pleasure to record the assistance received from staff at Watford Central Library, Paddington Library and the photographic collection at the Imperial War Museum. For permission to spend a day talking to the veterans of the Royal Hospital, Chelsea, my thanks to the authorities. A particular debt is owed to Clive Trebilcock at Pembroke College, Cambridge; H. Strachan, research fellow of Corpus Christi College, Cambridge; David Duguid of Penguin Books and my father. All went through the manuscript at various stages and saved it from the crassest errors of fact and judgement. Those which remain are due to my own failings. My thanks finally to Miss Eleo Gordon, adjutant to the project in its final stages.

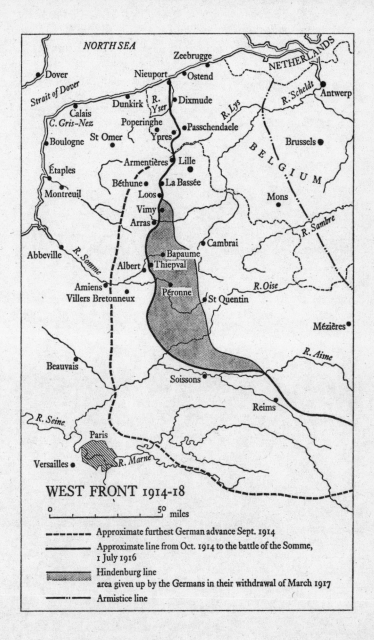

NORTH SEA

Dover

Strait of Dover

Zeebrugge

Nieuport • Ostend

NETHERLANDS

R. Scheldt

Antwerp

Dunkirk • *R. Yser* • Dixmude

Calais

C. Gris-Nez

Poperinghe • Passchendaele

R. Lys

B E L G I U M

Boulogne • St Omer • Ypres

Brussels

Étaples

Armentières • Lille

Montreuil

Béthune • La Bassée

Mons

Loos

Vimy

Arras

R. Sambre

Cambrai

Abbeville • *R. Somme*

Bapaume

Albert • Thiepval

Amiens

Villers Bretonneux

Péronne • St Quentin

R. Oise

Mézières

Beauvais

R. Aisne

Soissons

Reims

R. Seine

Paris

Versailles • *R. Marne*

WEST FRONT 1914-18

0 ⸻⸻ 50 miles

⸺ ⸺ Approximate furthest German advance Sept. 1914

⸻⸻ Approximate line from Oct. 1914 to the battle of the Somme,
1 July 1916

▨ Hindenburg line
area given up by the Germans in their withdrawal of March 1917

⸻·⸻· Armistice line

The smallest detail taken from an actual incident in war is more instructive to me, a soldier, than all the Thiers and Jominis in the world. They speak for the heads of states and armies, but they never show me what I wish to know – a battalion, company or platoon in action. The man is the first weapon of battle. Let us study the soldier for it is he who brings reality to it.

(Aron Du Picq, pioneer writer on the behaviour of men in war and Crimean war veteran who died in battle in the Franco–Prussian war)

INTRODUCTION

In the Great War more than five million Britons wore military uniform and were involved, in various capacities, in the war effort, for varying periods. But, both during and after the war, the individual voices of the soldiers were lost in the collective picture. Men drew arrows on maps and talked of battles and campaigns, but what it felt like to be in the front line or in a base hospital they did not know. Civilians did not ask and soldiers did not write. Just as in the Napoleonic wars or in our own time, Vietnam or Northern Ireland, the experiences and inner lives of the 'other ranks' were as private and unknown as those of Kalahari bushmen.

Just ten years after the end of the Great War it seemed that there might be a change. For five years, a number of memoirs were published, of which the works of Graves and Sassoon are the most widely read today. Then the public grew weary and moved on to think about unemployment or the dictators' growing power. The war could surely not have been so black? There must have been invention and exaggeration. From Oxford Cyril Falls, the professor of war studies, warned civilians against even the most reputable of war memoirs. He pointed out that a popular war writer like Montague was 'over-sensitive' and that Robert Graves, being an 'intellectual', had a mind less penetrating than that of the common man. Civilians came to agree with him in the thirties.

After thirty years of virtual silence, the fiftieth anniversaries brought renewed interest. This may have been due to the 'Great War' series on television or perhaps to the need to find a moment in time when the fatal haemorrhage and the decline from power began. Again the books began to flow. Compared with the thirties, there was one big change: the memoirs of generals and fighting soldiers were replaced by descriptions of battles and whole campaigns. Their bibliographies were generally brief and made up of the Official History of the war plus regimental and divisional histories. This may well have been a matter of abbreviating research. Equally, it may have reflected that distrust of '*le menu peuple*' so common among British historians. One of our best military writers,

Hubert Essame, remarked that 'poets are temperamentally unsuited for any form of service in the infantry'; while soldier writers are 'exceptional and rare' anyway; the majority of serving soldiers saw the war differently – and so on. What emerges are works which enlarge our understanding of strategy, re-create battles chronologically using the wide brush of unit movements and throw in vivid, action-packed vignettes to speed the pace of the battle accounts. The soldiers' war is at best relegated to a single chapter with colourful accounts of mud and vermin, bully beef and particular deaths in battle.

This neglect of the individual soldier and of the records he has left is a pity. Studied from the bottom and looking upwards, the Great War becomes less useful to staff college students and more meaningful to the layman – and to old soldiers of any war. The battles lose their structure and inevitability and change from mannered Jacobean tragedies to unstructured happenings in which action seems to relate little to script. The battles, moreover, lose their central position. The pleasures of the march, the company of mates, the prospect of good billets or of seven days' leave become more important. By rummaging in the great mass of memoirs – and in local papers – a picture emerges of a new sort of war: the infantrymen's war. It is made up of small details and large emotions. It is described by men who had little idea of time, place or importance. The only surprise is that the microscopic approach of the individual produces such agreement on which things were thought to be worth writing down and remembering and on what men thought of the various facets of their common experience as each made an impact. The framework of the army with its set daily and weekly routines provided all with a common memory on which to string their particular experiences.

The raw material on which to base a study of the front-line soldiers' war is abundant. With the massive response to Kitchener's call for men, no longer was the soldier drawn just from that part of society which read books like *The Temptress*, *The Lost Diamonds* or *Red Rube's Revenge* then tore them up to use as cigarette paper. Into the New Armies came a much wider cross-section of society, including many who thought it no shame to be articulate and not above their station in life to communicate in print. Even the simplest men, after the 1870 and 1902[1] Education Acts, were likely to be abler writers than their counterparts in earlier wars. There is therefore a vast library of memoirs, published and unpublished, in the Imperial War Museum.

Almost without exception, there is remarkable sobriety and simplicity in the writing. Maurice Bowra shows the mind of the veteran soldier well. As an Oxford don, his reputation was that of a man who was scholar, *bon viveur,* egocentric and unfeeling for all his ability as a raconteur. He presented a hard face to the world. But when, on one tour to the Middle East as resident intellectual, totem and lecturer, he saw a wreath thrown over the side of the tourist cruise ship as it passed through the Dardanelles, he needed to go below decks and lie down, so deeply was he moved. In his memoirs too the pages on his war experiences stand apart for their simplicity and humility. Such men, with the ability to be moved so deeply and with the memories of their dead comrades and friends looking over their shoulders, felt no need for pretence. Again and again memoirs reveal secret places with remarkable detail. Through them, a picture of the 'interior history' of the war – which Walt Whitman thought could not come out of any war – is possible.[2]

An event which involved five million men can never achieve consensus. Exceptional circumstances alone would see to that. Beale missed serving in the front line and was sent to the guns simply because size fourteen boots could not be found. Pennie, breaking his glasses *en route* to France, served one week in a vegetable garden and nine months in a cookhouse because the army could arrange neither for glasses to be supplied nor for a short-sighted man to be sent to the front. One of my uncles was kicked by a mule while embarking for France so spent the rest of the war invalided in England. Professor Willey trained as a signaller until January 1917, then was made prisoner by the first German soldier he saw. Private Williams served with the King's Liverpool Regiment. Being a farm labourer, he was chosen to serve as the colonel's cowman and spent the battle-of-the-Somme period milking cows tethered in a field at Carnoy, within sniper range. Rogerson tells us of a Newmarket stable lad who happened to be at Chantilly when the war broke out so served as a poilu in the French army throughout the war at five sous a day. Against such diversity, generalization must clearly have its limits.

Another factor which confuses any facile conclusions is that of the radically different evaluations men might make of an apparently simple situation. This might happen because of differences in intelligence. The perceptions of a man like Bowra or Willey could have little in common with those of 'Mary', described by Cook. With an intelligence too low for him ever to be able to grasp what was going on, 'Mary' exposed himself unwittingly and had his leg severed by a shell splinter below the groin. Dying, he tried to grasp the severed artery, with a puzzled look on his face, never understanding that he was dying.

Temperament might divide men as radically. Subalterns West and Jones may well have served together and spoken to each other, since both died in the Arras offensive of spring 1917. West was a Balliol open scholar in 1910 and a collector of books and insects. At Blundells he had been known as 'worm' and most enjoyed solitary walking. He had joined the war with distaste, noting the 'Prussian mood' in the country. After reading Bertrand Russell's *Justice in Wartime* he had determined to stay out. 'I question if I am of martyr's stuff,' he had said to himself. But, after the hesitation, he had joined up and hated every minute until he was sniped in April 1917. Jones of Dulwich had also won a Balliol scholarship and had been resident in Oxford with West. With just one-twelfth vision since the age of six, he had been rejected by the infantry but had managed to scrape into the ASC, whose requirements were less exacting. There he had worked his passage ruthlessly to the front line to become a subaltern in the Tank Corps. Five months later, in July 1917, he was shot. Always a lonely boy, like West, Jones on the other hand had found comfort and companionship in the war. In his last letter home he had said: 'I love all the men and simply rejoice to see them going day by day their own jolly selves, building up such a wall of jocundity around me.' Despite similar social backgrounds, such different personalities produced a very different awareness of the war. Even men of similar personality might gradually diverge from each other. Tubby Clayton,[3] founder of Toc H, wrote that even individual perceptions of what was happening changed as men were worn down by the stress of the war. He told of a signals captain with a Military Cross who at first thought of the war as 'a rough and amusing football match'. Later in the war the captain refused to go back to France and in 1920 entered Putney mental hospital.

Finally there is the problem that the Great War on the west front fell into three clearly demarcated phases. Men who served in one alone were radically divided from those who had served in others. The year 1914, for example, produced a pattern of war more closely related to the Mississippi theatre of the US civil war than to anything which followed. Until November 1914 the war had been mobile, the country virginal. At the battle of Aisne Private Brian had shot three mounted cavalrymen and then been chased by another two just as he might have been had he been fighting at Waterloo. Even when the trench line stabilized during the winter of 1914 there was a degree of improvisation which would have staggered the Kitchener men who only arrived in any numbers during 1916. Often there was no front line at all, just one strand of barbed wire in front of scattered breastworks. First time up to the front, Bruce Bairnsfather, later cartoonist and inventor of Old Bill, found it difficult to discover from men even where the line was. Food and clothing arrived infrequently, so that Burnley reckoned on getting quarter rations in the front line if he was lucky, supplementing what he got by pistol shooting in broad daylight. One day he got a rabbit and three chickens together with gooseberries and rhubarb from no-man's-land. Hawkings remembered men wearing puttees on their feet in late November when their boots disintegrated, while Clapham was without the seat of his trousers between January and July 1915. He was not able to change his underwear for a month at a time. With few inspections and fewer staff inquiries, a clean rifle was the only thing demanded by authority. If this could be achieved with vaseline and a bit of shirt, there was no comment. Fortunately perhaps 'there was not much fighting in those early trench days'. A few shells might arrive just before breakfast, lunch and tea while sniper action already called for slow head movement over the parapet and the wearing of a brown woolly hat. Only at Ypres was there sustained action, and even this had elements of Napoleonic simplicity. During 1st Ypres Paul Maze met an English civilian in grey flannels on the Messines ridge, who announced that he had just shot a German – 'a walking one'. The civilian was driving his own English sports car with a rifle mounted on the bonnet and had come from Antwerp and attached himself to Rawlinson's 7th Division. At the start of 1st Ypres, German bands came to within 200 yards of the battle front and Hyndson, watching the Worcesters make their famous counter-charge at Gheluvelt on 31 October, saw his own men shooting a German officer on horseback.

The middle period of the war saw the institutionalization of trench warfare. Specialized weapons appeared, like the 800,000 grenades ordered monthly after July 1915 and the 1,000 Stokes light mortars ordered in August. Already during the battle of Neuve Chapelle in 1915 more shells were fired in thirty-five minutes than during the whole Boer war. By mid-1917 guns would be set every six yards and deliver four and three quarter tons of shells per yard of the enemy front line before regiments advanced, in accordance with orders set down in foolscap files twelve inches thick. The war at this period was in a clinch. It was highly organized, with leave rotas, rest camps, training schools, but permeated with a sense of purposelessness and anomie, similar to the feelings of later generations about Vietnam – or Northern Ireland.

In March 1918 the war suddenly changed its character for the last time. The Germans had first discovered the optimum combination of weapon systems on the east front in 1915, tested at Caporetto in 1917 and finally thrown at us in spring 1918. At the end of the German offensive, the British had lost nearly half a million men, the French about the same. Both armies lay exhausted in improvised trenches. Then came the counter-strokes of July and August 1918, which lasted to the end. Again men fired from behind hedges, advanced by sections in the open, unlimbered guns without cover and communicated by semaphore. Those who saw only one phase could never have grasped that a war lasting just four years could contain in it the Napoleonic characteristics of 1914, a transition period in which the war looked like the eastern flank of the US civil war, then a final period combining the mobility of the start with the fire power of the middle period.

Nevertheless, when all allowance is made for the diversity of men and the changing nature of their war, there remains a strong impression that there was much more during the Great War to unite men than to divide them. When old soldiers of the war meet, they talk with unexpected warmth of their common experience so long ago. My first experience as a boy of the plasticity of adults was when my father and the next-door neighbour, both reticent men, used every occasion when 'gardening' to talk with animation over the garden fence, literally for hours, about the old days in Flanders.[4] So it was when Eden dined with Hitler just before the Second World War and both men discovered that they had been on opposite sides in the same section of front at Villers Bretonneux, axis of the 1918 actions. There followed a conversation and exchange of trench sketch maps on the back of menus which Eden valued to his death. The pensioners at Chelsea Hospital too tend to group today according to their wars, and, if details elude, common memories sustain relationships which common age provides. Shared experience and shared awareness recall a time when a man's life was at its prime and when men experienced closer friendship for the duration than they were ever likely to enjoy in civilian life after the war.

MORE MEN

ARE WANTED FOR

HIS MAJESTY'S ARMY

WHO MAY ENLIST.

All men who are 5ft. 3ins. and over, medically fit, and between 19 and 38, and all old soldiers up to 45.

TERMS OF ENLISTMENT.

You may join for the period of the War only if you do not want to serve for the ordinary period of the regular soldier. Then, as soon as the War is over, you will be able to return to your ordinary employment.

PAY.

Ordinary Army Pay (the lowest rate of pay is 7s. a week, less 1½d. for Insurance). Food, Clothing, Lodging and Medical Attendance provided free.

SEPARATION ALLOWANCES.

During the War the State, by the payment of Separation Allowance, helps the soldier to maintain his wife, children or dependants. The following are the weekly rates for the wife and children of a private soldier, including the allotment usually required from his pay:—

	Government Separation Allowance.	Larger Allotment required from Soldier.	Weekly Income Secured to Family.
For Wife only	9 0	3 6	12 6
" and 1 Child	14 0	3 6	17 6
" and 2 Children	17 6	3 6	21 0

For each additional child an additional Separation Allowance of 2s. is issuable.
Families living at the time of enlistment in the London Postal area are allowed by the State 3s. 6d. a week extra as long as they continue to live there.

Fuller particulars as to Separation Allowance, and as to Allowances to the Dependants of Unmarried Soldiers, and to the Motherless Children of Soldiers, can be obtained at any Recruiting Office or Post Office.

PENSIONS for the DISABLED.

Men disabled on service will be entitled after discharge to benefits under the Insurance Act IN ADDITION TO the Pension given by the War Office for partial or total disablement.

PROVISION for WIDOWS and CHILDREN.

The widows and children of soldiers who die on active service will continue to receive their Separation Allowances for a period which will not in any case exceed 26 weeks, and afterwards they will receive, SUBJECT TO CERTAIN QUALIFICATIONS, pensions at various rates.

HOW TO ENLIST.

Go to the nearest Post Office or Labour Exchange. There you will get the address of the nearest Recruiting Office, where you can enlist.

MEN ARE WANTED — ENLIST NOW.

PUBLISHED BY THE PARLIAMENTARY RECRUITING COMMITTEE, 12, DOWNING STREET, S.W.   Poster No. 56.

THE KITCHENER ARMIES FORM

The crucial decision which produced the greatest volunteer army Britain had ever put into the field was taken almost casually. Kitchener[5] had been summoned to speak to the Cabinet. In his abrupt, terse way he told the assembled politicians that he calculated on a three-year war, which would need at least a million men. The First Lord of the Admiralty, Winston Churchill, noted afterwards the 'silent assent' of the Cabinet. Stupefaction would have been a better word. Foreign Secretary Grey thought Kitchener's prediction 'unlikely if not incredible'. He thought that the war would be over before a million men could even be trained. If not, then 'of course' the million would be sent abroad. There the matter rested, with Kitchener lending the weight of his reputation and finger to the appeal for men.

The reaction of the country appears to have been as bemused as that of the Cabinet. A survey of newspapers of the time gives a uniform impression on this point. The Bradford *Daily Argus*, on 4 August, the day that war was declared, suggested that 'it will be in the kitchens that the pinch will be chiefly felt but that difficulty may be overcome by deleting the more dainty dishes'. Just ten days later the Catford *Journal* announced that 'what with the war and the rain, last Saturday was a most depressing day for the Catford cricket club'. The next day the *Sphere* counted 7,000 spectators at the Canterbury cricket festival, and in its section on fashion predicted that there would be a taste for military braid on coats and for cavalier capes with Napoleonic collars; 'rich though sober materials will be in the vogue with red the popular colour'.

There was certainly little hostile feeling towards the enemy. The *Sphere* on 8 August advertised a trip to Hamburg at 45s. return and a week later was still advertising German cameras. Germans were even allowed to return to Germany to join their army. On 4 August a Greenwich magistrate discharged a drunken and disorderly seaman to the latter's evident surprise, saying: 'I suppose you were thirsting to get back to Germany for a fight.' The Lutheran community of Dacres Park in South London were photographed three weeks after our declaration of war returning to Germany 'in accordance with the laws of their country'. Only in East London were these returning men intercepted, in a curious incident which well showed the perplexed attitudes of the time. The German government had chartered an English ship, the *Erna Bolt*, to bring back their reservists resident in Canning Town. A solitary policeman headed off the marching column with the order: 'Now then, fall in behind there.' The Germans protested: 'But we're going home.' 'No you aren't. You're coming along with me,' replied the policeman. The local paper observed that 'there was little disappointment among the sixty Germans captured by this one policeman. They sang ragtime and made cheery remarks to the watching crowds. These advances were mostly met with hostile looks.'

It is true that German waiters were boycotted while aliens became spasmodically unpopular with the news of U-boat sinkings or Zeppelin raids, but for the most part, if newspapers of the first year are a guide, the war was as marginal to people's lives as the Napoleonic wars had been to the generation of Jane Austen. Thus the Neutrality League were able to place their advertisement in most papers – 'Englishmen, do your duty and keep your country out of a wicked and useless war' – while Bernard Shaw's suggestion, in the *New Statesman* ten days after the war had started, that troops on both sides shoot their officers and return home was not challenged in public, though Asquith thought privately that Shaw should be shot. A letter in the Catford *Journal* on 21 August seems to have expressed the majority view: 'To be really at war I ought to burn with hatred. But the only two Germans I have ever spoken to were two of the nicest gentlemen I have ever met. We may be at war in the technical sense with the German emperor but with the German people – never. We must fight; honour demands it. But we must not lose our tempers.'

People seemed certain of only two things. The first was that the war would soon be over. The government's first credit note for £100 million suggested that they believed that the delicate structure of world credit would permit only a short, sharp conflict. In this spirit, the Swindon *Advertiser* carried an advertisement from the Dresden Conservatoire after a week of fighting. This announced the fifty-ninth year of Dresden's courses in music and the start of a new season on 1 April 1915. Prospectuses were available from the Directorium 'on the expectation of a speedy return to normal'.

The second prediction was of idle factories and of shortages.

As a young man at Oxford, the future Professor Woodward commented first on the remarkable absence of jingoism when the war was announced, then on the expectation of a great naval battle and of tobacco shortages. These feelings led to a fierce run on shops. The mayor of Swindon noted the panic-buying as 'an ugly feature of the perturbation' and appealed to 'a sense of patriotic duty' – with little apparent effect. As a St Albans shopkeeper put it, sovereign spenders became ten pounders. One of his best customers arrived by car on 8 August to carry away twenty-four tins of milk, twenty-four tins of corned beef, twelve tins of tongue, half a side of bacon and a hundredweight of flour. At a more practical level and on the obverse side of the buying and hoarding was the £4 million subscribed within two months for the Prince of Wales Relief Fund in anticipation of factory closures. Thus with sides of bacon in the larder and blood money paid out to workmen who had been ominously unquiet during the reign of Edward VII, many expected the quantities of each to be sufficient for the temporary disruption of the European war.

The reason for this inability to grasp the seriousness of the situation was the failure of the news media to communicate. Radio and television lay in the future. Even national newspapers had a relatively small circulation. The *Daily Mirror* in 1912 had become the first daily to sell a million copies, for people tended to read national papers only on Sundays. Thus the *News of the World* was selling three million copies by 1914, but then as now such Sunday papers dispensed little political information. All that people wanted, they got from the local press. This tended to be local information together with national horseracing and football results. *Titbits*, *Answers* and *Police News* might supply occasional relish. The relatively small number of those people with sufficient information to form a reasoned picture of world events and those without is shown by such circulation figures as *The Times* 150,000 and the *Kentish Mercury*, covering just a corner of South-East London, with 25,000 copies. One must remember too the even more drastic news starvation of the countryside. The village of Sibford received news twice weekly in the carrier's cart from Banbury, and this was not exceptional for a rural settlement.

This news scarcity was reinforced at the outbreak of war by rigorous censorship. The need for it had been learnt at the time of the Crimean war, during which Raglan, commander-in-chief, had remarked that the Russians required no secret service since they had only to buy *The Times*. Even *The Times* admitted that 'it had gone to the verge of prudence'. In 1914 therefore John Buchan's department of information was amongst the earliest war organizations. Only in June 1915 did it relinquish its monopoly of military news, even then only admitting authorized men with the rank of temporary captain. Little wonder that a cartoon in the East London *Advertiser* late in September 1914 was captioned 'Let me have your poster [to a newsboy]. It's got more news than your newspaper'.

The only way in which men at home could find out about the reality of war was through the letters of serving soldiers published in the local press. Many papers published few and stopped altogether after 1st Ypres in November 1914, but some went on until the censor caught up with them in mid-1915. The following are typical of the more alarming letters: 'The Boer war was a picnic to this' (Whitby *Gazette*); Private Downes, commenting on a night of artillery fire at La Bassée which caused 836 casualties in his regiment, since the Germans were able to use searchlights with impunity, 'it was a night of terror I will remember as long as my life lasts. We had a very happy Christmas. It was murder. It's dreadful out in the trenches' (Catford *Journal*). The Evesham *Journal* in October 1914 summarized a letter from Private Blakeman:

> the fighting he describes as very exciting work and sometimes the slaughter is terrific. It is often impossible to bury the dead and the stench from their decomposing bodies is very bad indeed. Sometimes, after what he describes as a 'stand up', the bodies lie on the ground over the space of a mile as thick as sheaves after the self-binder in the harvest field. Sometimes explosions lift men eight or nine feet into the air and then they simply go to pieces.

On the other hand, and to confuse the majority viewpoint, there were always the optimists, like a correspondent of the Watford *Observer*: 'We went into action on Monday morning . . . We killed them in heaps like flies on paper. It was terrible work but we glorified in it. We gave them a couple of bayonet charges. Their pluck lasted until we were about fifty yards off then they were off. It would do you good to see our little chaps who were laughing and shouting and chasing the big fellows. You wouldn't think it was war.' Such levity would confuse readers but, whatever judgement they made, these letters were just vignettes from humble men submerged in trenches. What was happening in the war overall or how serious the general situation was, there was no way of knowing.

It was probably for this reason that there was no great rush to join the Kitchener armies and save the country. Men joined when they had settled their domestic business and not before. The patriotic exaggerations of the press, together with the lack of facilities for processing recruits, had made the influx of the first two months seem greater than it was. Only in 1923 were the figures[6] published which showed the gradualness of the response, bulging somewhat just at the start and after the news of defeats at Ypres and Loos:

1914:			1915:		
	August	300,000		January	156,000
	September	450,000		February	88,000
	October	137,000		March	114,000
	November	170,000		April	119,000
	December	117,000		May	135,000
				June	114,000
				July	95,000
				August	96,000
				September	71,000
				October	113,000
				November	122,000
				December	55,000

A casual and rather easy-going attitude to the war began to change towards the end of 1915. At the start of the year the distinguished surgeon Cushing contrasted London unfavourably with empty and serious Paris. He could see little khaki, while cockneys stood with pipes in mouths and hands in pockets listening to recruiting bands. City work still started at 9.30 am, leaving plenty of time to shave and read papers whose front pages advertised for domestic servants and whose back pages were filled with soccer news. Cushing noted how afternoon tea remained the life-stopping ritual it had been before the war. With the bad news of the battles of Neuve Chapelle and Loos, with the shell scandal and news of U-boats, the *Daily Mail* wall maps with their little coloured marker flags were put away. Previously the war had been regarded as a limited liability affair peculiarly suited to unattached young men. Those not of the status sympathized in a spirit of *noblesse oblige*. London buses and cinemas had been made free to men in uniform, the Imperial Hotel in Russell Square served 1s. lunches to soldiers, while Ellison remembered an ex-Boer war surgeon, medals on his dressing gown, inviting men into his house at Whitstable, saying: 'I shall be proud to have any soldiers in my house provided they are all clean men and will not spit on the wallpaper.' By the autumn of 1915 the war was seen to affect everybody. There was daylight saving, petrol rationing, meat-less days, bread at 10d. the loaf, woollen clothing unavailable and trousered women in the streets. Hardships coming on top of bad war news transformed the general mood, so that a feeling of rising too slowly to some crisis developed. By mid-1916 only fried fish and ice cream could be bought out of shop hours and Monash thought Britain one large factory living in a mood of hysterical anxiety.

One form taken by this hysteria was the paranoid suspicion that a large number of young men were dodging their duty. Sir Frederick Milner expressed an opinion that press gangs on race courses would soon fill the New Armies and that discipline with active work would regenerate the sort of men who gathered there. Whether these gangs were to work in the members' enclosure he did not say, but he did believe it useless to appeal to a sense of patriotism. Local newspapers appeared to fill in the detail behind Sir Frederick's assertions. A recruiting sergeant in the Whitby *Gazette* wrote:

> It's very slack this week. I don't understand it. I have talked to twenty fellows this morning and I don't think that one of them has any intention of enlisting. Only two were married but the feeling amongst them is that they're not wanted. One hefty chap said that when he was needed, he'd go, but not before. I'm just beginning to get on alright now, he said. The fellow above me is a Territorial and I've got his job. Others told me to mind my own business.

Major Pike in Tintagel had similar shocking revelations to make at a recruiting meeting, recorded in the *West Briton*.

> He had been told about two young men who had been willing to join up, but their mother sent them away for the day – 'that was a common spirit in the county of Cornwall'. His sergeant had met with many rude remarks. Some had said that the English were no better than the Germans or that they didn't want any

– soldiers billeted upon them. Speaking of holiday visitors to Tintagel who came with their chauffeurs, 'he did not think they were quite playing the game'. People should make life unbearable for those who were not going to the war, he thought. Anyway, without the support of people, the major found it 'a weary and rotten game going round in search of recruits'. Major Pike's sergeant then followed by backing up what the major had said. He too had received few promises and many impudent answers. At that point a young man in the audience called out: 'It won't make any difference to me if the Germans come.' 'It is a disgrace for you to say such a thing.' 'I think you ought to apologize for what you said.' 'Certainly not – not for one word.' (Applause of audience.) The young man then sat with his back to the platform. Commented Major Pike, he would not take that man even if he wanted to join up later. (Applause.)

As stories accumulated which seemed to support the view of widespread skrimshanking, a whirlwind campaign began. By the autumn of 1915 fifty-four million posters had been issued, eight million letters sent and 12,000 meetings organized. This seemed insufficient and so in January 1916 Kitchener brought in conscription, stating that he had given the fullest and fairest trial to the system which he had found in existence.

Going back over the figures today, it is clear that there were relatively few men hanging back in the years before conscription was brought in. The numbers of men joining up each year were as follows:

1914: 1,186,357
1915: 1,280,000
1916: 1,190,000
1917: 820,646
1918: 493,562

Since about half a million men would have become eligible each year as they reached the military age, conscription had clearly been unable to unearth a significant number of dodgers.

This was not to say that individuals were not playing safe. The tribunals appointed to examine objectors in 1916 have left a mass of cases. The Leeds tribunal, for example, heard 120 cases daily and kicked about half of them into the army. One reads of men like Lincolnshire farmer Fred Cannock, who slipped recruiting sergeant

Costello a sovereign to delay his call-up until October so that he could get the harvest in. He was duly fined £25. Abraham Josephs of Hackney, 'a tall, muscular fellow', swore he was forty-one until examination at Somerset House revealed his true age to be thirty-one, and so a fine of £2. A Leeds man claimed exemption because he had to bring his wife tea in bed and had just started a course of hair tonic which would require three months to show results. An eighteen-year-old carrier from Hackney claimed exemption on account of 'expansion of the lungs', until Captain Fisher told him to expand his chest to fit his lungs (laughter in the tribunal). 'I don't mind if I do,' said the carrier, laughing as well.

If there seemed to be many young men still in England despite the demands of the war, there must have been explanations other than shirking, given the relatively few scoundrels caught by the tribunal net. Despite 244 separate circulars sent to these tribunals to close every conceivable loophole, they were obviously unable to find as many recruits as people thought were still at large. In the end Bottomley thought typical recruits from the tribunals to have been of no value even as agricultural manure. The bottom of the barrel had been reached much earlier than expected, in fact.

The two reasons for retaining so many men of military age in England were unexpected even by military men. The first was economic. Mining, farming and transportation all needed able-bodied men. Thus 1,670,788 were kept in these reserved occupations to back the front line. The French had shown us the way here when they called up initially one-third of the Le Creusot ironworkers and had to send them back again when production slumped disastrously. The second reason was to do with health. A check on conscripts in 1916 found that, of every nine men examined, only three were A1 fit. Two were of inferior health, three incapable and one a permanent invalid. Overall 41 per cent of young males were given the bottom health classification of C3. All this reflected a state of affairs which a hundred years of health legislation and prosperity was supposed to have changed. Malnutrition was part of the cause. A diet of bread and margarine, tea and condensed milk conspired to produce state-educated children five inches shorter than their public-school leaders. In Leeds in 1904 a check found 50 per cent of the schoolchildren suffering from the malnutrition disease of rickets. Squalid living conditions reinforced the effects of poor diet. Twenty per cent of babies in 1914 Cornwall died in their first year of life, while in Hackney in the same year 119 died of scarlet fever, fifty-three of diphtheria and sixty-nine of tuberculosis – all of them the diseases of poverty.

The problem of the historian is not therefore to explain a vast initial rush to join up or a rapid decline of early enthusiasm; it is rather to suggest why so many joined a war voluntarily when few people thought the war to be of great importance and when there was relatively little pressure from the public for them to join up.

So complex a happening can have no simple explanation, but a clue to the chief single explanation is perhaps provided by the fact that only 16,000 men registered as conscientious objectors, while of these only 1,500 refused to do any work connected with the war effort. It would seem therefore that few men doubted that war was a fully acceptable job socially. The accepted image of war was even an honourable one. Henty, Marryat and the *Boy's Own Paper* reinforced the ideas of Darwin to such an extent that, even after the great blood-letting, Watford Boys' Grammar School celebrated Empire Day in 1918 with three Rupert Brooke sonnets on war, Kipling's 'Fringes of the Fleet', a recital of Seaman's '*Pro Patria*' and then presented prizes for essays on Clive, Nelson, Cook and Gordon. In such a society it needed very little to send a man to war, particularly when so little was known of its unpleasant side.

The high status of war nationally was reinforced by traditional responses within the social groups which made up the nation.

As in Napoleonic days, the greatest response came from the richest men as leaders and the poorest as followers. Those with a stake in society maintained only by constant effort lagged behind. These were chiefly the self-employed and professional men, who became the chief victims of the tribunals.

The greatest response was at the top of society. Cricket and racing were ended for a time, cars were laid up and evening dress at the theatre became bad form. The fierce squires in tweeds and plus-fours gave way in the pages of *Tatler* to uniformed, sad-eyed young subalterns and, though the *Ladies' Kennel Association Notes* remained, photos of volunteer nurses soon came to outnumber those of debutantes. By the end of 1914 the dead included six peers, sixteen baronets, six knights, ninety-five sons of peers, eighty-two sons of baronets and eighty-four knights' sons. Thirty-nine of the fifty-eight home international rugby players of the 1913–14 season had joined up within two months of the outbreak of war. Winchester, typical of the public schools, sent no one to Oxford in 1915, while 531 of the 594 leavers of the six months previous to the war were in khaki before conscription was brought in.

As with so many serving soldiers after the war, very few of these rich young men examined in detail their reasons for joining up or felt the need of a post-Freudian generation to look for the worm in the rose. Nevertheless two ideas seem to stand out from the writings of those who did reflect on the earliest days. The first was a sense of adventure. Wrote Harold Macmillan: 'The general view was that it would be over by Christmas. Our major anxiety was by hook or by crook not to miss it.' 'What fun we meant to have,' wrote Andrews in that public-school way, which made a jest of the serious and reduced all conflicts to the scale of a house rugby match or steeplechase.

The second impulse of the rich was patriotism of the Rupert Brooke kind. To serve one's country was to make a free choice untrammelled by a sense of duty or obligation, for the generosity of the gentleman was that of medieval knight or Athenian freeman: they considered the privilege only. Carver wrote to his brother:

> The grand obstacle hun hunt is now open. There is no charge for entry. At present we are sitting and looking dubiously at the first obstacle. It's a devilish stiff one and lots more like it to follow. However, if one does take a nasty toss, there's always the satisfaction of knowing that one could not do it in a better cause. I always feel that I am fighting for England – English fields, lanes, trees, good days in England, all that is synonymous with liberty.

After his death in 1917, the parents of Subaltern Jones noted that the words 'honour' and 'sacrifice' were the most frequent words in his letters home.

Reading through the letters and memoirs of the well-to-do, one has the strong impression of men oriented in the past and responding in the style expected of the country houses of England, leading their tenants into battle with the ethics less of the chivalric knight than of the Cambridge undergraduate doing a vacation stint in the college boys' club in London's East End.

A vigorous response, if not relatively as great, came from the bottom of society. The first historian of the Kitchener armies thought that men joining early on were of the same social class as those who had joined the Regulars in the past. Rowntree tells us about them. In 1900 1 per cent of recruits had come from the servant-keeping class, 7 per cent from shopkeepers and clerks and the remainder were manual labourers. A spot check on Smiths in volumes 7 and 13 of the *National Roll of Honour*, which relate to the working-class area on either side of the Thames in East London, shows that 70 per cent of those eligible had joined up before conscription was brought in.

Patriotism played a part in this. Cook, a printer's apprentice at 12s. a week, started buying the *Daily Mail* and marking his map of the front line with pins. When he saw 'Britain at bay', he joined up. But the patriotism of the working man was usually different from that of the subaltern. Simple men thought of themselves as being worked on by society rather than as playing an equal part in a national enterprise. The words 'duty' and 'obligation' are most frequently used. Letters to local newspapers often noted patriotism in this way. 'I never had any doubts as to my duty to fight in this Great War for all that I held in my life most dear.' 'It's murder to be in a bayonet charge. You really don't know what you're doing. A mortar shell blew our lance-corporal to pieces. I got some of his brains on my arms and in my tea. Another cup of tea wasted I said. Ah, it's a bad thing is war and I don't want to go back but then, it's duty you see.' 'The eighteen months I have been at the front have been like years. In a night bayonet attack I thanked God for guiding us back to our own people. It was a night of hell. I know it is hard for you but when duty calls, one must obey.'

Patriotism features in many letters home like these. It might even spur a man into joining up. Seventeen-year-old Rhondda miner Kingsbury felt that he was letting his mates down. Though he was getting a sovereign a week when his brother and friend joined up, he felt a pressure, conclusive when he read news reports of hard-pressed men. Dawson felt the same. Initially he was merely angry when he heard a portly lady dressed as Britannia singing at the Leicester Square Empire: 'I wasn't among the first to go but I went, thank God, I went.' But then followed a film of the German entrance into Brussels. A Belgian soldier in the audience who had lost both his legs began shrieking and most of the audience left before the end. Shortly afterwards, he saw two Mons men at the tailors and thus joined up with the growing conviction that he was needed out there.

More important than patriotism in whatever form it took was the more traditional inducement of financial pressure and an awareness of the limited possibilities for improvement in the future. In the past the army had offered a few years' excitement and a full belly before settling down behind the plough's tail. Now it did the same for many. East Ender Henry Winter was earning 10s a week from a London clerical job in 1914, and working from 9 am to 6.30 pm for six days a week. When he joined up, he got 5s. a week from his firm, 7s. army pay, 14s. 7d. ration allowance and 3s. 6d. uniform allowance. The total amounted to three times his peacetime salary, with the bonus of a break in routine. Ellison's memoirs also talk of 'a chance to get out of a rut'. Wrote Griffith: 'I cannot remember that I ever thought of soldiering as anything but a better way of life than sitting at a desk. None thought of it as a noble calling – it was what your friends were doing.'

The close link between working-class enlistment and the economic situation is well seen in the contrast between Leicester and Nottingham. For the first time in history the Boot and Shoe Operatives Union recorded no unemployment when army contracts began coming in. Leicester was our leading shoemaker and during 1915 on average only 124 Leicester men joined the army as against 432 from neighbouring Nottingham. Birmingham, traditionally prosperous with its small engineering workshops and after 1914 with its armaments links, largely ignored the Willingness Forms sent out during 1914. In May 1915 a circular was sent out in Leeds to all in the distributing trades, assuring men that their jobs would be kept open after the war. Immediately 355 of the 833 men involved joined up. Good wages and a secure job were therefore the first priority for most manual labourers. Deficiencies in both areas seem to have been the chief propellant into Kitchener's armies of working men.

When the tribunals began operating, it was mainly the self-employed and the men who had gained hard-won respectability who came before it and resisted the call-up. Only men who could afford a solicitor and professional counsel were likely to think it worth their while to confront the state's whipper-in. Reading tribunal accounts, one meets most frequently men like a mineral water manufacturer of Penzance, who in March 1916 said that one son at the front was worth £3 a week to him and that, if another son went, he would be broke.

Any account of enlistment would be incomplete without mention of that large minority of men whose reasoning defies categorization.

Some men were forced into the army. John X was interviewed by *New Society* during May 1975 after fifty years in a mental hospital. 'When I was sixteen,' he recalled, 'my foster parent got me a job in a big mansion. I went as the gardener's potboy. I was paid half a crown a week and the woman used to give me a shilling till I joined the army. I was then 17. What made me join? The estate agent said: "There will be millions wanted in this war. I think you'd better go first." So I thought about it and did so.' In a similar spirit, landlord Slater took his footman, cowman and forty-three-year-old butler to enlist at Maidstone. Bert Warrant joined the 10th Londons after robbing the Hackney Empire of £300. Private Jenkins took similar evasive action from police in hot pursuit after he had looted German shops in Billingsgate. Men arrested after the lootings of 17 October 1914 in Deptford High Street, which were aimed at German shops, were given the choice of eighteen months' hard labour or immediate join-up.

Some got into the army by chance. Rogerson's servant Parkin had seen his friend off to the front, got drunk and was claimed by the sergeant next day, to his own surprise and his wife's annoyance, since he had apparently accepted the king's shilling unawares. Heath got a commission without even contemplating joining the army, just because his cousin was the director of military training.

Some were escaping from private dilemmas. Graves so dreaded going to Oxford University that he delayed the ordeal by joining a war which he thought would be over in six months. Reith, forced by his father to be an engineer, looked upon war as an escape route. Surgeon Keynes, unhappy under his superior at Barts, wanted a break in the same way. At the other end of society Fred Eagle, a Norfolk blacksmith, joined up in June 1915; since he was a father of sixteen children, all living and only one old enough to fight, one assumes that domestic circumstances were crucial. Private Silver went into the army after deserting from the navy. Aged sixteen and a half, he had twice refused to learn to swim and had been beaten with an inch-rod, the ship's company lining up as witnesses while his castigator took a ten-yard run up to complete the job with nautical punctilio.

Some joined up against their better judgement. Poet Philip Thomas joined the Artists' Rifles after thinking hard about Robert Frost's offer to join him in the USA. Barnes wrote of horrible doubts and inertia before his conscience prompted him to act. The Cornwall *County News* of October 1915 tells the story of thirty-three-year-old widower Richard Hicks of Fowey, who had joined the engineers at the start and been sent to Chatham. Summoned to France, he was given a home leave. Wrote his father: 'I last saw my son alive at bedtime on Tuesday. He was quite cheerful. At 8.15 next morning I found my son dead with a rope around his neck, the other end tied to a bed post.'

Kitchener's volunteers were therefore as diverse as several million young men taken at random can be. Few had rushed to join the ranks but most who were able to fight had volunteered to do so. Looking at themselves and at the men who had stayed behind, they would have been surprised to hear themselves later considered as the best men of their generation. If they had known how many would be called upon to die, they would equally have had little to do with any melancholy over a 'lost generation'. They had chosen to do a practical job which gave a break and a change. The permutations and nuances of their motives were many. In the end all they had in common was their total ignorance of the rigours which lay ahead.

2

THE TRAINING OF 'OTHER RANKS'

For the first two months of the war, the handling of personnel provided the chief difficulty in the formation of the Kitchener armies, for men in such numbers and from such diverse backgrounds had never entered the wildest plans of the old army. The movements of Private Cain were therefore not unusual for these early days. As a boy bugler just four feet eleven inches high, he had sworn his oath of loyalty standing on a box to make the legal requirement of five feet three. In order to get to the front earlier, Cain had switched battalions on his own initiative. When a War Office telegram announced the discharge of all boy soldiers, within the hour Cain went off to Wigan drill hall, memorized the eye test and joined up as a band musician. Only the fleetest of army clerks could have kept pace with such movement. Even when individuals had been integrated and were where they were supposed to be, birth pains might not clear. The 2nd Dorset Yeomanry, for example, began as infantry, then after three weeks were registered as cavalry at forty-eight hours' notice. Thereafter, they became bicycle troops, infantry, cavalry before stabilizing as bicycle troops. Commented Bridport's local historian, without a trace of humour, 'they seem to have been able to do anything'.

By the start of October Kitchener was able to report that the problem of personnel had been replaced by that of the scarcity of materials. Housing, feeding and clothing could not keep pace with the growing armies. Barracks, for example, were completely full after just a fortnight's recruitment. Kingsbury of the Somerset Light Infantry was lodged in civilian billets at Topsham. This was the commonest temporary arrangement. Food was another matter. Since it was not supplied, he and his mates had to walk into Crediton to buy it from their own pockets, and were driven at times to eat snails. Not until the early months of 1915 had these problems been solved. Parker joined up in September 1914. His last piece of kit and his service rifle came only during January 1915. By that time the half million huts ordered in the early days had been supplied and tea could be drunk with sugar and milk, bread with butter eaten on plates with cutlery.

Even in 1915 the deepest intractabilities within the civilian army remained. The first was the peculiarly English difficulty of social class. Not since the early railway days in Victorian England had there been such a throwing together of social classes and occupational categories as in the months after August 1914. Hankey wrote that the middle class were as conspicuous in the New Armies as a Norfolk jacket at a dinner party, and told himself that he did not mind when the manual workers called him 'mate' or cheeked policemen on route marches. Newspaper reporter Andrews was even more startled by the uninhibited behaviour of the Glasgow poor in the Black Watch. The blueness of the language, the body lice and the violent games of soccer in the drill hall were beyond his comprehension. When his boots were stolen, a sympathetic NCO could only say to him: 'You've got to watch yourself, laddie. They'll steal the milk from your tea.' The Pals regiments, each made up of men from a particular town, got over these frictions by excluding manual workers. Time solved the social problems of other regiments as men in France moved up the ranks or joined unofficially segregated regiments. In this way, of Watford Grammar School's ninety-seven dead, only forty died as privates while twenty-seven served in the more select rifle regiments.

Obedience was the second intractability, for in a civilian army it was never instinctive. Powell remembered his Major Gale complaining that there was too much discussing of orders, followed by the RSM complaining of first names being used between different ranks. At the very least, he insisted, privates must stand to attention when being addressed by NCOs. In the Suffolk regiment, Heath wrote of the taciturn peasants of remote villages turning up five minutes late for parade because they had been shaving, while the 7th Royal Scots Fusiliers began by smoking on church parade and eating blackberries while on their assault course. Even when army norms had been established sufficiently to make it clear to all that only an officer was allowed to think and decide, followed in descending order by sergeant and corporal, there was a tendency for the better educated to acquiesce in the humorous absurdity just for the benefit of a particular officer who was clearly a 'sportsman'. The less well educated went on grumbling and remained suspicious to the end, or so J. B. Priestley thought.

Looking back, it would seem that volunteering provided most of the answers to its own problems. Men who had balanced the odds and freely chosen a radical change in their own lives could all take devotion and understatement for granted. No man was more immersed in army behaviour than Kipling, but even he could barely grasp the idea of an army in which there was no lying, no crime. When Kingsbury and his mates were eating snails in Devon because Army supply had broken down, they were also buying puttees and cap badges from their own pockets. This era of good feeling lasted until men entered France and became divided by the test of explosive and particular deaths. Thus the mayor at their port of exit from Britain commented on 'the earnest yet cheerful demeanour of the men and their excellent behaviour'. They had, after all, joined up to do a particular job and, in their common anxiety to get on with it, they were prepared to shed those civilian quirks and crotchets which might interfere with their preparation for that task. These were the heroic days, when the outlook of a regiment was that of a sporting club.

The basic training which provided the civilians with their military skills had an air of unreality. This was nothing to do with the time factor for, although the training was completed in ten weeks, it had been the traditional opinion of the territorials before that war that, while it took a year to make a gunner, twenty days sufficed for the more primitive skills of the infantryman. Rather the unreality related to what was taught. One-third of the time for a start was given to drill alone – 'we sloped, ordered, presented, trailed, reversed, piled arms and did everything possible with them except fire them,' wrote Noakes. 'With rifles we marched, counter-marched, wheeled right and left, inclined and formed squads and about turned until we were streaming sweat and weak in the knees with exhaustion.' It was hard to relate any of this to the needs of a soldier in battle, particularly since the platoon training which was fundamental in this region entered the schedule only in the tenth and final week.

Even when the battle training made its belated appearance, it was until late 1917 based on tactical concepts obsolete even at the time of the Boer war. The idea was that lines of men would approach the enemy in leapfrog style, each line supporting the next with covering fire until a line was 200 yards from the enemy. Then would come the crucial orgasm of the bayonet charge. 'All ranks must be taught that the aim and object is to come to close quarters with the enemy as quickly as possible so as to be able to use the bayonet. This must become a second nature.' The words were written into training manuals at the close of the Somme campaign, and repeated with just one significant exception the official handbook of 1914. Missing were the words 'close with the enemy, cost what it may'. This was the only minor adjustment made in battle training in Britain after the disasters of 1 July 1916, the first day of the Somme.

The role of the bayonet and the emphasis that was put upon it is worth a closer examination, for the values associated with it by the army suggest the real purpose of the basic training.

The bayonet was supposed to have been the greatest glory of our old army. The capacity to fight at close quarters which it implied was supposed to distinguish the British with their professional traditions from the amateur Germans. One training book remarked that grenades were better suited to the bovine and passive enemy. The only problem, not noted, was that just 0·03 per cent of wounds on the battlefield throughout the war were inflicted by the bayonet. In a war dominated by high explosive, close-quarter bayonet fighting, which would have been admirable against the Spanish tercios of the sixteenth century, even against Napoleon's Imperial Guard, became the least common mode of fighting.

It is hard to escape the conclusion that the 'discipline' required by bayonet work was thought of as an end in itself. No other weapon required to such an extent the subduing of individual fear and robot-like obedience to orders. Practical knowledge of map-reading, trench survival, the characters of particular weapons, what to do to avoid machine-gun fire or deal with a pillbox was thought to be secondary to this. As long as a soldier could be guaranteed to obey all orders, he could be considered 'trained'.

This limited objective and the methods used to achieve it caused much bitterness. In studying war memoirs, I was constantly surprised by the flashes of anger. Graham wrote:

> I used to think courage, verve and idealism the real power of the army in war. But we all of us soon learned that the uniform betokened hard bondage and duty. Though men were generous in offering themselves to fight for their country, there was no atmosphere of generosity and national gratitude but rather an atmosphere of every man expecting his neighbour to shirk what he could. Private soldiers were all passive. NCOs were active and drove privates to do what was required. The real driving power lay in the brutal word and thought and act. I noticed that men,

who in themselves were not brutal, cultivated brutality to get the army tone. The characteristic word of command was not merely enforced by firmness, by loudness, by peremptoriness. The vital thing in it must be menace. It must be an intimidating bawl; it must act on the nerves. Soldiers must be driven by frightening them all the way. The RSM was like a big farmyard dog. He rushed forward and barked menacingly at everyone who appeared in his line of vision.

Such harsh comment is typical. It refers not just to the practical side of drill. Most recruits seem to have thought drill useless and no more. Rather it refers to the nature of the relationship with army authority which accompanied the drill and whose aim seemed to be quite simply to break a man, then to rebuild him in his new army role as a servant, pliant and totally subservient.

This process began when a man joined up. As a new entrant to the RFA in 1917, Bowra had to be up by 6 am and clean out the stables with his bare hands before burnishing his steel spurs for thirty minutes and blacking the instep of his boots. Private Graham had to polish his ration tin with a bath brick daily, as well as polish dummy cartridges and his rifle pull-through four times daily in the Guards. There followed drill, less important for what it imparted than for the way in which it was carried out. 'It is impossible to think much of yourself when a sergeant has bawled out before the entire squad, "I think you're the ugliest thing that has ever dropped from a woman" or "fancy a decent woman having children from a man like you". This constant humiliation and the use of indecent phrases took down the recruit's pride and reduced him to a condition where he was amenable to any command.'

Off the drill square, the unimportance of the individual was constantly emphasized. Men ate from enamel bowls without knives and forks, and then only after a free-for-all in the stampede to the cookhouse. Mail was censored. Feet and rectum would be inspected. Irrational demands, like the insistence that all blankets be folded in one way only or that nails on boot soles be polished, multiplied. As a constant reinforcement of these shaming conditions, there would never be explanations or apologies.

Above everything else came constant fatigue.

From reveille at 5.30 am until lights out they had been driven and harassed and bullied for weeks to the strain of 'Look to yer front there. 'Old yer 'eads up can't yer? Them tanners was picked up on the first parade.' The fatigue of continual over-exercise was severe to men fresh from sedentary lives or stiff from the workshop. They were sore all over. He remembered one awful day. They had been drilled and marched, drilled and inspected from dawn to evening on a baking autumn day. Then at 7 pm there had been three hours of night operations. At midnight they had been wakened by a false fire alarm and had had to turn out in trousers and boots.

Richard Aldington's tone of protest is echoed in many other memoirs.

The end product of all this was the 'soldier'. He had become a man identical through uniform with every other man. Every minute of his day was fitted into a prescribed timetable with each day identical. His movements as a 'soldier' had to be jerky, like a marionette or mechanical toy. The individual with a mind of his own had been replaced by a number and rank which could with impunity and without protest be addressed in the loud, impersonal tone a schoolmaster uses with children beneath his contempt. A beautiful example of the army's concept of the 'soldier' can be found in the drill book of the Cameronians:

> The musicians are expected to do their best to perfect themselves in the use of their instruments. This can be done only by the most careful attention to the advice and instruction of the bandmaster, whose orders they are always most implicitly to obey. They must take the greatest care of their instruments and any damage done by carelessness or neglect will be charged against the man in possession of the damaged instrument . . . the bandmaster is a warrant officer but will rank junior to the sergeant major.

The assumption here seems to have been that army musicians could learn nothing without the tuition of an NCO, would not practise unless ordered to do so and would attempt to damage their instruments then blame someone else for the damage if given the slightest excuse. One wonders how a symphony orchestra would function under such a regime.

If individuals stepped out of the line of uniformity, then the army was backed by a formidable list of punitive measures. For a minor infringement, the offender would be put on a charge then brought to Company Orders. Unshined boots would get a man three days confined to barracks. Coppard got four days for blowing a raspberry on parade. Weightier cases would go before the colonel, who could stop pay, strip rank or give field punishment number two. This meant a note in the pay book, pay forfeit, sleeping under guard and the performance of such fatigues and pack drills as could be crammed into the day. All the while the offender would be on a diet of water and biscuit. Worse, he would not be allowed to smoke during any of the twenty-eight days' punishment. Field punishment number one hit harder. A man here might be exposed in public, handcuffed to a waggon wheel and spreadeagled for two hours daily. Lucy remembered how men would avert their eyes from the evidence of how far the army was able to humiliate them. Punishment was not so easy on active service, but Lane wrote of the Guards in 1915 obliging a field-punishment-number-one man to pick tins from the top of the parapet and dust sandbags and firestep.

Serious offenders faced court martial. A major, captain and lieutenant would judge the prisoner, with the prisoner's own adjutant prosecuting and a company officer defending him. During the war 304,262 of our men were court martialled with 86 per cent convicted. Three hundred and forty-six were admitted to have suffered the death penalty, though ten times as many had the sentence commuted. The unfortunate were shot in a secluded place with men of their own unit as witness. Twelve men chosen at random would be issued with a mixed live and dummy dozen of bullets to ease their consciences. Each death was reported simply as a casualty on active service. The proportion of officers to men who were thus executed was one to a hundred.

What was the effect of all this severity on the individual soldier? It seems in the main to have beaten him. Many memoirs reflect a bewildered acceptance and silence in the face of an antagonist holding all the aces – 'I am only a little man. What can I do?' Faced with the impossibility of sustaining dignity in a situation so often degrading, most accepted the official line and compensated with that sad or boisterous humour and vulgarity which pretended that such an acceptance did not matter since it did not touch the real man and related only to a temporary and unimportant phase of the man's life-span.

Left, right, left, right,
why did I join the army?
Oh why did I ever join Kitchener's mob?
Lor lummy
I must av been barmy.

A few responded by not admitting any humiliation. To them the demands of the army became the only possible demands and could in fact give dignity. Self-respect was thus salvaged by identification. These became the smart saluters, the brisk and bustling men, who might well become NCOs.

Vignettes of passive acceptance appear constantly in memoirs. Watching a firing squad, Coppard observed that 'the code of slavish obedience to orders given, no matter what, was as strong in me as in all volunteers then'. Similarly, watching a firing squad at Neuve Chapelle, Graham reported that battalion snipers refused to shoot a 'shellshocked' deserter. Reveille next day was sounded an hour earlier than usual and the men, in full battle order, were lined up around three sides of a hollow square. The condemned man strolled to the execution post, smoking, and was shot unbound. 'Our mutiny was only in the heart, such was the power of discipline.' Another old soldier, Evans, looking back, was surprised that it never seemed to have occurred to him or his mates to question army wisdom if the brigadier and the commanding officer were content to accept it. The most apposite observation I came across was from German intelligence officer Nicholas, who wrote: 'even after they were captured, the English retained their strict discipline. Maintained by a severe code of punishment, it was in their blood.'

There is something displeasing about all this. How can the practical requirements of war justify such severity? Should volunteers have had their individual wills so crudely broken? There would appear to be two grounds for defence. Some thought that the discipline instilled by drill was necessary to keep men facing the enemy, while others added that the army way was the most efficient way of bonding a large, amorphous group of men.

Taking the first point, that great French soldier, Du Picq, a generation before the Great War, had laid it down that 'trembling must be taken into account in all organizations, manœuvres, modes of action'. Battle is terrible, so his argument went. Men will only fight under great disciplinary pressure. Thus did Trotsky, manipulating a civilian army also, feel it necessary to give a soldier the choice between possible death if he went forward and certain death if he went back. After serving in two world wars, Gort believed 'you want something to help you over your fears and, if you can get control over your fears as you do in drill, it helps drive the man forward in war. The feeling of unison, of moving together is a help.'

Concerning the second point, it was argued that, if all relationships were stereotyped by drill, something more than the conquest of fear might be achieved. The individual might arguably be assured that he was an integral part of the conglomerate and might have specific if limited expectations, while a leader would be aided by having a simple standardized role, which could compensate for possible deficiencies in personal charisma. Overall a simple script for interaction would be easily comprehensible to all. Complementary responses could be guaranteed where all men could assume a behaviour peculiar to each niche in the hierarchy. The end product was probably a shared pattern of perceiving, interacting and doing, which stabilized mutual expectations, eliminated personal relationships to a high degree and minimized friction by formalizing authority relationships. In the final analysis the rigid structure may further have given a margin of safety where an emergency situation demanded prompt and exact obedience, quick and uniform thought. Even Liddell Hart thought that this might often have been the case.

Against this defence there are some fundamental objections. The most important is that Second World War[7] studies strongly suggest that fear is not the chief impetus in battle. Respect for leaders, a personal philosophy of seeing the job through, ideological conviction all play a part. The most vital driving force, however, would seem to be loyalty to mates. That being the case, platoon training with a view to socializing, rather than punitive drill with a view to breaking individuality, should have been the chief priority – as it was in the colonial armies during the war. Militarily too the use of men in small, self-contained units was one of the ingredients in the successes of 1918 on both sides.

Punitive drilling moreover seems to have had the side-effect of eliminating an important military element – that of initiative. Major Fuller contrasted the Tommy unfavourably with the poilu in this regard. 'I found it unnecessary to teach the French soldiers, for they taught themselves, explained things to each other and were wonderfully intelligent compared with British soldiers.' He reinforced his impression with many anecdotes. Arriving once at an Arras rail-head 'I found the sentry walking about in a brisk and soldierly manner. On seeing me, he presented arms and shouted, "Guard, turn out". At the station, 200 yards away, shells were falling and three trucks of flax were blazing and a large stock of rations was on fire.' While Fuller arranged for a group of men to uncouple the blazing trucks and move them away from a petrol dump, the sentries continued their beat while the station master hunted desperately for the rubber stamps which had been scattered by the original shell blast. Fuller might be regarded by the conservative as a brilliant but critical observer. Yet even Wavell, a more establishment figure, looking back on active service in both world wars, found the British soldier low in cunning and a non-starter in situations requiring independent thought, for example dealing with his own camouflage, the enemy's booby traps or just retreating. That enterprise might have been stimulated by a different type of training seems to have occurred to few high in authority before 1918.

Another objection to our training concerns the best way of bonding a large, hierarchical organization. One way was to insist on the precise relation of bandsman, bandmaster and sergeant major, then back it with the full weight of impersonal rigour and army punishments. Even during the Napoleonic wars Moore thought he could get more out of his riflemen by giving them the status of respected colleagues taking part in a dignified and worthwhile job. 'Old Officer' had backed him anonymously in 1795: 'It is highly dis-agreeable to hear an officer preface his orders with, "Damn your blood, sir, I order, etc." This is very unbecoming from one man to another and is language I would not use to my horse. Men love to be used as men and not with such outrageous treatment.' In short, an army could be bonded more surely with more respect and less fear.

Colonial troops supply a contrast to our men and suggest how an alternative concept of training might have served both with regard to battle motivation and army organization. Though they came mostly from rural societies with a frontier ethos, colonial soldiers were sufficiently close in temperament to ours to make comparison possible. During the late Victorian age emigration from Britain was running at 200,000 per annum. Many 'Canadians' were Britons who had 'discovered' Canadian relatives, and this entitled them to enlist at Liverpool with the Canadians and thus qualify for a dollar a day rather than a shilling. Colonials were therefore closer to Britain than they are today, which probably explains their response to the war. Thirteen per cent of Australians and 19 per cent of South Africans eligible enlisted voluntarily compared with 24 per cent in England and 6 per cent from Ireland. One could hardly imagine such a response since the Second World War.

The colonial soldier insisted on higher status and individuality than his British counterpart expected. This came out in many ways. Even during the Boer war Australian buglers received 4s. 6d. a week and sergeants 8s.; in the Great War they outbid everyone. Their men would slam a twenty-franc note on a canteen counter and say cavalierly, 'Say, pard, cut that out,' while Thomas Atkins boggled. Duties and fatigues were kept strictly within bounds. Fuller remembered the first Canadians refusing to handle their own kit at Southampton docks. Ironically Kitchener men were brought in to do the porterage. Smith found that Canadians did not bother how engineering material was unloaded from a train provided that it was unloaded. There was no attempt to dress mules from the right or set men to polishing the railway lines as the British army would have done. Even the uniform stood apart. The Australians' was of pure wool, dusty grey in colour and with vast and useful pockets. A bush hat, brim curled in a variety of ways and with home-town badges fastened to it, set the whole thing off.

Their relations with authority were totally different from those of the British. If a colonial officer tried to enforce the old-world view, he was likely to be briskly dealt with. Joe Winter still recalls a delightful picture of Australian privates throwing their officer over the parapet of a bridge. Instead an officer was expected to put himself on the same level as his men. Aldington writes of a Canadian major sitting on a double-seated latrine, chewing gum and chatting with an adjacent private. Even generals weren't immune. My father heard corps commander Birdwood called 'Birdie' and warned of a low spot in the parapet where snipers could be dangerous. When Carton de Wiart picked up an Australian for not recognizing Birdwood, the reply came: 'Why the hell doesn't he wear a feather in his tail like any other bloody bird would?' This did not mean that there was no professional respect. Though colonials refused to join in the St Vitus dance of saluting back at base, they would still salute their own officers. Further, as Monash pointed out, 'very stupid comment has been made upon the discipline of the Australian soldier. That was because the very purpose and conception of discipline have been misunderstood. It is, after all, only a means to an end, and that end is to secure the coordinated action among a large number of individuals for achieving a definite purpose. It does not mean obsequious homage to superiors nor servile observance of forms and customs nor a suppression of the individuality.' Quite so. To the end of the war, colonials remained the enemies of pomposity and humbug. Bowra wrote of the vigour of their complaints; one man in particular who stepped forward three paces on parade to fart, thereby challenging the smallprint of King's Regulations. It was not merely that the colonial soldier was allowed to remain an individual, hierarchy was limited to the conduct of professional matters and was not allowed to become the sole cement of an army.

These colonials, serving in units which allowed them so much more individuality, became our best soldiers. When the Anzacs came into the west front, they made nineteen attacks in their first forty-five days to lose 23,000 men; by the end of the war 68 per cent of the force had become registered casualties. Germans regarded the presence of Australians as a sure indication of forthcoming offensive action. By the last months of the war it was the non-Britons who had lasted the strain of war best. Between 25 March and 5 October 1918 the Australians took 23 per cent of all prisoners and suffered one-sixth of the casualties before they were rested. There was no reply when an irritable letter from Monash appeared in *The Times*, protesting about lack of publicity for Anzac achievements. British junior officers were poor, wrote Monash, brave but unskilful and few British divisions first class. The spirit of the Anzacs was well shown towards the end of the war by Chaney. When shelling started, the colonials left their trenches without orders. As things quietened, so they returned with sharpened bayonets. Said one to the other, 'How about it, digger?' 'Right-o matey,' and off they went across no-man's-land in the dark, returning with bloodied steel. 'Just had ourselves a barney, matey.' Chaney was duly horrified and commented sourly on their absence of 'discipline'.

Colonial troops had only national reinforcements, whereas British battalions might receive drafts from any regiment; the Australians and New Zealanders entered the war on the west front only in 1916; colonials were probably bigger men physically, from a more open society – all these objections might be made to the superior fighting strength of colonials. Fierce and continuous fighting, however, really began for the British Expeditionary Force only in July 1916, while nearly all of the colonials were front-line men, since their support was given by British troops. They therefore tended to fight for longer periods. In short, colonials man for man fought better, were better adapted to the longueurs of trench fighting and supplied the storm troops of the BEF to the end though trained in a manner totally different from the Kitchener men. First in battle and with proportionately nine times the number of men in military prison than had the British, in the words of John Terraine, a recent apologist for our commander-in-chief, 'Haig's admiration for these notable soldiers grew, although they never ceased to puzzle him'. They puzzled others as well, for it was only from across the oceans that a citizen army came, trained to use the virtues of a citizen army. Our soldiers, until the last year of the war, continued to be trained as blockishly as had been Wellington's men.

3

COMING TO TERMS WITH THE ARMY

Training completed, civilians became soldiers. In the eyes of the army they therefore had become 'men'.

'Man' to a staff officer was a being like a chess piece – 'Send three men to sap A and tell them to hold it at all costs'.

'Man' to a quartermaster was an envelope of skin consuming food, needing a billet.

'Man' to a subaltern out of the line was a shadowy creature. Even a dedicated officer like Chapman had to write:

They used to tell us, 'Get to know your men'. It was hammered in at training schools. 'Know your men, young man, and they'll follow you anywhere.' I have an old platoon role before me; three pages of numbers, names, trades, next of kin, religion and so forth. Faces come back out of the past to answer these barren details. Here and there rise memories of their habits, their nicknames, the look of one as he looked at you, the look of another as he spoke to you. Husky voices re-echo endless talks held over braziers. 'Was you ever at 'atfield? Ah, that's a fine 'ouse.' 'Na, don't know that side o' the county.' The faces of the talkers have disappeared. Only the shabby outlines and voices remain. Did any of us ever know you? No. As you would have said, 'Gawd knows but ee won't split on a pal.' So you remain a line of bowed heads and humped shoulders, sitting wearily in the rain beside the roadside, waiting, hoping, waiting – but unknown.

Below the subaltern was the NCO. 'Man' to him was a being tending constantly towards evil. Only constant harassment would keep tunic buttons fastened and restricted areas restricted.

March in fours means keep step and dress off correctly. Parade each evening at 5.30 and on Sunday afternoon. Men are not to pull the pig's tails. Men are not to clean boots on the dustbins. Offenders will be severely dealt with. Stand still on parade there. Can't you understand English, damn you. Hold your shovel properly that man there. Take that man's name and number. Half an hour's extra shovel drill this evening.

'Men', in short, were like those nightmarish characters in a Kafka novel, unable to achieve recognition of their individuality or even of the fact that they were human.

Added to this low status were the discomforts beyond number; coarse trousers sagging at the waist and billowing round the buttocks, bound with unevenly laminated puttees; beds of verminous straw on stone floors, with latrines made of stinking poles suspended over stinking pits; meals of cold bully beef mixed with jam; cold and tiredness so acute that they seemed to replace the membrane round the brain. The list grows steadily as one reads memoir after memoir. So many of the reminiscences are recalled in a tone of cold anger, even towards the end of men's lives, that it would seem natural to assume that soldiers did what their country required of them but hated the army which was that country's spokesman and all things associated with it. But this was not the case. I have the enduring impression that most men did find a satisfactory home within the army, accepted the conventions of its hierarchic attitudes and even managed to hold the army in some regard.

Talk to any Great War veteran today and show him photographs. He looks for cap badges and shoulder titles to establish the regiments involved. He reads off rank from that bewildering permutation of chevrons and crowns, which placed a man within the complex army hierarchy. Stripes below the elbow on the left arm showed an old army veteran. Length of service could be checked below the other elbow with yellow stripes showing the degree of danger to which a man had been subjected. Veterans remember all the bugle calls and the order of parade, for all these things showed the historical dimension of the army, that dimension which gave to men a feeling of dignity and importance as surely as it does to workers in an old firm or students in an old public school or university.

At every point a recruit was aware of tradition. The day he enrolled he became 'Mr Tommy Atkins' to civilians. This name went back to 1829, when Wellington chose this name as an example for the account book of the soldier. The recruit would then put on his khaki uniform. This dated back to the Indian Mutiny of 1857, when the former uniform had been boiled in water with mazari palm to make it less hot, less conspicuous. The puttees which gave him so much trouble were of Indian origin as well, just like the officers' breeches, copied from the Rajputs. The weapon he was given was the 'hipe' –

as if higher command were reluctant to acknowledge the passing of the pike two centuries earlier. The regiment a man joined was likely to have a long history. The 1st Battalion Glosters wore a bronze sphinx back and front of their caps to commemorate a gallant stand in Egypt; the KOYLI's wore a white rose in their caps on 1 August to remember Minden in 1759; the Cheshires had oak leaves on their helmets in memory of Dettingen; the Norfolks had always been 'the holy boys', the 51st 'the coalies', the Royal West Kents 'the dirty half hundred'; rifle regiments wore green with black facings just like their Jäger and Chasseur counterparts abroad and marched faster, without colours, fingers through triggers, with leather harness rather than webbing as they had done since 1797. Even men who joined new Kitchener regiments would participate in these rituals, since at some time they would probably serve in old regiments, as war casualties were so great that men were shuffled round into depleted regiments like cards in a pack. The ninety-seven dead of Watford Grammar School, for example, represented fifty-eight different regiments.

The high value put on old traditions is illustrated by the speed with which Kitchener men took over the old jargon. Recruits became Knocker White, Bogey Harris, Spiky Sullivan, Dodger Green, Pincher Martin, Tug Wilson or Wiggy Bennett, as they had always been. From the Indian army came Blighty (England) chit (slip of paper), dekko (look), rooty (bread), cushy (comfortable), dixie (cooking pot), wallah (chap); from Egypt came bundhook (rifle), bint (girl), buckshee (free). Graham put the end product beautifully:

> Because of the famous deeds, the name of the regiment is whispered in awe. But look at the men off duty with their caps off so that you see the narrow foreheads lined with suffering, the blank eyes. Off parade the warriors are working men but the tradition of the army prevails. They do not desire to enter unions. They think in the army way and they talk in the army way. The man whose name is Smith becomes inevitably dusty Smith. The bread is called rooty and the fat is gippo. The guard room is the spudhole and if you are looking smart, you are looking posh.

Thus did most civilians find a narcotic charm in aspects of an institution so large, so all embracing, so old.

The second great positive bonding force was provided by the various niches in the large organization within which men could find an identity. The simplest of these was occupational. Bombers, mortar men, machine gunners, Lewis gunners, all had their own units almost completely detached from the bayonet men. They marched at the rear with their own handcarts and limbers, claiming the privileges of witch doctors within their tribes, adopting the gun-fighter's sandunga. The signallers were also separate and a good example of these tribes within tribes. With eighteen in a battalion under their own sergeant, they had their own billet out of the line and were exempt from fatigues. They went up the line an hour before the rest and just carried their own equipment. Most of trench time was spent in their own dugout, testing lines and sharing private jokes on technicalities with other 'iddy umpties'. Each quarter hour they would buzz all lines and, if there was no reply, the course of action expected gave them the prestige they enjoyed among the bayonet men. Under the heaviest shellfire, and in pairs, they went out to run a finger down the line, clothed and muffled to the ears in goatskins and comforters, chatting and whistling in their casual way. It was their duty, too, to dispense tea from frowsy dugouts and keep anxious-faced NCOs waiting in the vicinity, for they were the 'news wallahs', first into action and last out, propelling their out-rageous handcarts packed with musical instruments, braziers, kettles and blankets, at which the greatest martinet would turn the blindest of eyes.

Apart from occupational categories, there were the various units into which the army was officially divided. These were based on numbers rather than on particular skills, and a soldier was a member of each simultaneously. They were:

a section under a lance-corporal – of about 15
a platoon under a subaltern – of about 60
a company under a captain – of about 250
a battalion under a major – of about 1,000
a regiment under a colonel – of about 2,000
a brigade under a brigadier – of about 4,000
a division under a major-general – of about 12,000
a corps under a lieutenant-general – of about 50,000
an army under a general – of about 200,000[8]

The largest unit meant little. Many veterans today are hard pushed to recall in which army they were fighting during a particu-lar period of the war. As Feilding remarked, 'I remember being

asked on leave what the men thought of Haig. You might as well
have asked the private soldier what he thinks of God. He knows
about the same amount on each. I have only seen my army commander on three occasions in three years – Plumer twice and
Birdwood once.'

Corps was an equally shadowy unit, for the corps commander had
no real independence. Divisions passed through his hands in battle.
With fluctuating personnel, all the corps commander could do was
to show 'keenness' and 'put on a show' probably at the expense of
the men he handled.

Division was a different matter, for this was the largest self-
contained unit which moved about as a single unit. Bath-houses,
cinemas, concerts and canteens all existed under the aegis of the
division. Despite the size – a moving division occupied twenty miles
of road and needed 188 lorry- and waggon-loads of equipment a day
to keep it functioning – most men knew each other by sight.
Veterans today of both wars value their divisional histories, and my
father was most struck by the memorial to his 58th Division in one
of those tiny villages, tucked away in that loneliest part of France –
the old Somme battlefield. This surprises an outsider. How can a
unit of 10,000 men be their home in any way? But so it was in those
days.

Below division was brigade. This, like corps, was something of
an administrative convenience, and even regiment below it lost
lustre when so many of the linked battalions became separated.
Company, however, imposed itself on men. Each week the captain
signed a man's paybook. Company NCOs detailed parades, ration
parties, fatigues. Thus company and division were the most practical
of the units, though it was the battalion which tended to give a man
his prestige as a fighting man and certainly a position on the leave
roster. In civilian parlance, division and company were like school
and form. One gave position in the world with a common uniform
and awareness of belonging to a single unit, however different the
constituent parts; the other gave the more personal touch as the
largest unit within which the soldier was known to authority by
name. Both units, however, were too large to be loved, too large for
a man to open his own privacy and share himself. Such intimacy as
there was within the army was in platoon and section. Within those
two units men were on first-name terms. The section in particular,
with corporal and his men, would often survive like the lifeboat of

a shipwreck in time of emergency. The men of the section would be all sorts. Harry Ingham's diary gives the addresses of a Scottish butcher, an Exeter schoolteacher, a Cheshunt barber, a Bolton chemist, a St Helens plasterer, a Scottish student and a Cambridgeshire farmer. Of such small units Priestley wrote:

> out of any ten men chosen at random for you to live with, I decided that, unless luck was running hard against you, one of them would be your sort, a man you could call a friend, often pure gold. The next eight would be average decent fellows, conventional, timid, a bit shuffling perhaps but capable of responding to a reasonable appeal. The tenth would be no good except to a saint or teacher-leader of genius. He would be twisted somewhere inside, a man who wanted some kind of authority and power over men.

Arguably the small group unit was the strongest single sustaining force in the war. Studies during the Second World War suggested this, and Manning hinted at it when he described a discussion in which men haltingly tried to find the reasons for going on. All agreed ultimately that they were fighting for themselves and each other. Many writers remarked on the power of comradeship. Feilding wrote of 'the spirit of camaraderie the like of which has probably not been seen in the world before'; Liddell Hart that 'the fellowship of the trenches was a unique and unforgettable experience'. 'The fact remains that, terrifying and uncomfortable as they often were,' Rogerson observed, 'the war years will stand out in the memory of vast numbers who fought as the happiest period in their lives. And the clue . . . we were all comrades . . . we saw love passing the love for women of one pal for his half section.'

The rationale for all this was practical utility. The group helped each carry the guilt of killing, allowed the pooling of verbal aggression which eased the burden of dependence and fear, rewarded too conformity to new norms of conduct which gave such security in war as was possible. Above all, the group allowed a sense of purpose not present in the actual war situation and which permitted men to impose a sense of time upon days and years which seemed otherwise featureless and endless. This purpose gave mutual support on the battlefield. United by a common jargon, by shared secrets and experiences, by common discomforts and grievances, by deep fears and by common laughter, by shared prejudice against other

units and common authority, by sudden violences and long still-
nesses, as David Jones put it, men belonged to platoon or section
as to no other aspect of their war life. In the end, collective personality became so pervasive that men on leave felt like deserters,
would eat meals for dead comrades, internalize the values of dead
comrades and become reticent about their private lives, so as not
to weaken the bond. Captain Thomas Kettle MP indicated the
power of the group in his last letter back to his brother just a day
before his death:

> We are moving up tonight into the battle of the Somme. The
> bombardment, destruction and bloodshed are beyond all imagina-
> tion. I have had two chances of leaving my Dublin fusiliers – one
> to take sick leave and the other to have a staff job. I have chosen
> to stay with my comrades. Somewhere the choosers of the slain
> are touching as in our Norse story they used to touch with in-
> visible wands those who are to die. I am calm but desperately
> anxious to live.

To an outsider the strength of the small group might easily have
been missed. The dead appeared to be quickly forgotten, certainly
in conversation. Often bickering would flair up with as little rational
reason as in a flock of feeding starlings. Coppard wrote:

> We would often quarrel violently over nothing. We would rage
> over little things. Our life was dominated by small, immediate
> events. Bad weather and long working hours would provoke out-
> bursts of grumbling. A sunny morning and the prospect of a
> holiday would make us exuberantly cheerful and some would
> declare that the army was not so bad after all. A slight deficiency
> in the rations would arouse mutinous mutterings. An extra pot of
> jam in the ration bag would fill us with a spirit of loyalty and
> patriotism. If an officer used brutal words, we would loathe him
> and meditate vengeance. If he spoke kindly to us or did us some
> service, we would call him a toff or a sport and overflow with sen-
> timental devotion to him.

Men would turn upon each other as lightly.

There appeared to be little gentleness or consideration. Hope
recalled going down a dugout in support.

> The air is foul with a mixture of stale tobacco smoke, smouldering
> candle wicks, brews of Oxo cubes and strong tea flavoured with

the more human stinks of an overcrowded dugout. It doesn't look as if an extra twelve could possibly find resting place. Our methods are anything but gentle. 'Beg pardons' or 'by your leaves' are neither expected nor given. We merely choose a spot and fling down our equipment and sit on it regardless of sprawling legs. Nobody takes offence at our uncouthness. It is a hard life we live and the ability to look after oneself and rough it are assets. Softness is played upon. Firmness and rough handling when the occasion demands it are taken for granted.

An outsider who overheard the talk within a small group might have further doubts about the strength of the relationship. Men kept a careful social distance and maintained intimacy without warmth. The independence of each man was carefully avoided. Men never thought of each other as husbands or fathers. When a man said, 'I have lost my eldest boy,' his mates would all be surprised. So it had been in the Napoleonic wars when Harris's riflemen only knew each other by surnames.

Within the limits of a professional relationship, close friendships might wear a calloused surface off duty but, when danger appeared, men looked after each other with a rough, protective care. If there was no enthusiasm, there was little shirking. The wounded were treated with the utmost gentleness and the weak and soft were guarded too. If a man's behaviour were off-beat or windy, the group sheltered him like a mascot or teddy bear. That gentleness in human relations so much missed in France, a country in which there were no intimate relationships with women or children, turned men towards each other. 'They had every excuse for turning into brutes and they hadn't done it. True, they were degenerating in certain ways. They were getting coarse and rough and a bit animal, but with amazing simplicity and unpretentiousness they had retained and developed a certain essential humanity and manhood.'

Within the group there were three particular types of relationship which are best examined in ascending order of formality. The most intimate and intense was the friendship of mates, closer even than the small groups of men who would mess together. Private Willcox wrote:

I met Ira by a shellhole. For months we campaigned together. The happiness we had managed to drag out of those dreary months, we shared. The sorrows we shared. The parcels from home we shared.

On those blessed days of rest we had flung bits of poetry to each other. We thought that after the war we would quit the monotonous life at home and we would go adventuring. We had mapped out what we would do, where we would go. They knew us in the Royal Sussex as 'The twins'. 'If you fall, I shall stop. Hell to them all, I shall stop.' But we were separated before we began. He was attached to another platoon. I saw him as I went over the top. He was well. He laughed as he swore: 'What a bloody mess.' We said good-bye; God be with you. I never saw him again. Later I wrote to him. The letter was returned undelivered. The mark of a rubber stamp was on the envelope – Killed in Action. Just that. A country's regrets to me that my friend was dead.

Drinkwater tells us of a friendship as close. The men were Roper and Middleton, who did all their duties together, took leave together and were both killed by the same rifle grenade. Serving with the West Yorks at Hooge in 1915, Cooke wrote of the twins Hugh and Jock Campbell. Both were coalminers. They went into battle holding hands. Only Hugh came through.

Less intense than these pair bonds was the shared esteem that men of the group had for valued individuals within it. The status of these men found no reflection in official army rank. They were the men to whom others looked for personal reassurance rather than for specific directives of any sort.

One type of reassurance came from men who provided an active example. Plowman tells us of Corporal Side.

A man less like a soldier than any I have seen in France. He is short, cross-eyed, bandy legged and has a preference for boots and shoes and clothes too big for him. In civil life he is a rag-picker and the character of his profession adheres as it will to a man. For parade purposes he really ought to be smuggled among the cooks. The other day we were in a sap when an idiot set the rumour running that the Germans were coming over. 'Coming over are they? 'ere. Gimme me rifle,' and he went up the sap apparently intending to put the Germans back in their places singlehanded.

Kingsbury wrote of Private Grey of the 1st Devonshires, a fisherman by trade. On sentry he would sing sea shanties and beat out the rhythm using his whole body. Private Ting in Chapman's platoon once was the company scallywag. A newspaper vendor with twelve children, he was constantly demoted to the ranks for conduct out of battle then promoted for his conduct within battle. 'Fritz, yer old sossige,' he would shout. 'Come out ternite, Fritz, and I'll give yer –'

Such linchpins of cheerful normalcy gave constant support but so too did the calm and settled men, solid and reliable, punctual in their duties and always with a clean rifle. These were men like Corporal Holroyd of the engineers, a man over forty and an Oxford graduate. He would wash his feet regularly regardless of danger and sit for long periods whether in rest or under bombardment reading his pocket dictionary. Another such man was the divisional intelligence officer described by Paul Maze.

> I was told that he lived somewhere near me on the Ypres salient but I had never been able to find him. One evening I struck a patch of fresh vegetables and flowers in the midst of a desolated shelled area. I found him sitting up in bed, a shelf full of books beside him. He had built up for himself a life completely detached from the war and to this he returned every evening after his work. His pride was his vegetable garden. He was perhaps the only man in the salient who supplemented his rations with home-grown vegetable. We would meet at night and, while we talked, we would watch the salient being shelled and the everlasting fireworks over the distant line. His mind always wandered back to Spain where he had lived before the war and whither he longed to return. His descriptions of the wild Spanish country with snowtopped mountains defined against an everlastingly blue sky contrasted with our own surroundings and would refresh his mind.

Men like this officer or Holroyd were men whose social adjustment before the war allowed them calm during it. They were men able to adjust to any authority and whose inner world was so clearcut that it eliminated the tiresome interruptions of reality. Their example to more perturbed men was constantly soothing and reassuring.

The last of the three supportive relationships within the group was that between the men and their officer. Out of the line, the officer was a man apart. He never visited the estaminet of the men and they had to stand to attention when addressing him, and could get an interview only by written note to the orderly room. Then they would be marched into the officer's presence, cap in hand, sergeant in attendance, and standing to attention all the time.

In the line all was changed. Trappings like insignia, saluting, social distance gave way to survival and were largely omitted. Instead the officer was seen constantly by his men, checked trench stores, detailed men for wiring parties and sentry, critically assessed men's capacities in various situations. It was now the despised subaltern who took over from high command and was seen to speak with authority. As Alec Waugh remarked, it was rare to see authority above the rank of major in the front line, and even then few majors appeared. Hardy, the VC padre, summarized the result: 'The line is the key to the whole thing. Work in the front line and they will listen to you. If you stay back, you are wasting your time. Men will forgive anything but lack of courage and devotion.' Speaking for padres, he was in fact speaking for army authority too. If the gentleman subaltern shared high explosive with his men, then men accepted the demands of the army more readily.

Battle capped this acceptance, for the officer's function had always been to lead towards the enemy, cossett leading his flock or, as it must have seemed more often to the subalterns, the tup lamb leading the flock to the slaughter house. Mottram worked out that, in his regiment, officer casualties were five times those of other ranks. Pound further calculated that, in the first week of the battle of Loos, eighty-four of the 106 officers who died were under twenty-six years old.

The manner of death was clearly visible to their followers and deeply moving. My father remembers his Captain Hall

leading the company into the attack by driving a golf ball with a club in front of him. He was hit by a sniper and died the same afternoon. This ridge before Hangard wood was deadly. It was so broad and flat that German machine-gun bullets skimmed an inch above the ground. So many of our men were hit that Colonel Symonds became uneasy. 'Cawston, I must go up to the ridge to see what's happening.' 'I wouldn't go if I were you, sir. There's no need for you to expose yourself.' 'There's something wrong with our position. My men are out there, Cawston, and I want to know what's going on.' Symonds was a bulky man, slow and elderly. He was hit. It took four men to get him down from the ridge. He died later that day.

In the high-stress situation of front line and battle, men tended to transfer their loyalty to the officer as an idealized figure who might be able to control danger. The officer, too, drew strength from the close relationship. Said Captain Ian Campbell:

Back in the billets I hate the men with their petty crimes, their stubborn moods, their continual bad language. But in a difficult time, they show up splendidly. Under heavy shellfire it was curious to look into their eyes. You perceive the wide, frightened and rather piteous wonder then the patient look turned towards you. Not 'what the bloody hell is this?' but 'is it quite fair? we cannot move. We are little animals. Is it necessary to make such large shells to kill such feeble animals as us?' I quite agree with them but had to put my eyeglass fairly in my eye and make bad jokes. And, looking back, I blush to think of the damnably bad jokes I did make.

Many officers found the relationship of the front line a moving and close one. 'What a wonderful people are our infantry and what a joy it is to be with them. When I am here, I feel I should never go away from them.' Feilding wrote this just after his men had insisted on repairing a trench, though the spot had clearly been ranged by an enemy mortar. A rather more enthusiastic sentiment was printed during the war in the national press:

> Oh never shall I forget you
> my men who trusted me.
> More my sons than your fathers'.
> They could not see you dying
> or hold your hand when you died.
> Happy and young and gallant
> they saw their first-born go
> but not the strong limbs broken . . .

Often difference in ages made the relation a paternal one. Fleming-Bernard wrote of his colonel, John Allardyce, about an occasion the colonel was on leave and in McVitie's shop in Edinburgh. 'My mother was ordering a parcel to be sent to me at the front when she was prodded in the ribs by a thick, blackthorn stick. Turning round indignantly, she found herself confronted by a large, fierce and surly-looking individual who said, "And who are you to be sending parcels to one of my boys?" He was a rock of sanity to us all and we loved him.' And so it often seems to have been with a platoon, loved collectively with a protective, possessive emotion like that between father and son. If not quite love, there was always mutual respect. 'I shall never think of the lower classes again in quite the same way after the war,' wrote Carrington in his war diary. A future cabinet minister, Boyd Orr, thought similarly: 'The Sherwood Foresters were mostly miners from Nottingham and Derby. They were a very congenial, clubbable lot, helping each other in difficulties and sharing the parcels sent from home. When we took prisoners, they showed no great enmity. It was as if a cricket match had been played and won. Ever since, when there are troubles and strikes with miners, my sympathies have always been with the men.'

There are as many such references from Other Ranks. Writing of an officer sniped while looking for souvenirs, Moran described him as 'a lovely young fellow'.

He came to us from Armentières and straight from Oxford. He was a quiet lad of the best type. From the beginning, the men looked towards him. He was buried after dark on the edge of the wood. The men were half kneeling, their eyes on the ground. Barty Price was standing a little apart, appearing extraordinarily tall and thin against the sky. He looked up: 'You have lost a good officer, men.' And then, after a moment's silence: 'Put him with his head towards the enemy.' He read a short service, stumbling as he failed to make out the words in the gloom by the aid of a torch. Then we got up and went away and no one spoke. Before we were relieved today, I walked over to the grave and found that the men of Stirling's company had been working on it overnight. They had planted it out with stones and had planted moss and a few wild flowers that drooped before they took on fresh life.

Enclosed within a historic institution, given a precise place within the complex hierarchy of rank and unit, offered some of the most emotional relationships a man would know in his life, the individual civilian in Kitchener's armies was given as many reasons to come to terms with his new status as he was given reasons to hate it. If this paradox was a difficult one for the soldier finally to come to terms with, then it fitted in with so much else that awaited the soldier in France.

4

TRAINING THE OFFICERS

The old professional army had drawn its officers almost exclusively from the public schools, then groomed them in Sandhurst or 'the Shop' at Woolwich. With the enlargement of the army in 1914 and the fearful casualty rates during the war, the traditional sources could not suffice. By the start of 1917 a typical division needed fifty fresh officers monthly, and Nicholson guessed that overall about 10,000 replacements had to be found.

For some time, the public-school section of the community could fill the gap. The number of car-owning families gives an indication of the number of wealthy households in Britain. With a Rover 12 costing £425 or a Rolls-Royce Silver Ghost £950 plus the salary of a mechanic who might double as a chauffeur, cars were a luxury in Edwardian times. The number stood at 132,000, so an annual officer requirement of 10,000 should have been found from these regions with little difficulty.

On leave in November 1914, Haig had identified this source. 'Send out young Oxford and Cambridge men as officers,' he had written. 'They understand the crisis in which the British empire is involved.' The university men might well have an army background in addition. Haldane in 1907 had created the Officers' Training Corps despite the protests of Ramsay MacDonald, who saw it as a class divider. In the first seven months of the war, the OTC had vindicated traditionalists like Haldane and Haig by producing 20,500 commissions. Distinguished public schools might even bypass the universities. Marlborough sent 506, Eton 350, Charterhouse 411 sixth-formers straight to France as Second Lieutenants. At first sight, therefore, it looked as if the social distinctions of the officer had been preserved together with the traditional outlook. Before the war, cavalry regiments had demanded a minimum income from capital of £1,000 per annum, the Guards £400, the Cameronians £100. Early Kitchener subalterns seem mostly to have been of this financial calibre.

As the war progressed, casualty rates meant that even university men could not keep pace, so the army had to go outside its selection pool. By the end Graves judged that about one third of the officers had come from OTCs while two-thirds had been promoted in the field. Hutchison checked the backgrounds of his company commanders, and the result was fairly typical. One had been the son of a Scottish miner (MC, DCM with bar). Another had been a wool salesman (MC and bar). A third was an ex-medical student (DSO, MC) whose adjutant was the son of a land agent (MC and bar). None of these were of the public-school section of society.

The problem facing the army was therefore a dual one. On the one hand, it had to teach the role of authority in a short time to soldiers who were unlikely to know many of the cues from hearsay or family tradition. On the other hand, younger men of higher social class, already familiar with authority, needed to be taught to think as 'soldiers.'

At first sight, undergraduates should have been the most tractable of material. In 1914 there were only 10 per cent the number of students that there are today and none had assistance grants. A poor student might just get by with some coaching, but a student needed at least £160 per annum to survive and then had carefully to avoid tradesmen's debts. These young men were hardly likely therefore to resemble their namesakes today, though they seem to have done as little work – Donaldson at Magdalene observed that 25 per cent of students left Oxbridge without taking degrees. The knowledge taken from university was knowledge of common dress, common manners and common speech rather than devotion to academic excellence.

Making officers, however, proved less easy than social background suggested. Old regular soldiers like Lucy were appalled at the Kitchener subalterns. 'At the end of 1915 the civilians took over. They were undersized, they slouched, they were bespectacled. They wore their uniform in a careless way and had a deadly earnestness which took the place of our *esprit de corps*. They saluted awkwardly and were clumsy with their weapons. Their marching was a pain to look at and the talkative methods of their officers and NCOs made us blush.' He might have added that they insisted on carrying their own valises, on addressing each other as 'Mister', while reading books and tempering authority with tact, all things unheard of in the old days. Faced with such non-military conduct, senior officers protested. Max Plowman recalled his colonel first addressing his assembled subalterns: 'The discipline of the battalion is damnable. Some of you officers don't know your job at all. You think the men will respect you because you wear a belt. You've got to command these men before they will respect you. I have seen officers talking to men as equals. I won't have that. In future, such men will be reduced to the ranks. You can go.'

This discrepancy from expectation was something more fundamental than just youth and non-military bearing. Experience in business or at university tended to produce men more mature and complex than the army had had to deal with before. Postponed commitment to social roles had allowed experimentation with various types of behaviour and produced a man more multifaceted and playful than the traditional Sandhurst subaltern. With high status outside the army, such a man had less need to identify with army values. Coming into the army, he had other ways of doing business compared with what was now expected of him. Two anecdotes well show the sort of strains that civilian subalterns could introduce. When a suggestion was made by Boyd Orr that water be carried up to the front, contrary to regulations, under an ambulance seat, the Regular officer replied, 'By God, sir, I will have you sent home.' Playing bridge at Villers Plouich, Dugdale said to General Pulteney, 'Why on earth did you not lead the heart, Sir?' In half-serious manner Pulteney contrasted this familiarity with pre-war days and thought insufficient respect was being shown him.

The problems of getting a man promoted from the ranks to become an officer were more straightforward. A personality moulded around deference and obedience had in short space to be reversed. With a task so clearcut the old Army, in contrast with the public-school or university men, was better able to cope.

The most important element facilitating the transformation of clay into gold was the limited nature of the new role of 'officer'. During peace the officers' function had always been conceived of in the narrowest terms. NCOs trained and managed the men. Only when they were fit to respond to the word of command were they put in front of the officer, whose duty it was to regard them with total lack of friendliness or apparent interest. The officer directed, supervised, inquired, but it was the NCO who knew and acted. In war, too, the officer was assumed to have little discretion. 'Old Officer' in 1795 had written in his book of advice to officers that in battle they should 'be very attentive to orders. Here you have nothing left to your judgement. It is only required of you to obey.' So it turned out in most engagements in the Great War. Army commanders briefed divisional and brigade HQs, who then passed on a synopsis to colonels. Subalterns might or might not be briefed, according to the personality of the colonel. Fielding learned of a counter-offensive at Loos only through the *Daily Mail* though he has been just 200 yards from it.

The two functions expected of a subaltern by the army – man management in the limited sense of personifying authority or acting as a longstop for the NCO at most; a channel for the communication of orders – are well summarized in two documents. The first was the officer's actual commission: 'George by the grace of God . . . to our trusty and well-beloved . . . we, reposing special trust and confidence in your loyalty, courage and good conduct, do by these presents . . . you are at all times to exercise and well discipline in arms both the inferior officers and men serving under you and use your best endeavours to keep them in good order and discipline . . . given at our court of St James's . . .' This was the longstop. The function in war was laid out in a handbook of 1917. In it the officer was just expected to be 'cheery, punctual and well turned out . . . to be blood thirsty and forever thinking how to kill the enemy and help his men to do so'.

An officer therefore did not need much specific technical knowledge. All he was thought to need was 'authority'. Any schoolmaster or shop steward knows just how quickly the tricks of that particular trade can be acquired. The end product might be a cold eye, a jutting jaw, an assertive body position and a loud voice; it might be a relaxed but purposeful approach, quiet-spoken but eschewing all appearance of self-doubt or hesitancy, but either way a short course with rites of initiation to help the repudiation of an old identity, time to consolidate extra self-confidence and the support of the hierarchic army structure, could make the change.

Up to mid-1915 the course for prospective officers lasted just one month with final selection made in games of rugby or soccer according to the respectability of the violence displayed and quickness of reaction generally. Then came a short trench tour with the new subaltern carefully kept away from Other Rankers who had known him as a private soldier. In time, the course became more professional and lasted three months with a long spell of leave before going back to the front line. The end product was remarkable. Gibbons observed, with many others, that, when the public-school officers were killed, working-class replacements were just as good and soon acquired the same mannerisms. My father, a wary old socialist, had to admit the same grudgingly. Only a Military Medal ribbon would allow a quick check on the ranker background of a new officer.

Once in France, trained, the officer was much assisted in his new role and dignity by the dress and physical separation which traditionally went with his position. In the past, officers had been selected exclusively from the 'gentlemen' class to exercise authority in that capacity rather than in a professional sense. It was just therefore that the officer should take with him those appurtenances of distinction which marked the authority of a civilian gentleman.

Dress was the first trademark. While 'Other Ranks' wore the shabby garb of the artisan, the officer equipped himself at his own expense in the khaki equivalent of hunting dress. Riding boots and breeches marked remoteness from physical labour and the Sam Browne belt identified the officer as a member of the sword-bearing class. Pope and Bradley in 1916 offered officers' breeches at £2 12s. 6d. and the tunic at £1 7s. 6d. No private could buy his own kit in this way.

Dressed as a gentleman, the circumstances of the officers' daily living were approximated as closely as possible to those of the country house. A gentleman without servants was unthinkable, so the officer was given batmen of one sort or another. Medical officer Keynes was astonished in 1915 to be given the services of a batman, an orderly and a groom together with three horses. Personal living space was awarded in proportion. At base camp, officers slept two to a tent in comparison with Other Ranks at ten. Feeding was similarly selective. Other Ranks ate their last meal at teatime just like manual workers in peacetime; officers sat down to their main meal in the evening. It was no bad meal either since, when the rations came up, officers' servants had the first pick – after the ASC. In addition canteens would sell ham, cheese, sardines, olives, wine to officers, while men went round the back for their cocoa and biscuits, according to Manning. Officers' parcels weekly from Harrods further supplemented ration fare and were safer from pilfering because of marks of rank indicated on the address label. Passes were freely given to officers, enabling men like Bairnsfather to consume the *table d'hôte* at the Faucon d'Or just thirty minutes after leaving the front line. Charley's Bar in Amiens was particularly favoured by subalterns on a pass. There they could buy Old Orkney whisky at

2s 6d. a bottle and take it back to their dugouts. Food parcels of Other Ranks, on the other hand, had to be opened in the presence of an officer according to the regulations so that alcoholic contraband might be seized. Only officers were allowed spirits in war.

Conditions of service were lightened for officers. Better housed and better fed, the officer was higher paid and was able to bring home-comforts with him without any personal effort. If brave in battle, reward was more certain. Indeed the very condition of an award was officer witness of the deed. Punishment, on the other hand, was less certain. During the war only three officers were admitted to have been shot for cowardice as against 400 men. If the officer was worn by war, then exit was easier. One thousand four hundred were sent home for one reason or another, and few Other Ranks could have been in the position of Eton schoolmaster John Christie, whose mother could write personally for the release of her son and get it. If he did stay, then the bonds of the front line were looser for an officer. The officer could write home when he wished and 'of course' censored his own mail, as Chandos remarked. Married officers could meet their wives in Paris, while leave was more frequent. Major-General Macdougall had twelve home leaves during the war and got home for each Christmas. Private Ellison got three leaves in contrast and seems to have been typical of Other Ranks in this infrequency of home leave.

The special treatment continued if the officer became a casualty of war. Wounded on the Somme, Latham pointed out at Boulogne that he was an officer. Immediately the R.A.M.C. sergeant was as one transformed, jumping to attention and getting a sprung ambulance to take Latham to the Duchess of Westminster's hospital at Le Touquet. On the third day he was asked whether he wanted to return to England or not. In the same hospital, after the first gas attack at Ypres, officers were fed on whole chicken, milk puddings and oranges. Subaltern Rogers tells of breaking his foot playing hockey in France. He was sent home at once and lodged at the Central Hotel, Marylebone, which had become the Prince of Wales Hospital for Officers for the duration of the war. There were two to a room and a Harley Street consultant in attendance. General Jack found similar treatment when he caught a chill during 1916. For four days he was given champagne and port at meals and the use of a hot, private bath by the Field Ambulance unit. Even in death there was distinction. Cushing noted that officers' coffins were of seasoned wood with a planed top compared with the un-seasoned green elm used for Other Ranks.

When these privileges were added to the training, it would seem that few officers rejected the role which the army gave them. Small discrepancies there might be, but these could be worked on by senior officers from the old regular army. The first historian of the Kitchener armies, Kipling, noted the constant harassment of subalterns. Ewart wrote of a 'kit *strafe*' in 1915, in which the adjutant went through valises, removing hair oil, light-coloured shirts, deck chairs and collapsible wash stands. Books of any type by any author were inevitably declared to be contraband. In 1916 Evans suffered a similar visitation. Surplus kit had to be returned via Cox's shipping agency. In that particular inspection, helmets and bullet-proof waistcoats were declared within the forbidden category. King's Regulations might cover such harassment at a pinch. It hardly justified the contempt of sour colonels. Bridges wrote of an Irish private knocking down two Kitchener officers and getting away with it – 'Arrah, Colonel, y'know them's not officers,' he had said. My uncle remembered Major McGrath, his superior officer, ordering the young subalterns not to give orders to his sergeant for six months – 'You think you know something. You don't know anything.'

Tempering the blandishments that went with higher rank by constant reminders of relative insignificance within the army hierarchy, the army proved that officers could be manufactured as easily as Other Ranks.

5

OVER TO FRANCE

The journey to France might begin at any time for individuals who had completed their training. Henry Winter remembers the selection of men for a draft to reinforce the regiment's first battalion at Gallipoli.

The Brigadier just walked along the ranks, pointing to this man or that. He pointed to Charly Taylor next to me. The name was noted by Sergeant Butler. Not a word was spoken. With his aggressive Kipling moustache, Taylor was like Brecht's 'soldier of La Ciotat' – silent, immobile, perfect. He neither complained nor criticized; never expressed an opinion because he had none to express or words because he had few of those to spare. He drank as he worked – in a passionless silence. He ordered his first quart then took it to a remote corner of the pub and drained it in one draught. Then he immediately ordered another. With this second quart, his silent evening's drinking began. On his return to our hut after such an evening, he would be unusually garrulous, addressing the hut in general – 'bit chilly . . . turned cold . . . dark night . . . beginning to rain.' He was everyone's friend, ready at any time to swop a guard or cookhouse fatigue with anyone who wanted the evening off. Odd that the brigadier should read all this in a glance and select him to die for his country. Three weeks later he did die, leaving a wife and three children behind him in Hackney.

The battles of Neuve Chapelle and Loos might all have taken individual men while they were still training in such a way. More usually the men went *en bloc* in the groups with which they were preparing. The moment would be long expected, even hoped for. In correct army fashion, the colonel would announce the open secret:

'NCOs and men of the 8th Upshires. Er, you are, er, proceeding overseas on active service. Er. Er. I, er, trust you will do your, er, duty. We have wasted, er, spared no pains to make you efficient. Remember to keep yourselves smart and clean and, er, walk in a soldierly way. You must, er, always maintain the honour of the regiment which, er, er, which stands high in the records of the British army. I . . .' A faint murmur of 'bloody old fool', 'silly old bastard', 'struth', too faint to reach the officers' ears, came from the draft. The alert CSM caught it and he cut short the colonel's peroration with his stentorian 'Stand still there. Stand steady. Take their names, Ser'ant 'Icks.' The last person he saw was the little colonel standing at the extreme end of the platform, standing very erect, standing rather tense and emotional, standing with his right hand raised to his cap, standing to salute his men proceeding on active service. He wasn't a bad little man. He believed intensely in his army.

A common addition to this scene of departure sketched by Aldington was a crowd of cheering civilians or the regimental band. But few men later to write their memoirs thought it an important scene at the time. Minds had already left England but as yet without anything known or specific to focus on. It was a time of emptiness, anxiety, waiting, like new boys going to big school for the first day.

The port of departure was invariably Folkestone. From camp, men would follow that steep, narrow path down the cliffs, today planted with rosemary for remembrance and carefully kept as a war memorial. Below them, the men would see the grey-painted channel steamers, which would look to us more like Thames pleasure steamers. Standing on the quayside, the men would be subdued as they looked at the plane and destroyer escort – first sign of the insecurity of war. Standing near them would be men returning to the front after their home leave. These would be studied with intensity for clues about the future.

He [Aldington] was immediately struck by their motley appearance. He and other draft members were spick and span, buttons bright, puttees minutely adjusted, boots polished, peak caps stiffened with wire, packs mathematically squared, overcoats buttoned to the throat. The men returning from leave were dressed anyhow. Some had leather equipment, some webbing. They put their equipment together as it suited them. None of them had shined or polished for months. Some wore overcoats, some goatskins. The skirts of some overcoats had been roughly hacked off with jack-knives. The equipment which weighed so heavily on the shoulders of the draft seemed to give these soldiers no concern – they either wore it unconcernedly or chucked it onto the deck with their rifles. He noted with amused scandal that the bolts and muzzles of their rifles were generally tightly bound with oiled rags. Their faces were lean. They were still curiously drawn though the men had been out of the line for a fortnight. The eyes had a peculiar look. They seemed strangely worn and mature though filled with a kind of energy; a kind of slow, enduring energy. They looked barbaric, not brutal; determined, not cruel. Under their grotesque wrappings, their bodies were lean and hard and tireless. He had been waiting eagerly for these men to get away from their time-honoured jests and speak of their experiences. But he was disappointed that these men spoke in such a trivial and uninteresting way. He felt they ought to say important things in Shakespearian blank verse, something adequate to their experience and the intensity of the manhood he instinctively felt in them and admired so humbly. But of course this was ridiculous of him. Part of their impressiveness was their very triviality, their complete unconsciousness that there was anything extraordinary or striking about themselves. They hadn't tried to think it out. They went on with the business, hating it, because they had been told it had to be done and believing what they had been told.

Once the police had checked all papers, the men would embark and put on life jackets. Gawn recalled the complete and apprehensive silence of the men during the dash across the Channel. This was only broken when another steamer passed them, heading for England. The Australians on it, bound for leave, were singing, 'Take me back to Blighty' and gave Gawn's draft three cheers. Paper formalities at Boulogne would take over an hour while men hung about, glancing nervously up at circling airships, looking at the white-painted hospital ships with their green bands, reading the warning notices '*Taisez-vous. Méfiez-vous. Les oreilles ennemies vous écoutent.*'

Landing at Rouen or Boulogne the men would have to march in full equipment to the base camp. Étaples was the biggest of these, a hard day's march distant, a huge grassless field of sand, holding tents for 100,000 men. It had an atmosphere of its own, for, if the wind were strong and from the east, the distant sound of gunfire could be heard. Owen wrote:

It is a vast, dreadful encampment. It seemed neither France nor England but a kind of paddock where the beasts were kept a few days before the shambles. There was a very strange look on all faces in that camp; an incomprehensible look which a man will never see in England nor can it be seen in any battle, only in Étaples. It was not despair or terror. It was more terrible than terror, for it was a blindfold look and without expression, like a dead rabbit's. It will never be painted and no actor will ever seize it.

The routine was fixed. Breakfast was at 5.45 am with the men going onto the 'bull ring' at 7 and staying till 5.30 pm. There would be platoon drill and unarmed fighting with boots, teeth and knees – neither having been taught much in England; there would also be the army bullshit of bayonet training and uphill running on sand-hills with supplementary kit. The most novel side of it all was the manner of authority. In England nothing had been savage in its severity. There had been little foul language. This now changed into a fierce, vindictive atmosphere. Memory of base made Burrage angry for a long time. The purple, pompous, strutting dugout officers and the brazen-voiced NCOs clinging to their safe jobs and yellow armbands seemed to take pleasure in insulting the fighting men. All places were out of bounds, all authority jumped on undone greatcoat collar-hooks. At the end of training there was a rush as in a wild-west lumber camp for the first meal sitting. Gladden wrote recently of the tables covered in filth from earlier meals and of the stench of stale food and human sweat. Truly the years do nothing to sweeten the taste of contempt and indignity for soldiers as well as schoolboys. At the end of the day last post was blown over the encampment, over the railway line which cut through one corner of the camp, over the cemetery in another corner with its 12,000 graves. Aldington wrote of the shattering and heart-rending effect as 'the inexorable chains of rapid, sobbing notes and drawn-out piercing wails' swirled over the camp.

Thinking the matter over with hindsight, some men realized that there was bound to be a degree of harshness at base. The drafts were new and uncooperative, while NCOs did not know the men or feel any pride in grooming for a particular regiment. The softening force of acquaintance which worked in England had no place in France. The men moreover were likely to be tense and on edge, tetchy as invalids. NCOs would also be aware that men destined for the front would regard the 'canaries' with a degree of contempt as men training them for savage encounters which they themselves had chosen not to face. Men in convalescence further expressed the scorn, demanding special privileges, neglecting uniform regulations and talking back to non-combatant officers. Base NCOs felt under attack and were likely to make the most of the capacity for pre-emptive strike which army discipline allowed them.

After the stint at base, the railway took the men towards the front line. To a generation with visual memories of the railway lines running into Hitler's death camps, tense faces peering from cattle trucks, there is something disconcerting about the imagery of this journey from base camp. The soldiers went in waggons of the same type, forty of them in each waggon, kit hanging from hooks in the roof. Death was a high probability for both generations of travellers in these cattle trucks, but the earlier generation was offered those elements of Keystone comedy which the army so often served up. Loading took five and a half hours – though by the end of the war this had been cut down to one and a half hours. Once the mass of men had adjusted themselves sufficiently for the forty men to be able to lie or sit, they realized that they had no idea where they were going or how long the journey would take or where food would come from. Often the train went so slowly that men could exercise by walking beside it, defecate in tranquillity by the line or walk up to the engine to beg hot water from the driver to make tea. Most men, like Gladden, were 'annoyed beyond endurance by the inconsequential aimlessness' of the journey. They came to dislike the vast engine with its innards draped along the boiler, the engine driver in his baggy blue overalls and goggles, the country with its low rises and long views, its settlements secreted in folds and unseen, a country desolate as the *meseta* and seamed with poplars like jugular veins – it all overwhelmed a man with emptiness and grief. How could a land just an hour and a half from the Kentish coast be so empty, so different? Would battle dead lie forgotten in this country seemingly on the other side of the earth?

Meanwhile time passed, as men ate iron rations against orders, smoked and threw track ballast at the green glass insulators of telephone poles or sat on top of the waggons if the weather was warm.

Arrival could only be sudden and unexpected. Then after hours of lassitude, forgotten apparently by the army and the war, all became hassle to de-train within a rigid and tight timetable. Burrage tells us of the difficulty of disgorging a well-fed train within the limit allowed. Four or five men would be left on as the waggons began to move off. They had to jump off with 60 lb. of kit on their backs, at best crashing onto the track, at worst meeting a train moving in the other direction.

The men would stand idly around at the railhead, their predatory instincts carefully watched by the commandant and his police. Then they would be formed in fours by platoons in company columns. Each brigade was given just 5,505 yards of road so that the division would occupy just fifteen miles, a great millipede of babel with 12,000 men and 6,000 horses and 1,028 waggons taking five hours to pass any spot.

At the time men regarded the thing with impatience, a chasm to be crossed in getting from A to B, a journey between events. Only in looking back did they find in the march one of the three unique trademarks of their war – the march, barbed wire, howitzers wheel to wheel. So much else – weapons, kit, attitudes – were repeated in the Second World War, but the march and the songs that went with it were like an umbilical cord which joined survivors and linked them too with the wars of Wellington and Marlborough. Of all the photos I showed my uncle, that of a straight, cobbled road, steeply cambered and poplar lined was the only one that drew a smile of remembrance from him.

When the column started off, full discipline applied. With the order 'at ease' when the rhythm had been established, rifles could be slung; and with the order 'easy', men could smoke and sing. The routine never changed during the whole war. Men marched for fifty minutes in the hour, covering in that time three miles, and twelve to fifteen miles in the day. Each regiment of four in the brigade took its turn at the head of the column, enjoyed setting its own pace and marching outside that cloud of dust which settled over the column and hung about it, shot through with tobacco smoke and the buzz of conversation and music. The right flank was changed each hour while officers on horseback led the men and NCOs took the rear to measure the gaps – seven paces between platoons – and check on men falling out. Each fifty minutes the whistle blew and men collapsed, slackening their belts and sliding forward at the roadside to use their packs as a pillow. In advance four trenches would have been dug with a urinal for each battalion, marked with yellow flags. The facility would be used only when the worst of the march spasms had been cat-napped away. There seems something hermetic about the wisdom of the army on the march, the wisdom of an institution with an ageless knowledge of the few strengths and many weaknesses of its followers, a wisdom which avoided the big overall aim and settled on the minute and shrewd details by which people are governed.

There were some pleasures in marching. Cloete's thoughts when he was injured in hospital strayed back to the march, to the ring of boots on cobbles, the chinking of bayonet against entrenching tool, the smell of sweat and the sound of song spread over the battalion. As men smoked and talked, a comforting sense of comradeship suffused the column. With all worldly possessions on a man's back, the cookers behind and no sense of responsibility for getting to an unknown destination, marching became a joy – provided the march was not too far. There was something bigger than just comradeship in this sense of pleasure. No civilian had seen so large a mass of men – except perhaps in the working-class ritual of the Saturday soccer match, although soccer fans were less similar in dress, thought and task. Here therefore was the grandeur of being a small part in something large and impressive. The worries, anxieties and traumas of the individual, beaded on the rosary of memory, were lost in the mass. They were not lost for the future; just overlain by tendrils from men totally responsive towards each other. A marching man was cut off too from the task orientation of his army role when marching. Only in rest was he ever similarly cut off from either fighting or preparing to fight. Marching men were thus neither rambling civilians, though something like, nor fighting soldiers, though like them too. Instead they achieved the warm security both of personal anonymity and professional rolelessness.

The void in the identity of the marching man might be filled with whimsy and fantasy. Perhaps he was going home or away from danger or nowhere. The army to which the man belonged was certainly treated with derision or ignored altogether. Men sang the songs of home and songs of derision. With the songs from home, the column would quieten as each man retreated within himself to savour the profound sense of loss. They would emerge to join each other again in derision of their present condition. There would perhaps be ribald songs with topical verses about the idiosyncrasies of the colonel. 'The nearest officer pretended not to hear while he concentrated on memorizing them so that he could give a spirited rendering of it in the mess that evening.' The excreta of officers' chargers would be leapfrogged with cries of mock alarm. Then would follow the retaliatory search for tunic buttons undone by NCOs barking their meaninglessnesses: 'That man there. Put yer 'at straight. Pick em up. Left, right, left, right, left.' If a column of men passed in the other direction, then there would be banter: 'What mob are yer? Wrong direction, mate. Cockney rabble. Nasty smell 'ere, Bill.'

These were the pleasures of the march. Its pains were more tangible. The problem of problems was the weight being carried. John Parr, a victim of the first day of the Somme, wrote:

> The halt just pulls you round and the first twenty of the fifty minutes go fairly easily. Then time begins to drag and the last ten minutes are done by sheer physical force. It feels as if your neck muscles are being pulled out with pincers and your boots are soled with red-hot iron. You push your cap to the back of your head and the colonel riding down the column calls out, 'Put your cap straight that corporal there.' And all the time you have to smile and joke because all the others round you are joking when they aren't swearing and you know that many of them are worse off than you. I have seen nothing of the country as my eyes have been fixed on the heels of the man in front. Oh, blessed hour's rest and tea. The longed-for whistle just in time as the men were beginning to waver and sag. Oh, what should we do without tea here. A million blessings on the head of Walter Raleigh or Isaac Newton or whoever it was discovered its gorgeous refreshing properties. In the evening I would lie on the straw of the billets for an hour before I felt I could stand again.

The weight of the pack was not without precedent. Corporal Wheeler in the Napoleonic wars had written of himself as 'half beaten before he came to the scratch' with his 60-lb. pack with its four days of bread and biscuits, flour for seven days and sixty rounds of ball. The British pack in the Crimean war weighed 64 lb. No two accounts agree on the weight of a Great War pack but the following gives an indication:

clothing	11 lb.	14¾ oz.
rifle	10	11¼
100 rounds	6	4

trench tools	2	9¼
webbing	8	4¾
pack	9	12¼
rations/water	5	10
Total	55 lb.	2¼ oz.

The officer's kit is put by the same source at 42 lb. 10¼ oz., but such was the magnetism of his position and the ingenuity of his batman that a cart could usually be found to secrete the lion's share of this weight. It was never so for Other Ranks. For the common man there could only be more to carry. Verey flares, periscopes, wirecutters would all be distributed among the ranks. In addition men would hope to carry spare underwear, their own razors and toilet paper wrapped in a home-knitted cardigan or comforter. Any spare tea, cigarettes, or matches, a family bible and photographs would all be stuffed into the haversack. Under this weight, strong men staggered, only gradually picking up the rhythm of the march. Weaker men hunched their backs like camels and staggered on. Perhaps they would carry a note scribbled by a corporal to present to the assistant provost marshal if they fell out. Perhaps mates or NCOs at each elbow carried them through. Drinkwater recalled a march with Captain Davies at one elbow and a stretcher bearer at the other, while his own mind went back to his schooldays and the rugger field. Allen recalled the world receding into the outer distance and the landscape taking on an odd grey appearance. How much worse it all was for the over forties, the crippled and the slightly gassed.

Second to the weight of the pack as a source of tribulation to the marching soldier were his boots. After their first route march, men would often fall over when they started walking in their own shoes again. Unlike the German, the British boot did not extend up the leg but was still of that size which gave to the soldier an impression of brutality. Made ideally of Indian roan leather, it was equally ideally a tight fit forward and loose at the rear with the heel low for downhill marching (were all destinations at the bottom of valleys?). Read thought the standard Blücher boot superb for marching, but with the explosion in the size of the army and two million boots bought from Canada in June 1915 at a cost of £1½ million, art was submerged by private profit and a poorer fit. The old soldier did his best. The boot would be fitted after feet had swollen from a long march and then with the thickest sock in addition. Before marching, a man put wet soap on his feet followed by two pairs of socks. Boots were never taken off till feet had cooled down, while swollen feet would not be bathed till they were to their normal size. Nevertheless it was a lucky man who avoided side effects from the long march. Blisters followed friction, and callouses followed pressure. Doctors even coined a new phrase – footslogger's nodule – for the nodules three-quarters of an inch wide and half an inch thick which came from the pressure of laces on tendons.

Lastly, the marching man was assaulted by a number of physical irritants. Except where roads passed through villages, where there would be cobbles, roads were frequently unsurfaced. In wet weather they would become rivers of mud; in dry they would dissolve into clouds of choking dust. Then there was the steep camber, which tended to tip men after the weariness of a long march towards the ditches. The long, straight sections, so satisfying to the motorist today, fatigued the eye of the walker of those days by giving it nowhere to rest and tended, in the open, treeless deserts of northern France, to stretch one kilometre into four. If dust and heat added thirst, then there was little to ease it. Wells by the road were most often dismantled by the peasantry, who would only sell water for cash. To drink from the quart waterbottle during the march without permission was an offence punishable by field punishment number one.

Thus, by train and on foot, a man came towards the front line and the reserve camp. One must imagine men unused to prolonged exercise, constipated and suffering from boils, the flat-footed and the sick, sedentary office workers and clerks, all fitted into army boots of standard sizes, all moving slowly and wearily to the sound of the guns. Experience thus far had been of anxiety and pain, fatigue and companionship. Fear was still to come.

6

TRENCH LIFE

The trench system, in which men saw their most dangerous service, ran without break from the Channel to the Alps. Only an airman like Billy Bishop could get an overall view of it.

At 600 feet, we were free of most earthly noises and again I looked down. For the first time I saw the front line as it really was, mile upon mile of it. Now running straight, now turning this way or that in an apparently haphazard and unnecessary curve. The depth and complexity of the German trench system surprised me. No-man's-land, much wider in places than I had realized from any map, looked like a long-neglected racecourse by reason of the distinctive greenness of its bare but relatively undisturbed turf. Far behind, in enemy territory I saw factories with smoking chimneys and pleasantly normal villages. The view was so extensive that I counted six plumes of steam from engines of equally normal trains.

The front-line system was made up of three parallel lines – the fire trench, the travel trench at twenty yards, then the support line, close enough to reinforce in case of a raid. All three lines were built in dog-tooth shape with bays five paces wide separated by hiccups in the line designed to minimize bomb blast and prevent enfilade fire should an enemy raiding party get into the trench. The depth of the trenches was about four feet with a built-up wall of sandbags as a parapet to allow men to stand upright. The power of the bullets they had to keep out is suggested by the official widths laid down for these parapets – eighteen inches for loose-packed earth, thirty-eight inches for oak or seven feet of turf. At the bottom of the trench ran a drainage runnel leading to sumps and covered with lengths of wooden ladder called duckboards. Facing the enemy was a step – the firestep – which brought rifles tucked into the shoulder up to ground level. Ideally wire or wooden-plank revetting completed the structure by checking the constant tendency of the trench sides to collapse, but usually this attention to detail was found only on the German side of the line.

The support line was rather more complex, since less risk allowed greater comfort. Kitchens, latrines, stores and mortar positions were dug at the end of short lead-off trenches. Dugouts above all were the trademark of support. Fifteen-foot shafts led to caves about five paces square and six feet high. Shape would be kept by wooden beams and wire netting, while Greenwell thought that most were as well furnished as his rooms in Oxford – green camp chairs, gramophones with records from the latest London shows, Kirchner pin-ups stuck up with marmalade, and hampers from Harrods, apart from a miscellany of greatcoats, gumboots and rifle magazines would fill the space as effectively as the warm fug of sweat, tobacco smoke and the fumes of a coke brazier. These havens were for officers mostly but would attract an envious flow of runners and errand runners with their prospect of buckshee tea and warmth. Drinkwater thought it worth getting into dugouts under any pretext. Just how safe they were was another matter. If the roof was an iron sheet and a foot of earth, the dugout was just shrapnel-proof; only eight feet of earth would deter a six-inch shell.

To dig a front-line trench system took 450 men six hours per 250 yards, covered by marksmen, watching constantly for the arc of sparks which preceded a bursting star shell at night. Once built, sappers maintained it, for the whole ants' nest was sustained only with constant effort in the face of explosives and the weather. Even without violent extremes, larkspur, honeysuckle and forget-me-nots always threatened to take over, while mud fed voraciously on an assorted diet of wood and iron. Eberle recalled that a brigade's system needed daily ninety six-foot duckboards, thirty-four nine-foot iron girders, nineteen prefabricated dugout frames, 300 feet of board and three hundredweight of nails.

Individuals served in this trench system relatively rarely. Of the 20,000 in a division, only 2,000 were in the front line at any moment. The Black Watch once served forty-eight days in the line unrelieved, while the 31st Queenslanders prided themselves on a fifty-three-day stint at Villers Bretonneux, but they were exceptional. Few men fought for long periods. Noakes reckoned a typical month as four days in the front line, four in support, eight in reserve and the remainder in rest. Carrington gives us a detailed breakdown of a year from his diary of 1916. He was under fire for 101 days – sixty-five of these in the front line and thirty-six in support – with 120 in reserve and seventy-three in rest. This left two and a half months to account for, made up by ten days in hospital, seventeen on leave,

twenty-three travelling and twenty-one on courses. During that
year Carrington was in action four times and was in no-man's-land
six times with patrols or working parties.

One still needs to make further allowance. The section of front
where a man served was crucial. Anywhere near Ypres was always
bad. If a man served near Festubert after 1915, however, the war
passed him by. Trenches there were like a drawing-room with
grenade boxes in pyramids, polished gas gongs, rubbish bags on the
parados and men everywhere dusting and polishing like house-
maids. Alec Waugh served in autumn 1917 north of Bapaume,
where no-man's-land was a mile wide, and his company sustained
not a single casualty in one month. Dugdale at Villers Plouich wrote
of both sides walking around on top of the parapet by day, daylight
reliefs and an order forbidding men to shoot game in case men were
hit. 'Such things should not be allowed,' he thought. 'There was a
war on.' Ellison served on the Somme in the autumn before the
great battle. He found the whole area as intensely green as the
South Downs, while Germans from Curlu and British in Vaux cast
a blind eye on each other when they went duck-fishing with floating
rat-traps. Often a German military band could be heard. In this
way some men serving in the front line might be hit fearfully hard
while others might come through unexpectedly lightly. The 7th
Royal Sussex between June 1915 and January 1918 served on
twenty-one sectors, of which sixteen were quiet; the 2nd Royal
Welsh were on thirty-nine sectors between November 1914 and
December 1916, fourteen of which were quiet.

Once training had been completed at base, a unit would be intro-
duced briefly and in small groups to the front line, attached to
seasoned men so as to learn the ropes. Their first impression was
bewildered and confused. Mottram wrote:

Enormous noise. Continuous explosion. A deserted landscape.
Complete immobility of everything. Men were eating, smoking,
doing odd jobs but no one was fighting. A few were peering in
periscopes or looking through loopholes. I tried, but could see
nothing but upturned empty fields. Then suddenly there was a
terrific crash which flung me yards. I picked myself up and did
my best to laugh. Near by a man lay with a tiny hole in his forehead
and close to him another limped with blood pumping out of his
leg. They were both carried away. A casualty was not a matter for

horror but replacement. I regarded the incessant bombardment as temporary and expected every moment to see men going over the top to put the guns out of action. Nothing happened, however. That was how I first saw the war.

Out of the line during this period, daily life was likely to be difficult. Old hands resented the latecomers, who were thought to have been enjoying civilian pleasures while front-line men suffered. There would be an element too of informal initiation. The capacity to maintain a friendly façade, behave in a soldierly manner and be treated as a dependable team man would all have to be tested. Time above all was required to be able to share that common experience which bonded the fighting soldiers. 'Stunt' troops would give newcomers a particularly hard time. My father found the KOYLIs, and Gladden the Northumberland Fusiliers, particularly virulent. There would be pointed references to the dead, jeers at effete southerners. The new draft would get more than their share of fatigues and probably have to forage for themselves till they came on to the ration strength. On the other hand, a common situation of danger produced much practical communication. Gillespie and his men were taught about shell sounds and snipers by Black Watch veterans of Tel el Kebir, while Ellison took comfort from the calm and self-possession of all regulars. Men were taught the important little things – how survival might depend on a match: 'No bleedin' lights. Let old Fritzie see a light. 'Ello, ee says, blokes in billets an over comes an arf dozen shells knockin' yerall ter blazes.'

Induction completed, the unit would take over a complete section of trench. This would be done under the cover of twilight at either end of the day. Men would prepare carefully for their ordeal. With packs left behind, haversacks would be stuffed with chocolate, candle ends, four-by-twos and with cigarettes in every pocket or cranny. If the weather was cold, sheepskins, jerkins, extra cardigans and fingerless leather gloves jostled for place with periscopes, sandbags, bolt cutters, chain saws and other material for trench stores. The men looked like explorers to a remote part of the globe – as indeed they were. Like explorers, none of the soldiers would take off any clothing for at least a week. MacBride in late 1915 once spent forty-two days without taking his tunic or boots off.

The tribulations of the feared journey in the semi-darkness are well remembered. Noakes recalled:

The leading files, anxious to get to their destination, were apt to hurry along too quickly. Owing to the way in which the communication trenches wound continually around sharp traverses and corners, it was seldom that one could see more than one or two men one was following, and it was absolutely necessary to keep in touch in order to avoid taking the wrong turning. If one stopped for a moment to shift one's rifle or ease a cutting pack-strap, it was easy to lose sight of the man in front. There were frequent obstacles to negotiate on the way such as slack wire under foot, sagging telephone wires overhead which caught in the piling-swivel of one's rifle, unexpected holes in duckboards. It was an unwritten law that the leading men should pass back word of each obstacle as it was encountered. The word often transmitted faster than we moved and would be forgotten by the time the obstacle was reached, leaving us to be half throttled by the wire. Each mishap would delay the file behind. 'Nuvver 'ole. Pass it back. Big 'un an' all – lookwhereyergoing'. Men would accelerate their pace to catch up, whereupon there would come frenzied appeals from the rear. 'Go easy in front for Christ sake.' Thus we would be pounding along at a killing pace with our heavy equipment swinging and clattering, stumbling and cursing in the darkness as far as our breath allowed, sweating profusely, longing for rest or drink but unable to stop for a breather until our destination was reached.

The only chance for a break, in fact, came if the guide lost his way. This was often done, for the boards with trench numbers and map references were often used as firewood and, where shells had fallen, the ground seldom matched map or memory. In the twilight certainty itself wore a blurred edge.

When the detachment arrived at the front, officers would go straight to the battalion HQ dugout. Dugouts, telephones, stores, water and latrines would be quickly indicated on a rough sketch map, so that sentries and gas alarm men could be immediately appointed. Relieved men would usually dash off with immoderate haste, leaving newcomers to inspect the company HQ logbook at leisure and get the general feel of the area – work in progress, state of the wire, enemy shell and sniper activity, patrol routes and so on. Other Ranks would have done the job more quickly. 'Any shit about?' 'Oh, he's been shelling X trench at 12 and Y trench at 5 and look for the minnies over there.' If the previous unit had lost many men, there would probably be no maps, no inventories, desultory trench stores. The enemy would then probably know more about the set-up. Throughout the war tapped D5 wires would result in welcoming boards being posted on the enemy's parapet with raucous crowing greeting the bantams or a highland fling on mouth-organs for the 51st.

The trench timetable was fixed. Day started with stand-to half an hour before dawn, when all men waited with rifles on the firestep. Officially the enemy was then at his most dangerous but, as Noakes observed, 'it is the time we feel safest from disturbance for Jerry undoubtedly knows about this invariable routine'. He would think twice about attacking a defended line with fifty men in pockets of five every 200 yards. Meanwhile the orderly officer would come round checking fields of fire, condition of trenches and stores. Men were stood down at dawn with just one sentry per platoon left, while the others filed towards a dugout to get their rations and the officer composed a report for battalion HQ.

Following the tension of the night, breakfast was a great relief. 'Conversation is discursive and trivial but generally good-humoured though most language would hardly pass muster in a drawing-room,' Noakes recalled. 'Rifles would be cleaned. Three or four men would squat round and play nap. One or two would go over their tunics to catch lice in the seams. Some might start to sing quietly and others would join in.'

After breakfast came the officers' inspection. Then the platoon sergeant would detail jobs. A third of the men would be on sentry with relief every two hours and spaced out every twenty-five yards. A third would go back for rations. The remaining third would 'rest'. The word had its army connotation. 'There was always something to be done involving a movement and a standing about,' wrote Griffiths wryly. 'Digging, filling sandbags, carrying ammunition, scheming against water, strengthening the wire, resetting duck-boards. These duties seemed of such importance that they absorbed one's entire stock of energy. A bombardment seemed a troublesome interruption of the serious business of life in the trenches.' Drink-water remembered a fixed pattern during the day of one hour work, one hour rest and one hour sentry. Finally, the day would end with a flurry of activity after the stillness of the afternoon, as men stood to at dusk and the ration parties arrived under cover of dark. Parties of outsiders might come up with the rations to do fatigues – a welcome supplement for strained men.

Night was the most active time of the twenty-four hours, for war reversed the normal time sequence. That part of time which in England went unnoticed, in France rose and fell like a guillotine quantifying danger and marking time survived.

Night was silence and isolation and fear. Noakes recalled the experience with unease.

I shall not easily forget those long winter nights in the front line. Darkness fell about four in the afternoon and dawn was not until eight next morning. These sixteen hours of blackness were broken by gun flashes, the gleam of star shells and punctuated by the scream of a shell or the sudden heart-stopping rattle of a machine-gun. The long hours crept by with leaden feet and sometimes it seemed as if time itself was dead. In the darkness we were prey to all sorts of unreasoning fancies. A tree stump, a hummock of earth, a coil of wire took on new and menacing forms and in the light of a star shell, could seem to be moving towards us. No one, of course, admitted to being windy and would have denied the charge indignantly but I am sure that few were entirely easy during these long vigils.

Night could be violent activity in short spasms too. The tension which built up in the long periods of silent waiting added to the impact. Evans described one of these spasms on the Ypres salient.

One night the quiet was broken by heavy shell fire. We all went to the top of Clapham Junction to see what was happening. It was worth it. About five miles away, near Langemark, a raid or something of the sort was taking place. Each side was sending up a fine display of coloured rockets. Artillery from both sides was firing hard. Their flashes made the night sparkle. We could see the flames of the shells as they fell and hear the crump of the explosions. Gradually the panic spread. The whole salient woke up. More rockets, nearer now. Artillerymen left their dugouts, wondering what it was all about. Artillery observers in observation posts thought they had better order a few rounds to be put over. Machine-gun crews in the line on both sides fired a belt across no-man's-land just in case. Wires were now busy to various HQs, inquiries were made, men were hustled from dugouts to man trenches. In fact, the whole salient, always nervous, was thoroughly awakened. The mania reached our front. Behind us a battery fired salvo after salvo. The German batteries replied. A raid had been carried out by troops to the right of Langemark. One prisoner had been taken. In half an hour all was quiet again.

Sentry duty in these tense conditions tested the nerves. Plowman noted that all men liked to be visited on night sentry and even the normally taciturn would open up. Perhaps they needed to be visited as well. 'All quiet, chum. Bugger all to report? Kipping mate? Christ, mate, you'll 'ave 'em all over.' It was left to the platoon sergeant to keep the sentries vigilant, going round each hour and beating on the soles of men due to relieve on the hour.

An early warning of enemy activity came from listening posts in no-man's-land. These might be at the head of saps from the front line; more often they were in isolated shellholes, heavily wired in. At any moment a German patrol might hit the post; all the time the listeners heard German activity, louder in the night silence and more sinister for being unseen. These loud whispers reminded old hands of stalking in the African bush. They would overhear the hacking coughs and the snuffling Germans with their head colds; they would hear feet on duckboards and the night wheel noise, like a river in flood grinding the boulders on its bed. Bradley tells us of such a post at Hamel in late 1916, in which six men were unrelieved for sixteen hours. Using two dead South Staffordshires as a seat, they passed the time whispering of walks in Surrey. When the men were relieved, one tried to bayonet the relief and another had to be forcibly held down.

Night patrol was probably an even more severe test. The aim of the men crawling about in no-man's-land was to check enemy patrols, to see whether the enemy was gathering for activity. All patrollers were volunteers. Two was the ideal number, four a menace and five an army. Phlegm and ruthlessness were necessary. Evans particularly valued Privates Grant and Thomas, stolid cut-throats who would stab fast even if they met the devil in no-man's-land. The men who made up these patrols were usually well-known to each other, comrades in arms.

Pockets would be emptied, faces blackened with burnt cork and bayonets dulled with a covering sock. These were the preliminaries. Next, men would equip with knives and clubs; grenades were for emergencies only, since noise in no-man's-land spelled star shells and machine-guns. Sentries would be warned; finally the men would 'move off'. Scrambling over the parapet, never knowing whether machine-gun fire might not sweep the lip, the patrol would aim for a marked gap in the wire, then take a compass bearing. Carrington recalled the details clearly half a lifetime later:

> One covered twenty yards in half an hour. One heard the stealthy coughing of the German sentries and their infinitely careful shuffling from foot to foot. One would hear the steady thumping of one's heart. If the night were quiet, one might well be lost in no-man's-land, human sounds coming from all directions until a well-known tangle of wire set one right. Best of all on clear nights was the pole star, on the left going out and on the right coming home. Where no-man's-land was wider, larger patrols like a game of poachers and gamekeepers might be carried out.

When the men came back to their own trench, there would be hoarsely whispered passwords, acknowledgment by sentries and the final tension of running the machine-gun gauntlet while rolling back into the trench.

The dangers of patrolling were always great. Belhaven thought that reconnoitring enemy wire was even more difficult than stalking impala. The first difficulty was the obstacle course of barbed wire. Detailed periscope observation by day could never imprint on one's mind a perfect picture of the gaps, so complex was the wiring system. Ten yards from the parapet was a low wire strung with cans to trap unwary Germans. Then came a high apron, both squarely and diagonally strung. There followed another trip wire, a low apron, another trip wire then finally another high apron. Strewn among this lot would be coils left by working parties, two-foot rings or 'gooseberries' to block shellholes and odd sections of concertina wire. Once through this lot, farts and belches from ill-fed men, the glint of a star shell on spectacles or a fall into a shellhole might each give the patrol away. Even on return, nervous or sleepy sentries might open fire. Sassoon was once shot in this way. It required an optimist like Graves to find a cheerful aspect – at night wounds would be less severe, since fire would not be aimed, and dressing stations would be relatively free.

Day or night the enemy was hardly ever seen. Greenwell was in the front line for seventy-one days before he fleetingly saw a German. Each side therefore built up a picture of the enemy just like blinded men. Patrol habits, working-party routes, machine-gun positions were all known. Sometimes men heard sneezes or a sergeant-major bawling out a man. Each morning they saw the blue smoke of breakfast fires. Shells would come over for ten minutes every three hours or a dozen at midday as much as to say 'we've got your range, so no monkey business'. All these pieces of the jigsaw would be assembled until a reasonably complete mental map had been built up from the sounds of physical movement.

Though the enemy was not to be seen, there was a sense of constant danger. Macmillan found trench life a greater strain than battle, for it was strain unrelieved by excitement. Drinkwater wrote of 'the nightmare . . . a stunning effect'.

Though in our draft only one was wounded and none killed, it was a terrible impression of the reality of war for the new men. 'I'm going to make my peace with God before I go up to the line again,' said Fitz when he came out. 'Each minnie coming at us was like a row of houses rushing through the air,' said another. 'Poor old K. was bobbing like a baby,' said a third. All seemed surprised by the war and scared as if they had never imagined the thing before they saw it. In each man's eyes were the signs of strain and shock. One very dull boy of eighteen who had once told a questioning CO that the Boer war had been fought in Egypt seemed suddenly to have been wakened though not to have become articulate. He now laughed like Charley Bates and said 'oo-hoo' and 'not arf' when asked what he thought of the front and did he find it bad.

The problem was that in training no one had been prepared for vigilant inaction, for the blinded feeling which followed being confined below the surface, for the demoralizing stooped walk, for the need to take constant care. Men were worn out by all these things and, released from the need to polish buttons and salute, they dropped their weapons, lost their kit, slept on sentry, urinated in the trenches, cried when put in a listening post, 'forgot' everything they were told, dropped cans and litter everywhere and fumbled with their gasmasks when speed was needed. In this mood of tension, accidents were always possible. Kingsbury remembered General Maude challenged with a bayonet in the front line; on another occasion he saw a wandering pig at night-time challenged and shot.

This tension and fear had a rational basis. Priestley at Souchez in 1917 saw his B Company go down from 270 men to seventy during a period of holding the line and without any battle activity.

Few of the lost men were shell casualties, for the front lines were too close together. Whizz bangs might creep forward to the support line, but they did so rarely. Peripatetic mortar teams would generate chaos, but they visited the front rarely. Machine-guns swept the parapet accurately, but the machine-gun was basically a defensive weapon reluctant to give away its position needlessly. The fixed rifle worked on exposed places. Watson wrote of such a gun at Aubers firing every two minutes like a Chinese water torture and of the throaty gurgles of men hit in the brain; but fixed rifles could be easily evaded by alert men. The real killer was the sniper.

Snipers worked in nests behind the front line, though a few were in camouflaged suits in no-man's-land. The mechanic might be of any age. Fielding wrote of a wounded prisoner: 'He was quite a lad and so frail and light and his face so pale and artless that it was hard to believe he was engaged on so dirty a trade. He died as I moved him.' The accuracy that snipers achieved was impressive. Jack recalled Lieutenant Fenton of the Cameronians looking twice over a parapet at the same spot and being hit the second time by two snipers at the same time. Eyre wrote of a Rhodesian farmer, Turner, hit in the aiming eye when moving the steel shutter of his sniper's plate and then dying without sound or movement. The only way to remove snipers was to get a rough bearing by sound and field of fire, then triangulate by using a helmet or dummy to draw fire.

For obvious reasons of personal safety, no German sniper has written his memoirs. Attitudes and techniques are therefore best guessed at from our own techniques. It would seem that the sniper was proud of his craft, whatever the infantryman might think of it. The first British exponent, Hesketh Pritchard, wrote, 'The smallest of big game animals do not present so small a mask as the German face, so sniping becomes the highest of all forms of rifle shooting.' The first thing was to get a decent weapon. On our side, the Ross was held in the highest regard, accurate as a Springfield to 600 yards though armourers had often to ream out the chambers, since only perfect ammunition was tolerated. MacBride thought the German Mauser better, since its higher muzzle velocity allowed accuracy to 1,000 yards. Next came the nest. Men worked in pairs, the observer using a 20 × telescope and working out ranges. Ammunition was hand-picked with each bullet carefully prepared. Only one shot was possible at a time and then with oblique fire for muzzle blast, 'smoke' in cold or muggy weather, or telescope flash, might give away the position. Snipers could fill a large bag. Belhaven wrote of one man killing six Germans and wounding ten in a week. MacBride's diary reads: 'December 9th, 1915. Hazy. Cool. One leaning against tree. *Tué*. One fifty yards right. Fell across log. Shot three successive helpers . . . December 16th, 1916. Clear. Fine. Good hunting. Sixteen good shots. Seven known hits and feel sure of four more.' Since German snipers were specially trained men and always stayed on the same section of front, unlike the peripatetic British amateur marksmen, it is perhaps possible that the man who waved a signboard '87 not out' to the fury of Andrews's companions was not far out. Even staunch patriot Carton de Wiart was prepared to grant German superiority in this area of the war.

The reaction of an old hand like Lucy to sniper fire and the other dangers in the front line was to adapt as best he could.

I gave the impression of being a cool hand. When shots fell in my vicinity, I stopped for a moment to talk to someone near by and I kept my eyes and ears open. I judged the direction of the gun, whether the strike was on hard or soft ground, the timing of the salvoes – when I managed to walk past the danger point keeping nearer to the parapet than the parados, moving swifter through open bays, checking at revetments for lateral cover and often adding to my chances of safety by stooping at the most dangerous places to pick up a cartridge or wind a puttee, thus keeping myself well down without giving the impression I was doing so. The safety catch of my rifle was always forward with a spare cartridge in the sling and anything I carried was slung clear of my hands so I could shoot quickly. I avoided batteries, mortar and machine-gun positions and kept away from strongpoints in our own line. All these places got more than their ordinary dose of shelling. I never put my head over the top twice in the same place and, when I moved before nightfall, I used the ground like a redskin. I went unconcernedly when bullets whistled but got on the move when they smacked in the air near my head. I always hurried in and out of the line, postponed my halts until I reached the greater safety of reserve or front line from the communication trenches. I skidded past trench junctions and never halted at crossroads even though they were miles behind the front. My cartridges were always loosened in their cases, my iron ration intact and my water bottle filled. I ate automatically and functioned properly except under prolonged shelling when I got constipated like everyone else. The pocket holding my field dressing was pinned not stitched.

By such devices men might increase their chance of life.

What is harder to grasp is that so many men voluntarily placed themselves in danger unnecessarily. Sometimes it might be sheer devilment. Cook described a sign 'Gott strafe the Kaiser' being erected at Louvain corner within sight of the enemy line. Result – eight men died in the ensuing mortar shoot. Hutchison's men signalled snipers' hits and misses by waving their Glengarries, and two of them blew themselves up, carrying an explosive-packed dummy into no-man's-land. Feilding once heard a band playing '*Die Wacht am Rhein*.' When the Germans shouted to demand an encore, a fusilade of grenades was thrown across with inevitable mortar retaliation.

The chief source of death for volunteers was planned at a higher level than these wild spirits. This was the trench raid, invented by the Canadians early in 1915. The aim originally was to secure a German shoulder flash, hopefully with the live German still attached. The theory was that, if new divisions were indicated, the Germans were planning activity. If we knew all about the German regiments, then the enemy was just holding the front. Though there were easier ways of finding out this information, the raid really caught on. Between 19 December 1915 and 30 June 1916 some 5,845 men died and 119,296 were wounded in these 'minor trench operations'.

There were various reasons for the multiplication of raids. At the simplest, Tommy's fighting spirit was thought of as a sediment in a heavy wine which, unless frequently shaken, would come to settle in the region of puttees or trouser seat. General Jack also thought raids 'a very valuable means of training and producing a school of daring and thoroughly competent leaders', which may have been the case if the officers managed to stay alive, though the simplicity of the tactics used in these forays and the speed with which they were over severely limited the experience gained. Lastly, Jack thought, 'we must worry the enemy to death and maintain by every means our fine fighting spirit so that all ranks may continue to realize that they are individually more than a match for the Germans'. This was more doubtful, since losses seemed to worry our side more than the enemy, while there remained little to choose between morale on both sides throughout the war. But this way of thinking was common just above that level in the army where officers actually needed to take part in a raid, that twilight zone where, Jack honestly noted, most raids were initiated. Of course they allowed commanders below HQ level to make a name for themselves as well.

Once a raid was mooted, volunteers were called for. Cooper remembers his colonel addressing the men and offering two weeks' rest and the chance of decorations. Ignorance, a desire for excitement in an action over in minutes, a ruthlessly short-term view or close links between pals never failed to fill the quota. Once gathered, the men would all adopt the uniform of privates, concealing rank badges beneath the coat collar. Faces were blackened so as to be able to tell friend from foe, then coshes, knives, sharpened bayonets, pistols and haversacks of bombs filled the hands of the gangsters.

Early raids were organized more like night raids on dormitories in public schools than serious exercises of war. In the collected papers of staff officer Major Barber, a raid on the Somme in February 1916 was planned on three sides of paper in a field notebook. The simplicity could be alarming. Cloete remembered men being sent on a night raid with a harvest moon shining. Feilding described a similar piece of lunacy at Kemmel in February 1917:

At 7.17 am three parties containing nine officers and 190 Other Ranks made a wild dash across no-man's-land without any preliminary bombardment. At the same moment our artillery opened up with a box barrage round the selected trench section to cut off reinforcements. But the wire was not cut. Private John Collins rushed recklessly towards the German trenches, shouting, 'Come on the Connaughts' – a cry which the enemy took up. Sergeant Elwin stood up and fired his rifle at the enemy until he fell shot through the neck. The enemy now began freely to expose themselves. After two hours' firing, all was quiet.

Professionalism increased as the war extended itself. By July 1918 Major Barber's file showed raids being planned on thirteen sides of close-packed foolscap. The ground had been photographed, maps issued with mortars and machine-guns precisely placed, with fields of fire laid down and timings given. Mine galleries would be dug and wire pre-cut. Timetables were worked out in intricate detail so that grenades, gas cylinders, medical stores, signalling apparatus and all the other bits and pieces would be readily available in sufficient quantities. Final aerial photos would be studied at length in order to notify the men of any last-minute changes. The men meanwhile would have been rehearsing for days, going over and over ground chosen as being as near as possible to the real thing. Flags and ploughed lines, drum rolls for machine-guns would simulate reality. The action needed to become reflex for, as Grant observed, during the raid 'everything became blurred though it was probably the most exciting moment one has ever had'.

After all the preparations, the raid might be a success. Herd was involved in a successful raid at Hooge, in which two German officers in British uniform were captured and their wine, cheese, coffee and cigars taken from deep dugouts. Germans on their knees, holding bibles and crucifixes, were taken prisoner. For all this, Herd and his men were promised six days' home leave by Allenby personally. This concession was the trademark of success for, if a raid were driven off and no identifications secured, no reward was given. As a postscript Herd wrote that, of the 650 men involved in the raid, just 194 returned safely.

Casualty figures could be much higher even than this, because the basic idea behind the raid was wrong. In a territorial war the very existence of no-man's-land showed that a war was going on, for if ascendancy on any scale had been achieved then either a war of movement would have resulted, or the war would have been over. No-man's-land stood for a balance between two forces, an area into which either side was committed to applying maximum force if threatened – and a raid from one side could only be the application of a very slender force. Indeed the more raids there were, the more difficult further raids would be, given the increase in snipers, mortars and counter-raids on the other side.

Lane, like many others in the ranks, could remember only one successful raid during his two years at the front. I made a quick check on 4th Army records for the four months before the Somme. Fifteen raids were listed, of which seven were scored as successful. Bearing in mind the smugness of such sources, their tendency to exaggerate here and forget there, the impression of failure is clear.

Even in well-prepared raids, so much could go wrong. That elaborate raid noted by Barber at Hamel on 8 June was given away when machine-gunners opened up fifteen seconds early. Chaos ensued, completed by two of our eighteen pounders firing short into our own men. Captain Peard wrote bitterly of a raid in which the tape layers got stuck in their own wire so that the raiders lost contact with each other. He was himself machine-gunned and fell first into a saphead filled with barbed wire, then dived into a shellhole filled with water. One raid I came across went wrong when a subaltern forgot to distinguish between true and magnetic north on his compass and led all his men into unbroken wire where they were all cut down. No raid better illustrates the futility than the one described by Rees at Hooge just before 3rd Ypres. Just before the start, he noticed that the Germans were shelling their own front line. Reasoning that they must have got wind of what was to come and pulled back, Rees contacted his HQ. Since a creeping barrage of 300 guns was planned, HQ replied that it was too late to alter arrangements. At the end no prisoners were taken and casualty figures were never posted. The divisional history states that 'there were no incidents of special importance on the divisional front' that day.

Civilians contemplating trench war today would tend to think of it largely in terms of artillery and sniping action, raids and patrols. When the old soldier looks back over the years to his trench duty, however, he remembers clearly how seldom these actions interrupted the prolonged inactivity. To him, the real enemy was the weather and the side-effects of living rough.

Cold was perhaps the greatest enemy. A man might wear long-johns, thick socks, wool vest and greyback, knitted cardigan and sheepskin jerkin, but still the cold seeped through. Though a man doubled his vests and added newspapers and oiled waistcoats, it seemed to make no difference. All winters were longer than city men could grasp and all nights colder just before the dawn than they would ever have guessed, judging by the physical distance from the south of England. During the winter of 1917, when there was one degree of frost in London, there were fifteen in Arras. Hot tea froze in minutes and bully beef became chunks of red ice. Bread acquired a sour taste and boots froze solid in seconds if they were taken off. Ellison felt after that winter that he would never be warm again: 'The cold crept under our clothes, our fingers and joints ached with it; it seemed to congeal our blood and kill the very marrow of the bones. Fires of any kind were impossible so we were obliged to rely on stamping and arm flapping. It was several weeks before I fully regained conscious possession of my toes.' Rickson during 3rd Ypres, like Ellison, wrote that he thought he would never be warm again, likewise Bartlett, crossing the old Somme battlefield during the winter of 1918.

Though these winters gave the men the most prolonged experience of cold, each night tested the men. Wrote Drinkwater: 'Anyone who has not stood all night in a muddy trench with sodden clothing cannot know the sheer ecstasy of the first gleam of sunshine. To feel its warmth penetrating one's chilled bones is something beyond my power to describe.'

Mud, like cold, enveloped men of the front line. As a farm labourer at 'Akenfield', Davie was a man used to hardship, but he was in no doubt about the importance of mud. 'Did you kill men, Davie?' 'I got several.' 'What was the worst, Davie?' 'Why, the wet of course.' Where rain met bare earth or shelled earth, it spawned feet of mud. Boyd Orr reckoned that forty Englishmen a night were drowned in it. Nicholson on the Somme saw a man stuck fast for sixty-five hours, with two men pulling on ropes finally freeing him though with his clothing sucked down by the mud. Against mud of this quantity and depth, little could be done. Smith lamented: 'Puttees do not prevent mud from getting into your boots if you sink in ten inches or so. Mackintosh and overcoat get saturated with mud, both inside and out. My writing paper and shirt are the only dry things I possess.' Perhaps the best counter-measure was the boot, gum, thigh. The drawback was that it gave little grip on duckboards, while it steamed and wrinkled the skin in preparation for trench feet.

Living next to the earth and the mud, vermin were inescapable. There were beetles, ants, caterpillars, greenfly and mosquitoes which could blow up a man's face to the size of a football, but lice were the greatest tribulation. Writing during a European war 300 years earlier, Simplicissimus had described soldiers seizing handfuls of lice from their bodies. In the Great War lice were the common possession of all. Sitting on a box latrine in rest, Abraham once counted 103 on his clothes and body. They looked like little translucent lobsters and fed twelve times daily by holding onto clothing fibres with their six feet as they drank blood. They laid five eggs daily, which looked like tiny grains of rice on the seams of garments, and these lice were hard to remove, since they could survive on just one blood meal in ten days while their eggs could resist all cold.

The injury lice did was largely in the mind. Sent from the front to Bradford war hospital, Gibbons wept when he found that he had not escaped from lice. Nevertheless the physical side was unpleasant, for the lice could be felt moving about and men could become so sensitive that, after a fortnight of infestation, each bite could be felt. Scratching, in the filthy conditions of trench life, risked boils, impetigo or ulcers particularly around shoulders and waist where clothing was closest to skin and activity most vigorous.

Some counter-measures were possible. Thumb nails were used to crack visible lice followed by a candle run up the seams of garments. The art was to coagulate the blood of the louse without burning a hole in the shirt. First came the outside seams, then the inside, followed by a once over. 'Crumbing up' was a highly social activity and took a couple of hours with much ribald comment and black humour. The lice were known as mickies, cooties or chats and, from this, 'chatting' has remained in our social vocabulary. Patent chemical cures might be handed round from out of parcels from home. Harrison's Pomade at $4\frac{1}{2}d.$ or $9d.$ went under the slogan, 'Kill that insect, Tommy!' Since it was designed as a specific against children's head lice, the body lice of the front line were only marginally deterred. Keating's powder was another favourite. 'Tykes the ginger out of 'em. Mine ain't near so lively arter you strafe 'em with this 'ere powder.' But in the end the only real check was the army laundry service and even this worked only for a time if all clothes were treated. In April 1918 the *British Medical Journal* came to the pessimistic conclusion that a 2 per cent lysol–creosol solution at fifty degrees Fahrenheit used for twenty minutes was 'quite effective'.

The soldiers' hatred of rats came second only to their loathing of lice. Just as on farms, when cats have enteritis, the rat population explodes, so on the west front, where cats were absent, surplus food liberally dropped and corpses lying in plenty, rats multiplied with amazing fertility. They were most numerous back at rest, though the price they paid for better feeding was being hunted more frequently. Cordite might be put down holes by bored soldiers, while packs of ferrets with a sheepdog at longstop backed by men with clubs were not unknown. Yankee physician Cushing commented that 'the British soldier doted on a sporting event'. In the trenches rats might go through bully beef remnants under duckboards or burrow through packs in dugouts. Cook remembered kicking rats every two paces in reserve trenches at Mesnil, and men slept in overcoats and puttees and reckoned to kill thirty a night each. Generally, however, rats preferred parapet sandbags to trenches and would burrow in the dead rather than risk the retribution of the living.

Most men never got used to rats but, as with any hated enemy, humour could reinforce group dislike and prevent the hatred from becoming obsessional. Today many memoirs relate rat stories with relish. Bland described an old stager called 'Georgie'. Cheese was put in the candlelight for thirty minutes while a revolver awaited Georgie's appearance. As soon as Bland turned his back for a second, the cheese was gone. One man saw his copy of the weekly *Times* disappearing down a rathole. MacDougall described 'a mouse known as Peter, a rat called Dawson and a cat called Michael in our dugout. The mouse lives just behind my head, the rat under the table and the cat in the roof. A feud goes on all day between the rat and the mouse but the cat takes the part of America.' One hears of rats as big as cats, of rats with bare patches of skin, of sneezing and snuffling rats, but all were regarded with aversion and only poison gas could deal with them effectively – for a short time.

Gas again was the only cure for the fly. Six thousand horses in an infantry division produced forty tons of manure daily and provided a breeding ground at an ideal temperature for these flies. The noise of them on a battlefield might even drown the noise of an approaching shell. Chandos once counted thirty-two dead flies in his shaving water and seventy-two from his shoulder to his wrist. Officers would send home for flypaper, but the quantity of the creature beat all human stratagems.

The cumulative weight of cold and wet, vermin and poor diet, meant a big sickness list. Infectious diseases like measles, diphtheria or mumps occurred only in the same proportion as among civilians, but most other diseases multiplied. A comparison between 1914 and 1915 shows how lengthening exposure brought more hospital admissions (figures are for incidence per 1,000 men):

bad teeth	1914: 13	1915: 41
breathing	24	52
digestion	56	114
frostbite	34	38
flu	0	75

The hospital admission list for 1917 shows how many casualties were claimed, unrelated to enemy action:

anthrax	8 admissions
dysentery	6,025
enteric	1,275
frostbite	21,487
meningitis	692
nephritis	15,214
pneumonia	2,157
tuberculosis	1,660
VD	48,508

It must be remembered that those entering hospital were only the most severe cases, since all but those actually collapsing would receive just a brisk aperient known as a number nine pill – 'medicine and duty', the cant formula. If men were worse, the army's next line of attack was punishment of the sick, just as in Samuel Butler's *Erewhon*. An example of this was the treatment of trench foot. The combination of a poorly fitting boot, alternate freezing and thawing, the standing for long periods in freezing water and the lack of exercise would produce a blue and inert foot and might even turn to gangrene. During the war over 70,000 men were classified and three-quarters had to go back to base for a time. The army made the disease a crime and insisted on regular bathing with whale oil, a stinking substance more often used as rifle oil or as fuel for trench stoves. Trench fever sufferers, which after the war proved to be a real affliction like typhus and spread by the excreta of infected lice, were put under a punitive regime in hospital. So too were sufferers from scabies, which by the end of the war was responsible for filling 6 per cent of hospital beds. The villain was the itch mite, which laid eggs under the skin, but the army suspected skrimshanking so imposed a 6.30 am parade for sulphur baths and a starvation diet as part of the 'cure'.

After the cold and wet, the vermin and the disease, there remained one last force to bludgeon a front-line soldier. It was a force so much taken for granted that many memoirs don't even give it mention. This was the mental depression and physical sluggishness which came from lack of sleep combined with a total lack of information, which added to the lack of a sense of purpose.

Speaking to Lady Shelley, Wellington had observed in an earlier war that 'nothing wears out the troops so effectively' as bivouacking, sleeping rough. In the front line of the Great War all Other Ranks slept in that manner. Officers usually slept in dugouts; the most the men could hope for were sub-parapet cubbyholes supported by official-issue wooden frames five feet high and four deep. Knees would be used as a pillow with legs safe from passers-by and a groundsheet giving some privacy. Probably the occupants would sleep in threes and take it in turn to be in the middle. At the back of the mind, though, was always the thought that a shell or mortar might bury one alive, while sentry-go prevented any sustained sleep and no arrangement of clothing could keep out the chilling cold of the early morning.

Griffith wrote:

To lie down for two hours on a plank half sinking into a dream-ridden sleep, half hearing every noise within reach of audibility, there was little rest of body or mind. On such a bed, flesh was no protection to the bones; it was a small envelope containing a jumble of crossing nerves. Bone pressed down and wood pressed up until the sting changed slowly into a dragging pain. Getting up was a process of re-assembling the members. Arms were stiff though near at hand. Legs had travelled further from control but feet were far away in a distant land. A queer lightness in the knees enhanced the weight of the foot. A waking man was a slack-stringed fiddle to be tuned up peg by peg into the full tension of self-command.

The cumulative effect of such rest was to wear a man down without break. Hitchcock thought lack of sleep the greatest strain in his own war, while Saunders was barely saved from a court martial when caught asleep on sentry. Only an alert corporal saved him by saying that he had lent Saunders a pencil just a few seconds earlier. 'I was tired. Dear God, how tired I was; we all were. We had been on duty for three days and nights. My limbs felt like aching cotton wool, my eyes smarted and I sat for a moment on the firestep. It was a real physical effort to keep awake. I felt I would barter my soul for a few hours of uninterrupted slumber.' Little wonder that Jack, fresh from his dugout, was so startled by the rankers' capacity for sleep at every moment and in the queerest places.

The effect of constant sleeplessness on a man may well have been more than just the sense of physical discomfort. All modern experiments on sleep deprivation show that the subject begins thinking irrationally and appears to have his dominant characteristics diluted – in short, becomes grey, sluggish and unpredictable. The reversal of day and night activity patterns would add to the problem, since any night shift worker knows how long it takes to adapt.

If sleeplessness gave to a man a Kafka-like sense of unreality and de-personalization, then his submergence in trenches could only add to it. Day and night merged and periods of time came to be delineated by meals, just as on a ship at sea. MacBride lost fourteen days in one tour of duty and only found them afterwards by working painfully back through a diary. During the German retreat of 1917 Bailey wrote in his diary speculatively that it must be April, since the primroses were in bloom. With his head below ground level, of necessity, a man might as well have been fighting in Kent or China. Even today old soldiers look on maps of northern France with surprise, as if the west front were a state of mind or a residue of experiences rather than a geographical location. All are surprised at the relative positions of towns and villages, for the army was totally cut off from time for spasms in the trenches, then moved at funereal pace on foot after intense preparation and deliberation, multiplying distances by ten and abstracting direction, since so few men had compasses. Even if men did change front, the same routine and attitudes and lack of purpose awaited him. Moran wrote of 'the awful sameness of those years of trench warfare'. Only at HQ did the war make sense. There all the threads came together. Newspapers were censored, the divisional newssheet was heavily loaded with bromide, and most men anyway only read 6d. novelettes by Elinor Glyn, Charles Garvice and the like. Rumours might fill part of the vacuum but more generally men subsided in pessimism. Major Barber once summarized a battalion commanders' conference of May 1917 '. . . stimulating details for the men? . . . whether they would take any interest in them if they got more? . . . chief interest of the men is when they are going to be relieved'. It was only in the Second World War, when subalterns became generals, that the physical comforts of the men were taken care of adequately and the importance of motivation by information supply was realized.

Set against this gloomy and lengthy list of discomforts and terrors, did the front-line soldier have any pleasures or comforts in his front-line service?

The prime comfort was food. Tea might be drummed up at any time. A two-inch candle in a bully-beef tin would boil water in a quarter of an hour, while a cigarette tin with whale oil for fuel and rifle flannelette for a wick would do the same in double the time. By 1916, Herd reckoned, most men had a commercial primus with them, so that sergeant-major's tea, sweet and strong, was in constant supply. Food was a different matter. By the end of 1915 company cookers were often in support with a ration party drawing rations daily. Dry rations would be put in sandbags. Tea and sugar would be shaken into separate corners and crudely tied in place. Tins of jam, Maconochie stew and bully beef would be added with bread and mail on the top. A label would indicate the trench section and there would be wet rations – stew and porridge – in screwtop containers strapped to men's backs. Men looked forward to an arrival, which would guarantee a breakfast of half a round of biscuit, a loaf between three, tin of butter between nine, tin of jam between six and half a mug of tea each. Lunch could be a Maconochie to four with half a biscuit and half a mug of tea. Tea would be two thick rounds of bread and jam with half a mug of tea, no milk.

This was the theory. Reality tended to break down in the last link. Transport vagaries, mud and enemy artillery action were all variables which might interfere with supply behind the trench line. Even in the final carry, bearers might fall into shellholes, adding the flavour of chemicals, excrement and dead bodies as garnish. Tea, cheese and meat would mix remarkably in wet weather. Tins shared between groups stretched gossamer thin unless heavy casualties increased the ration. Bully and biscuits would produce such a thirst that half mugs of tea were insufficient; the water anyway came in tins and was saturated with petrol and lime chloride. Men might improvise with shellhole water strained through a handkerchief, but the practice was not without peril. Harrison wrote of using the water of a particular hole for days until a dead German was pulled out from its depths. Food was thus always a hope and a joy, an improvisation and a scarcity, yet at its worst it provided a moment of good memories and companionship in the trench routine.

Rum was a more reliable pleasure. Out of the line, the brigadier might issue rum on the advice of a medical officer if the weather was deemed officially inclement. In the line, rum was certain on stand-down at dawn. It was issued in half-gill units out of an earthenware jar marked SRD (service rum diluted) and carried like the ark of the covenant through the trenches. It had to be consumed in the presence of an officer so that pooling was avoided. This thimbleful of rum was unlike the domesticated apology served today as 'rum'. Burning the throat, it half choked the soldier and made his eyes tear violently. 'It did go down good. Every shot seemed to warm a blood vessel and circulate the blood round the body.' Abraham termed it sunshine administered internally. Worden described the miraculous rejuvenation of one teaspoonful turning sullen and cursing men into a whistling, buzzing group in minutes. As a temporary restorative in time of stress, it was without rival. MacBride thought it the concentrated essence of army council wisdom. It showed the army's intimate concern with individual welfare, mediating between its own more obscure demands and their necessity. It was gain, too, at little loss, for the quantity was insufficient to corrupt the morals of a louse – as one grousing old private soldier remarked. Things could go wrong, however, as they did in one section on 1 July on the Somme, where a double ration was issued just before the advance. On the other hand, Cook remembered serving at 'the Bluff' early in 1916 under a teetotal quartermaster, who issued dry pea-soup powder instead of rum before action.

Supplementing food and rum were a host of minor comforts. Cigarettes would be stuffed in every pocket, haversack and gasmask holder so that there would always be a 'nob end' behind a man's ear to give two draws and a spit after stand-down and on any emergency. Most men too would have a sandbag among their effects. Its use epitomized the domestication of the intolerable. Extra tea, chocolate and biscuits would be carried up the line in it. It would cover the legs in cold or wet weather or reduce the glint on helmets when stretched over the surface. Out of the line, it would hold all the goodies and souvenirs which men could collect for sale in the back areas. Newspapers at home carried advertisements for various items which might be sent out to France and carried in a spare corner of a haversack. A drum of cigars or silver-plated Gillette razor in a morocco case with a dozen blades (21s.); a silver indelible propelling pencil (10s. 6d.) or Lotus waterproof boots (35s.); John Bull's upside-down pipe (2s. 9d.), said to be proof against sniper observation; trench quoits at 5s. 6d. or a solid-fuel Tommy cooker for a quick brew-up with 100 usings from four refills, weighing just 4½ lb. and ten inches square; Veno's trench cough medicine (11½d.) or Dr Cassell's tablets, 'most economical' and a sure specific against shellshock (3s.). Though never carrying the art of adaptation to the extent that the French soldier, that travelling tinker, did, nevertheless the Kitchener soldiers carried themselves with the condemned man's disregard for inessentials in that zone of high explosive where even King's Regulations took shelter.

A rare luxury but much regarded if available was the wherewithal for a wash and brush up. Some front lines had standpipes, but the most that could be hoped for was a two-gallon tin sent up from reserve. This would serve to clean forty men, the last few salvaging what comfort they could from the semi-solid mass. At a pinch, shellhole water could be heated on a Tommy cooker for shaving. But for the most part the men of the front line had to live with dirt, and the more so since the latrine sap looked so like a mortar position from the air that men preferred to use a pail or helmet and toss the material into no-man's-land when NCOs' backs were turned. Men in war seem to have an irrational fear of being under fire with their trousers down. For paper, the continental *Daily Mail* was ideal, but more often a handful of grass or the tail of a shirt would have to do duty. British troops were later to be astonished when the Americans arrived, to see toilet rolls not only standard issue but soft tissue at that. Such levity and comfort was not for Other Ranks in Kitchener's army.

The final minor pleasure of trench life came from nature for some. Animals had a particular place as pets in a zone destitute of women and children and those situations in which a man might reassure himself of the gentler side of his nature. Cats were easily domesticated and abundant in supply in a region of derelict farms. Lucy recalled a particular major who always carried a kitten in his pocket and held up the war whenever the mite wished to relieve itself. Some men would bring hardy terriers with them, but generally the dogs stood shelling much worse than the cats and so were kept back at the horse lines. Birds gave pleasure to most. The bared soil rich in nitrates from shelling and free from the attention of farmers produced a vast crop of plants, particularly of cornflowers and poppies. Attracting insects, these flowers brought birds in their wake. A letter in the *Daily Express* (27 October 1918) noted sixty species within two miles of Péronne. The resilience of these birds gave men hope, and the press published a succession of letters, like *The Times* (2 March 1916), which noted a nightingale nesting in the front line at Hooge. A nightingale sang on the Ancre three days after a mustard attack (16 June 1918) with comment from the *Guardian*. The *Daily Express* (5 May 1916) published a letter describing a blackbird laying four eggs and bringing up its young in the guts of a heavy gun in constant use. However harsh the barrage, birds never missed the dawn chorus. Drinkwater remembered a column of men moving up the line on the Somme involuntarily stopping to listen to a nightingale: 'It was the first decent thing we had heard for a long time. There was something infinitely sweet and sad about it, as if the countryside were singing gently to itself. One felt as if the nightingale's song was the only real thing which would remain when all the rest was long passed.' In this way birds, like men, abstracted what decency and normalcy there was from living conditions all but intolerable.

Trench life was an enduring memory for all men. Returning years later to a section of front he knew well, Mottram was able to pick out the exact position of a trench.

I feel with one foot for the sandbag step by which one used to descend into the support line. Against my right hand should be the board that directed one to the gas gong and, just in front of my knees, I peer for those cracks of light that used to shine around the edges of the groundsheet or blanket that marked the entry to the dugout. My ears strained for the tip-tap of the machine-gun, for the creaking rumbling that preceded big shells, the instantaneous hiss that accompanied the detonations of the small ones. If only the sound for which I wait and the searching odour of waterlogged decay and chemicals were present, I should step forward confidently onto the duckboard and grope for the sill of the dugout. Framed in those dubious wooden props and sweating walls, lit by a candle stuck in a bottle, the flame of which shivers now and then with the vibrations of the great guns, they crouch round the table. Amidst printed army forms and revolver cartridges they are playing cards or sitting, not looking at each other, waiting for an order for some minor operation that must be a death sentence for one or other of them. If they are writing home, I shall not look at them, for then their stolid, good-humoured English faces will drop their mask of good form and they will show how deeply they care for all they have left behind. I hope rather that they will have got a gramophone to this place, for then their eyes will shine and tobacco smoke wreathe, the disc grinding out 'Any old night is a wonderful night if you're out with a wonderful girl'. The irony of it all is unintentional. No, we shall never be able to forget.

The eyes of former Other Ranks who read this may smile at the luxuries available only to one-pip officers, but the visual memory of life from a front-line cubby-hole remains for each man as for Mottram. Memories return to the end of life with the sharp detail of a finely drawn lithograph, for men remember vignettes of their war with spasms of almost physical buffeting. The trenches where they endured and suffered so much provide many of the etched details.

7

THE WEAPONS OF TRENCH WARFARE

The Great War was the first war in which there was no close season. In the war zone, noise was incessant. From distant base camps men might hear the dull boom of the howitzers if the wind was in the right quarter. Then conversation would abruptly end as men listened anxiously. Their awareness was more of a compressed air punch on the ear drum than of a sound, the source distant as fear in childhood memories. Later, as men went up to the front, so the minor parts in the great orchestral show would be filled in progressively and added to the bass of the big guns. First would come the tenor of lighter artillery pieces assorted in drum fire. Then in the front line the typewriter clacking of machine-guns, the bonfire crackling of rifles and the hacking cough of grenades. Infantrymen would survey the panorama of sound with an attitude mixed with one part of curiosity, one of despair and eight of anxiety. They well knew that each sound could be translated into personal mutilation, and they grappled endlessly with a calculation of probability that never resolved itself except in doubt.

The infantryman's defences were limited to two personal weapons – the rifle and the grenade.

The Lee Enfield rifle was much valued as a symbol of security, an assurance that a man's fate was to a degree in his own hands. Veterans today still remember their rifle numbers, inscribed on a brass plate in the stock. The greatest taboo of all in the front line was against taking a rifle or rifle bolt, whatever else might be 'won'.

The final version of the Lee Enfield was a fine piece of engineering, weighing just over 9 lb. and fitted with magazines of ten bullets, reliable enough to carry on through the Second World War though conceived basically as a cavalry carbine during the Boer war. With careful handling, such a rifle might well have seen a man through his war service. Indeed careful handling was almost guaranteed by the frequency and rigour of rifle inspections. Since the weapon was composed of 131 separate parts, a soldier was under the strictest orders to touch no part of the body of the rifle, just to keep the barrel clear. The twin dangers here were that trench mud might get baked hard in the bore or that the bolt might become overheated and seize up. For this reason men would cover the muzzle and bolt with customized canvas, a sandbag or even an old sock. Rifle oil carried in the stock would be applied constantly, with bacon fat used if oil was not available. What most interested an NCO in rifle inspection was fouling white streaks from the bullet or pitting by heat erosion. To combat this wear, boiling water would be poured from breach to muzzle, followed by oil eased through by the four-by-two-inch rag pulled through by the weighted coil stored in the butt. This would also be done ideally after every use, to deal with combustion soot while the barrel was still warm.

Used by an expert, the rifle was a precision tool. The amateur soldier Cloete reckoned himself able to hit a five-centime piece at thirty yards with six bullets in ten at rapid fire, while official ballistic ranges thought distances up to 600 yards close fire – up to 1,400 yards effective fire.

There were several good reasons, however, for the ineffectiveness of most rifle fire at any distance. Firstly, the traditional policy of the army had been devised for colonial conditions, in which rapid collective fire to produce a wide beaten zone was the best counter to running hordes of Sikhs or Ashantis. Where the Germans attacked in that manner, 1st Ypres for example, they had been shot down as effectively as third-world warriors. Therefore the aim of producing men who could fire eighteen rounds in a minute like the men of the old expeditionary force was long pursued. The concept of accuracy was secondary.

Secondly, the mental and manual skills to fire as complex a weapon as the Lee Enfield would be thinly distributed in a randomly selected group of civilians. Oil in the barrel would throw the first shot wide. In still air a bullet would drift to the left, up to seven feet at 1,400 yards. The lightest breeze would add six feet at 1,000 yards, while rain would make the bullet fly high. Then there was the problem of range. Instructors laid down that, at fifty yards, mouth and eyes could be seen; dots for eyes at 100 yards; faces indistinct at 300 yards; head and hat seen separately at 500 yards, and so on. Few German heads ever presented themselves for long enough to judge whether head and hat were separate, and if the sights were set meanwhile it was an unusual and indiscreet head which appeared again at the same spot to be shot at.

Finally, the conditions of trench warfare (which stuck men in holes for long periods, limited training sessions and hid the enemy in his role as a target) tended to produce a generation of riflemen who, in the opinion of Croft, would have been outshot by the archers of Crécy. Boche at 200 yards he considered pretty safe except in the early days of the war.

The infantryman's experience of rifle fire came largely from sniping and was the more alarming because no evasive measures could be taken. The bullet came at a speed of nearly a mile per two seconds, twice the speed of sound, so, if heard, the danger was over. Men might learn not to duck, but this only seemed to produce a worse feeling of danger. And what a range of sounds there were. From the longest range they made a buzzing sound as if someone had thrown a spinning safety match. In the open a bullet made a steady phew-phew-phew sound. If the bullet flicked foliage, men would gasp at the sensation of speed and wonder what it would be like to be in the bullet's path. Swishing meant crossfire; whining a spinning ricochet. The most dangerous was the brief roar of a near miss. It was just like a violin string breaking, followed by the report of the rifle firing it, like a popping champagne cork.

If a man was hit, there was often little bleeding, just a bluish aperture with spots of blood. Spin would produce much bruising and contusion but again little bleeding, for shock reduced blood pressure and crushed blood-vessels would be self-sealing. The irregular motion of ricochets, the long-range wobbles of spent bullets or snipers' close-range work were a different matter. The *British Medical Journal* already in the first month of the war was noting five-by-three-inch entry holes made by sniper bullets. The wounds of such bullets could break the nerve of onlookers. Carrington tells us:

> Pratt was hopeless. His head was shattered. Splatterings of brain lay in a pool under him, but he refused to die. Old Corporal Welch looked after him, held his body and arms as they writhed and fought feebly as he lay. It was over two hours before he died, hours of July sunshine in a crowded place where perhaps a dozen men sat with the smell of blood while all the time above the soothing voice of the corporal came a gurgling and moaning from his lips, now high and liquid, now low and dry – a death rattle fit for the most bloodthirsty novelist.

In battle the twenty-one-inch sword bayonet would be added to the rifle. It had been conceived in the seventeenth century in case cavalry should get near the rifleman, whose musket in those days had too slow a rate of fire to stop enemy at close range. For most of the Great War it was simply an anachronism, useful as a toasting fork, biscuit slicer or intimidator of prisoners. In the confined space of a trench it was as likely to wound friend as enemy. Attached to a rifle, its additional weight made fire calculations more difficult. General Harper at the time and Brigadier Essame today insist that 'no man in the Great War was ever killed by a bayonet unless he had his hands up first'. This was not just a matter of clumsiness for, if there was a chance of escape, few would fight at close quarters with cold steel. The imagination was too lively to contemplate coolly a stand-up with bread knives at close quarters. But the memoirs of front-line men give the lie to the confident assertions of generals. At night, in fog, in a wood or whenever surprise and difficulty of escape coincided, bayonets were used and often. Depth of incision left few survivors, though, if a man was not killed initially, he stood a fair chance of surviving if a dry bandage was applied. Letter-writers describe the sensation of bayoneting as being like inserting a knife point first into butter, the only problem being that of extricating the blade, since skin and muscle closed on the knife. Thus the half twist which men in training were taught.

The other weapon available to the front-line soldier was the grenade. Much used by the British army up to the 1870s, grenades had then been phased out so that, when the Great War began, men had had to improvise grenades from jam tins – 'Tickler's artillery' – or from slabs of guncotton wrapped around detonator and six-inch nails – 'the hairbrush bomb'. But after the Heath Robinson days came the Mills grenade in late 1915. By the end of the war some seventy-five million of these had been thrown, and they had come to replace the rifle in the infantryman's mind as the chief offensive weapon. With a range of forty yards at most, a German seen in the open a hundred yards off was more likely to have a grenade thrown at him than a rifle bullet, for so long a period of trench and hole fighting produced a howitzer rather than a horizontal mentality.

Though all men in action could stuff tunic pockets with grenades, the specialists were hand-picked. The chief criterion seems to have been the nuisance these men would have been if left in the ranks. Parkes recalled being enrolled after he had used a bomb bandolier as a windbreak while drumming up tea. Initial training was to throw jam tins of mud while others were doing fatigues or rifle drill. Were there any threats to make bombers do such monotonous work, the reply would be fumbled or dropped grenades, with officious NCOs beating a rapid retreat. The final touches to the craft of throwing grenades would be imparted in a five-day course. Astonished men found out that an explosion represented the trans-formation of a solid into a gas occupying greater space, that ammonal was bullet proof, and so on. Grenade care was more practical. The bomb was to be held in the left hand and the base plug unscrewed to be put in the trouser pocket. With detonator in hand, the pin was to be checked for rust then oiled. Detonator was then to be held between thumb and trigger finger, clasped by the fuse and put gently into its small hole, the cap fitted, then the base plug returned to its place. This action always remained tricky, so men worked in small groups with plenty of space or deep trench bays between them. Greenwell records an RSM blown up by a grenade which detonated instantly. Fielding saw a man with his forearms blown off take twenty minutes to die. Parker wrote of Private Hoare dropping a grenade while adjusting his puttees and wounding forty men. Such a weapon was not to be taken lightly, and fighting soldiers always counted precisely the five and a half seconds taken to detonation after releasing the lever.

With this limited hitting power in his hands, the infantryman was further supported in the front line by Lewis guns, machine-guns and trench mortars.

Weighing just twenty-six lb. and fifty inches long, the Lewis gun was more a rifle than a machine-gun. Light in weight, compact and without recoil, a strong man could fire it from the shoulder. If the trigger was quickly squeezed, one shot was fired. If the trigger was held, it fired just so long as ammunition was left in the magazine with its forty-seven-shot capacity. In skilled hands, and with no jamming, 550 rounds could be fired in a minute. With four of these weapons per company by 1917, such a weapon gave great stopping power to the front line. The amount of confidence it gave to foot soldiers was another matter. In some ways it was a good enough piece of engineering to last to the Second World War. With just half as many parts as the rifle, it needed no adjustment. Being air-cooled, it required no spare barrel. The trouble was that the gun jammed alarmingly easily if there was mud about – and mud was not altogether unknown on the west front. Furthermore the weapon required great stocks of heavy ammunition. Six men with great bags of the cartridge pans were needed to keep the gun operational in action. These were considerable handicaps.

The standard machine-gun was a very different weapon. Its firing team would have carefully tested its springs before action, packed each of the 250 bullet belts by hand and fired one belt into a shell-hole to test both ammunition and gun, so that the gun could be brought into action within four seconds of an alarm. Once on its tripod, the brass tag of a belt would be pushed through the feed block, the crank handle twice pulled, the rear sight flicked up, then continuous action would begin. Graphs would previously have devised the cone of fire, quadrant elevation tables would have been applied together with slide rules by the machine-gun officer, so that the pre-set weapon would sweep an enemy parapet like a broom, or pile lead into a pre-arranged gap in the wire. This rather than speed of fire was the trump card of the machine-gun – accuracy. On its tripod the machine-gun became a nerveless weapon; the human factor of chattering teeth, dripping sweat and faeces in a man's pants was eliminated. A terror-stricken man could fire his machine-gun accurately even by night. Moreover the weapon, though with the fire power of fifty riflemen, occupied a front just two feet in length, and thus presented a minute target to enemy snipers or batteries. The end product was indisputable. Six machine-guns could hold up a brigade; one gun could halt two battalions before they had got 200 yards from their front line. In Liddell Hart's opinion it was the machine-gun above all other weapons which held the armies fast.

Certainly there were drawbacks. The weapon was costly in both money and men, for it cost £30 a minute to fire and needed sixteen men to sustain it. Its weight made it dangerously immobile, so that two guns had always to be working together, protected by infantry and with noise and flash muffled as well as possible. The problems of keeping up steady fire were substantial too. In practice the barrel needed to be changed after two belts unless the gun was to be sacrificed in an emergency. At any time faulty ammunition might jam the mechanism. The charge had to be precisely right to overcome the friction of the working parts, eject the empty case and reload the chamber. A fraction too much charge and the extractors were broken. Wet belts, badly filled belts, broken lock springs, broken condenser tubes, a sinking tripod, were all hazards to this intricate and temperamental weapon.

But the chief drawback from the English point of view was the lead that the Germans maintained in machine-gunnery throughout the war. After German observers had seen the power of this new weapon in the Russo-Japanese war of 1904, the Kaiser had ordered one gun per regiment and donated fourteen million marks to further research. Our Treasury in contrast had turned the weapon down in 1907 and, when a special school was established in 1914, the man in charge, Baker-Carr, admitted that he 'frankly and cordially disliked the weapon'. Even after the Somme the machine-gun never quite penetrated GHQ thinking. Booklets treated the Vickers and Lewis guns as synonymous and decided that both were 'weapons of opportunity', whatever that might mean, apart from being a reason for leaving automatic weapons out of all calculations. The machine-gun officer remained 'an adviser' in the division, and the machine-gun corps 'attached' men in excess of establishment. Meanwhile German guns cut our men down like swathes in a cornfield, sounding as harmless as the seeng-seeng-seeng of a canary, a curious metallic chirping.

The final weapon which assisted the front line from the front line was the mortar. Five hundred and forty-five mortar shells were fired by our men in 1914, six and a half million during 1916. The largest were 'toffee apples', spherical charges on a steel shaft three feet long and two inches thick, which came back like a boomerang when fired. The main ones, though, were Stokes mortars, named after the inventor, who had produced his weapon with a £20,000 grant from an Indian prince via Lloyd George. Costing only £40 per weapon, the mechanism was supremely simple. All a man had to do was to select a shell with a ballastite cartridge of the right colour, green for 300 yards and red for 450, drop it onto the spike at the base of the firing tube and his job was done. Such was the speed of fire that twenty-two shells could be fired in a minute, with eight in the air at any moment – pocket artillery indeed.

The mortar teams were taken from the odds and ends of the infantry and tended to get better rations with easier discipline. Luxuries could be hidden in the battery's handcart at the rear of a marching troop column. To be set against this were the dangers of crimping fuses in the early model of the gun, and the high priority which mortar teams enjoyed in the eyes of German artillery once they showed their hand. Their chosen positions were usually cut in the shape of an inverted E, with only two of the six in the team exposed at any moment in one bay with the gun. The gun would be laid with map and compass, a man glancing over the top to spot the ranging burst. Their position was most often in the support line, and their action initiated by a front-line request to pinpoint suspected sniper or machine-gun nests. Their relations with the infantry were therefore close despite suspicions that the mortar men blasted the enemy then scampered off, leaving the infantry to sample any retaliation.

The chief drawback of the mortar was that the enemy's version seemed more potent. Certainly it was larger in calibre. The German projectile was the size of a two-gallon oil drum loaded with 200 lb. of a wet, yellow paste, which smelt like marzipan and burst with a force that sent a wave through the soil for a mile, as if the soil had been water. The range was over 1,000 yards, and the crews were itinerant specialists. A typical mortar shoot from the enemy line would lay down one missile per ten yards at three-minute intervals. Sharp ears were needed for the whistles from the German line, which indicated firing preparedness. Then the canister would come, turning over and over in the air and making a 'woof, woof' sound. The leisurely descent was demoralizing, as observers shouted out their warnings and men made rapid dashes for safety before the final swerve to the right and a crater the size of a large living-room at the end of it.

Cooper echoed the feelings of most front-line men when he wrote that he never got used to mortars. 'I don't know why I'm shaking. I just can't help it.' Gillespie's mind went back to school cricket fields when he recalled fielding deep and waiting for skyers. Even when swallows swooped over the trench, he would duck, calling the reflex 'sausage eye', and involuntarily seeing his past life rising before him with every enemy shoot. Though there were a dozen bombardments for every mortar shoot, it was the feeling of exactness combined with the huge amount of explosive in each canister which triggered the fear. On the one hand was the sensation of cat playing with mouse; on the other, vivid images of bodies bursting and disintegrating.

Mortars completed the battery of offensive resources open to the front line. But surviving accounts of infantrymen mention them less frequently (or the enemy's counterpart) than shells and gas. In his own mind the soldier could never see his side making any impact on the war with their own front-line resources. The infantryman was object not subject. He saw himself as the rodent occupier of a pockmarked, grassless zone, whose forward limit was determined by the very limit of human endurance. What was he but the counter in a game, pushed this way or that according to the fluctuating balance of the explosives equation as if on a games board. Never was a man more aware of being that counter, that regimental number, whose reality he had never really accepted in training however much he might outwardly conform. To a greater degree than even in his youngest childhood, the order of life seemed beyond the comprehension of a soldier under barrage of gas and shells, the future greyer and more unthinkable, even if a man could gather himself to contemplate anything beyond survival.

The artillery, which destroyed the body and mind of the front line, was of two types; the gun, with its high muzzle velocity and flat trajectory, and the howitzer, firing a larger shell more slowly in a stately arc, niblick to the gun's driver. The early success of the German 5·9-inch howitzer, set against the superiority of the French 75 gun to the German 77, led to our men sampling the howitzer most frequently throughout the war. Since the keynote of the Great War was its static quality, a much heavier concentration of big guns was obtained than in the Second World War, where more rapid advances made heavy artillery pieces always liable to capture. Thus, for these two reasons, footsoldiers often came under the fire of guns of massive proportions. The German 420 (about 17 inches) gives an idea of what this might mean. The whole piece weighed twenty tons and was moved by nine tractors. The cutting and steel lining of the gunpit took four days. The gun itself took twelve men five minutes to load and fire, a light railway and crane getting the one-ton shell into position. Each shell went at 1,700 mph to a height of Mont Blanc, covered a distance of about six miles horizontally and made a crater large enough to enclose a house – as some of them still would on the Verdun battlefield, the large battlefield retained as a war memorial. The gun in comparison was a scalpel. Not until the instantaneous fuses of 1918 could it do the damage of a howitzer in a war of trenches. Instantaneous detonation with low lateral spread of fragments over 1,000 yards then solved the problem of mud. Before that, the gun was feared chiefly as a dispenser of shrapnel. With a puff of white smoke and a violent tearing sound, a cone 200 yards deep and thirty yards wide would smash over a line of men if the timing of the air burst had been judged correctly. Those

Hadfield shrapnel helmets which lie today on Somme fields with inch-square perforations show that shrapnel was always a danger and that the inclined head against a close shrapnel burst gave insufficient protection.

Artillery could be used in several patterns. The least feared were those shells which came over in bunches on the hour just to warn that the enemy was on his toes. A stage higher came those isolated shots intended for a particular spot. Aerial photography and balloon observation meant that each side had detailed maps of the other side which noted every sandbag, pump nozzle, mortar pit and latrine. If hostile action was suspected, then these sensitive spots would be saturated. At the highest level were the great barrages. One field gun per ten yards, and heavies every twenty, was found to be the soundest all-purpose concentration by the middle of the war – used again by the Russians in the battle of Berlin in 1945.

The agony of the men being shelled began well before the explosion. The skilled ear picked out each gun, noted its calibre, the path of its shell and the likely explosion point. The small field gun went off with a crack like a fat man hitting a golf ball. The shell took off like a jet plane and arrived with a screaming shriek. A keen pair of eyes might pick out the fifteen-foot gunflash, blinding even as a flashlight in daytime. The medium artillery piece sounded like a giant newspaper being torn, its shell a farmcart coming down a steep hill with its brakes on. The heavy gun rapped a man's head with a heavy cane then rolled in a leisurely arc across the sky, a man on a bicycle whistling slowly and pensively. For a time the listener felt he could run beside it. Then it speeded up like an express train rushing down a tunnel. Shells passing over woods and valleys echoed. Shells falling in enclosed places came with a double bang and no warning. A near miss would whistle or roar, with debris raining down long after the burst. The strain of listening for all these sounds did something to the brain. A man could never be rid of them.

The effects of the explosion were bewilderingly varied. Keynes survived an eight-inch shell bursting ten yards away. Fleming-Bernard saw an eight-inch shell land on a waggon. Limber and horse were undamaged though the driver, a Bermondsey milk-float driver, went off his head. The battery papers were found 200 yards away in one direction, the case 150 yards away in the other direction.

Nicholson writes of the 51st on one occasion belaboured by 104 shells arriving at four per minute but only wounding one man.

Every soldier could tell such stories. The cushioning of mud, the petal-shaped blast pattern of shells, the fact that most gunners searched a map square blind rather than aim their fire accounted for many quirks. Nevertheless all men who nervously told such stories with a tone of calculated whimsy well knew how explosive and jagged shell casings tore the bodies of men. Almost three-quarters of wounds by the end of the war were shell wounds. Men knew too how enduring were the effects. The wounds almost always went septic because of the foreign matter taken into the body with the splinters. Low-velocity missiles like these fragments also caused more severe tissue damage than bullets, making a survivor vulnerable to gangrene. Even if a man avoided missiles, blast would cause death by concussion at ten yards. Kidneys and spleen would be ruptured, though there would be no surface marks on the body. Men who escaped scotfree would be left with souvenirs. Chandos injury recalled a near miss driving the air from his lungs, while face and hands felt chapped. Ernest Atkins wrote of nose and ear bleeding from a near burst, with earth particles driven into his skin.

There was infinitely more to shells than their capacity to do physical harm, for, according to almost every memoir of the Great War, shelling was the greatest inducer of fear. A night raid might pump more adrenalin into the blood, while soldiers new to the front might regard a shellburst as an exciting and interesting experience with an element of danger for others not so divinely favoured as themselves. Nevertheless the cumulative effect gave a man the quickest test of how well he was wearing.

If a man were unstable and ill-suited to war, whatever he might consciously think, a shellburst would most effectively prick the lie. Drury remembered an eighteen-year-old trembling for twenty-four hours after a dud dropped ten yards from him. Fielding recalled a young, keen and loquacious sniping officer clutching his arm by reflex, just like one of his own children might have done, as a shell passed close over head. Close bursts would with more reason shake a man's confidence in his invulnerability. There might be blackouts, blankness in willpower, numbness, a desire to sleep, an overwhelming need for a cigarette. Even the best-adjusted men might have trembling eyelids, shaking hands, nightmares or black moods to show the price they were paying for their self-control.

'I spent an hour or so dozing after putting my company into position,' wrote Christie. 'I woke up when our bombardment started and came out of my dugout trembling and able to talk only with difficulty. For a few minutes I was quite unable to control my nerves. Very curious as quite honestly I was not in the least frightened. If I could have moved I would probably have been cured at once. I felt a fool but it was purely outward and not inward. Anyway, it suddenly stopped.' It is worth noting that Christie's body was a shrewder judge than his mind, since he was shortly to work for a passage back to England.

The real test was the barrage, the continuous stream. There was no time for a man to compose his mind. It was like a dentist's drill endlessly in a sensitive tooth without anaesthetic. Wrote Allen: 'A damnable night. About the worst I have ever known. Not for a single moment has the shelling stopped. Everyone is badly shaken and every line down.' Grant remembered smoking eighty cigarettes between 5 am and 11.30 pm during a June day near Ypres in 1915 when German gunners shot continuously except for a break of ninety minutes for lunch. In another barrage Burrage felt every blow as a punch to his solar plexus, shivering and whimpering, 'Oh, Christ, make it stop. It must stop because I can't bear it any more.' With the 10th Londons at Ploegstraat in 1916, and for the first time in the line, Bradley lay down on the duckboards and sang, 'Oh, for the Wings of a Dove' at the top of his voice. He believed that he was never so afraid again. Official historian Bean saw the Australians, toughest of soldiers, shaking like leaves and weeping at Pozières on their introduction to west front shelling after Gallipoli.

No one was immune. Some stared at their hands clasped on their knees in a state of catatonic fear. Some hid their heads in their greatcoats in a state of torpor. Others would sit in certain positions, touch particular objects, whistle so many bars of a particular tune to ward evil off with ritual. Some wept; others joked hysterically, But all shook and crawled, white-faced in dull endurance, 'How long? how long?' men would ask themselves again and again. Men had no choice but to last out, nerves pared to the bone. Griffith described experience under a barrage. 'After a thunderous crash in our ears, a young boy began to cry for his mother in a thin, boyish voice. "Mam, mam . . ." He had not been hit but was frightened and crying quietly. Suddenly he started screaming again, screaming for his mother with a wail that seemed older than the world. The men began to mutter uneasily. We shook him and cursed him and even threatened to kill him if he did not stop. The shaking brought him back.'

Moran summed up the inevitability and tragedy of shelling on brave men when he wrote:

> At the time of this bombardment I was not too much frightened. I was too stunned to think. But it took its toll later. I was to go through it many times in my sleep. I used to hear all at once the sound of a shell coming. Perhaps it was only the wind in the trees to remind me that war had exacted its tribute and that my little capital was less than it had been. There were men in France who were ready to go out but who could not meet death in that shape. They were prepared for it if it came cleanly and swiftly, but that shattering, crudely bloody end by a big shell was too much for them. All their plans for meeting death with decency and credit were suddenly battered down. Self-respect had gone out of their hands. They were no longer certain of what they would do. It frightened more men away from the trenches than anything else.

The only retaliation against enemy artillery available to the front-line soldier was from his own distant artillery. But, whatever they did, he would be pretty certain to disapprove of it. If British guns were active, the retaliation came down on infantry rather than artillery; if they were passive, then it would be bitterly noted that the Germans were being allowed to get away with it. Anyway artillery fire was always a speculative business. Gun wear, map inaccuracy, changes of temperature, wind and pressure as well as casing and powder charge differences made accuracy at any distance impossible. Apparently identical shots from a sixty-pounder at 10,000 yards might fall within a zone 2,000 yards long and about 100 yards wide. Little wonder therefore that artillery were sometimes erratic in responding to a front-line SOS flare, might kill their own men following close to a creeping barrage and would need 100 rounds to be certain of hitting an enemy pillbox once. Infantrymen knew nothing of the mathematical complexities of firing an artillery piece; they knew only the fragility of the human body compared with a shell charge and could but count the number of dud shells, which litter the old battlefields even today.

Physical distance also drove the infantryman's sympathy from his gunners. Field artillery was tolerated, since it lived round about the support line, but siege artillery was another species, beings almost as remote as red-tabbed staff officers or official journalists. Their guns came and went like woodcocks in the night, startling infantrymen with their thunderous reports and flashes from ruined buildings and camouflaged sites. The self-contained batteries of eight guns had their own supply and signal system and travelled about with not just telescopes and switchboards, OP maps and the electrics needed to illuminate their sighting posts, but also with armchairs, well-stuffed valises and extra blankets. To watching infantry, all their worldly possessions on their backs, such super-numerary comforts were a source of cynical comment. They were not to know how seldom gunners enjoyed rest so that, when a siege artillery observer appeared in the front line, even so conservative a soldier as Subaltern Feilding welcomed the chance to be rude.

If men got talking in estaminets behind the line, the gunner's outlook was seen to be very different from the foot soldiers'. The combination of public-school understatement and childishness with murder at long range produced a jaunty sang-froid which jarred on men who smelt their fear and danger at close quarters. Odd phrases litter the memoirs of gunner subalterns: 'quite the most interesting experience I have ever had', 'wonderful shooting', 'an amusing day', and so on. Fraser-Tytler commended his colleagues as 'good partners in the game of hun-killing' and described a 'gorgeous killing' when thirty Germans had been spotted going into a barn and were killed with a salvo, followed a quarter of an hour later with a second salvo which added sightseers and medical officers to the tally. Little wonder therefore that Casson and his men watched an artillery position burning for an hour with the most complete detachment, for all infantrymen knew that gunners fought a cushy war, distant from the action and with extra pay and rations.

What no foot soldier knew was the danger, particularly in the last three years when aerial photography, flash spotting and echo location made a distant gun position as vulnerable as a man moving in no-man's-land. Andrews tells us succinctly of No. 199 siege battery during 1918. During the first four days of the Germans' March offensive the battery lost nine dead, eleven wounded, one shell-shocked and one prisoner. The forward-observation man went into battle with the third wave of the attack. During a gas attack layer and setter could not wear masks. A hit on the position could ignite all the shells, while defective shells could blow up in the breech, or partially engaged breech-blocks would blow back. None of this was visible from the front line.

All men feared artillery. Gas was their other great fear.

Allen tells us:

With men trained to believe that a light sniff of gas might mean death, and with nerves highly strung by being shelled for long periods and with the presence of not a few who really had been gassed, it is no wonder that a gas alarm went beyond all bounds. It was remarked as a joke that if someone yelled 'Gas', everyone in France would put on a mask. At any rate, the alarm often spread over miles. A stray shell would fall near a group at night. The alarm would be given. Gas horns would be honked, empty brass shell-cases beaten, rifles emptied and the mad cry would be taken up. It sounded like the Chinese trying to chase off an eclipse. For miles around, scared soldiers woke up in the midst of frightful pandemonium and put on their masks, only to hear a few minutes later the cry of 'All safe'. Then they would take them off again amidst oaths and laughter. Two or three alarms a night were common. Gas shock was as frequent as shellshock.

With such dyestuff giants behind them as Beyer and Badische Anilin, the Germans led the way in every type of gas technology. Tear gas came first in January 1915, followed by the killing gases: chlorine in April 1915, phosgene in December 1915 and mustard in July 1917. The mode of despatch was from cylinders in clouds up to July 1916, and then in shells and mortar canisters.

Chlorine was an inefficient gas compared with those that came later. Easily smelt and visible to the eye, men could usually avoid its full blast. Even in the first attack Cook noted that, if a man put a handkerchief in his mouth and kept his head above the trench parapet, he survived with few side-effects. Men feared it nevertheless. Thirty parts of gas in a million of air caused coughing, while 1,000 brought death by destroying the alveoli of the lungs and the smaller bronchial tubes. A man would thus find himself unable to absorb oxygen and drown in the water generated in his own tortured lungs. Sixty per cent of the Canadians who took the full weight of the first gas attack at Ypres had to be sent home, half being still fully disabled at the end of the war. The faces of those who died where they fought were characteristically blue, their arms wide in terror as they ran out of air.

Phosgene, a derivative of chlorine, had eighteen times its power and could not be seen. The insidiousness was that, even when inhaled in fatal doses, it was not immediately irritating, just smelling faintly of mouldy hay and producing a slight sensation of suffocation. (The inventor of the gas was able to enjoy a late-night party after first sniffing his creation and before dying from it.) Then would come shallow breathing and retching, pulse up to 120, an ashen face and the discharge of four pints of yellow liquid from the lungs each hour for the forty-eight of the drowning spasm. Belhaven remarked laconically that phosgene casualties were dreadful to see.

Mustard represented a new concept in gas warfare, in that its aim was to harass rather than kill. To the chemist it was ethylene in a solution of sodium chloride; to the soldier it was an oily brown liquid which looked like sherry, and smelt of onions, garlic or radishes. Its power was such that small quantities in a shell could destroy fighting soldiers for days. If there was no sunlight and the soil was dry, in deep trenches or woods the liquid evaporated slowly, lying in wait as it were like a self-cocking man-trap.

The effects of the gas would be felt only two or three hours after exposure. Sneezing and copious mucus would develop as if a dose of flu were on the way. Then the eyelids would swell and close, with an accompanying sensation of burning in the throat. Where bare skin had been exposed, moist red patches just as in scarlet fever grew, the patches becoming massive blisters within twenty-four hours. Thereafter there would arrive severe headaches, rise in pulse rate and temperature, pneumonia. All this would follow from exposure to just one part of the gas in ten million parts of air. In more severe exposures men might cough up a cast of their mucous membranes, lose their genitals or be burnt right through to the bone.

Men recalled slight brushes with mustard vividly. Fleming-Bernard wrote of blistered lips, loss of taste and his pipe tasting beastly for a week. After drinking shellhole water with mustard in it, Hewitt remembered his wrists swelling and eyes bulging, as well as the prophylactic treatment of Guinness and milk pudding in hospital. Ashmead-Bartlett slept inadvertently on a pile of leaking gas shells and felt very slack and tired for days. Chandos wrote of sneezing for half an hour, contracting blisters a foot long and of blindness for three days. The problem in all this was the difficulty of detecting mustard amongst the odours of the battlefield unless a man had the good luck to see iridescent stains on the ground. A soldier might then try and avoid it, for he could do nothing to counter the gas. Counter-measures were never found. The nearest soldiers came to applying counter-measures was when the Scots wore ladies' knickers over their bare legs at Nieuport.

Fuller observed once that mustard was a humane weapon. Only 2 per cent of those visited died, and then by pneumonia from secondary infection. But humanity, unlike death, admits of degree. A six-foot man has 3,000 square inches of skin, and it was on this that the vapour worked. Consider two reports, one from Nurse Millard, the other from a doctor.

Gas cases are terrible. They cannot breathe lying down or sitting up. They just struggle for breath, but nothing can be done. Their lungs are gone – literally burnt out. Some have their eyes and faces entirely eaten away by gas and their bodies covered with first-degree burns. We must try to relieve them by pouring oil on them. They cannot be bandaged or touched. We cover them with a tent of propped-up sheets. Gas burns must be agonizing because usually the other cases do not complain even with the worst wounds but gas cases are invariably beyond endurance and they cannot help crying out. One boy today, screaming to die, the entire top layer of his skin burnt from face and body. I gave him an injection of morphine. He was wheeled out just before I came on duty. Where will it end?

The official medical history of the war gave:

Case four. Aged 39 years. Gassed 29 July 1917. Admitted to casualty clearing station the same day. Died about ten days later. Brownish pigmentation present over large surfaces of the body. A white ring of skin where the wrist watch was. Marked superficial burning of the face and scrotum. The larynx much congested. The whole of the trachea was covered by a yellow membrane. The bronchi contained abundant gas. The lungs fairly voluminous. The right lung showed extensive collapse at the base. Liver congested and fatty. Stomach showed numerous submucous haemorrhages. The brain substance was unduly wet and very congested.

From the battle of 3rd Ypres in autumn 1917 to the end of the war, mustard produced 90 per cent of gas casualties and 14 per cent of all battle casualties. Lung weakness remained with the men. How many veterans alive today do not cough badly? Eye weakness might develop only years later. In 1990 there will still be 400 men alive blinded by mustard. Perhaps the fear of gas was not as irrational as many observers thought.

The British response to gas had been surprisingly rapid. Within a week of the first use of chlorine, a third of a million gas helmets had been made. They were made of black gauze rags tied at the back of the neck, held between the teeth and soaked in sodium thiosulphate. An improved version two months later was of army shirt material covering the head, using mica for eyepieces and a remarkable nosepiece-cum-tube for the mouth. The eyepieces soon broke or steamed up, while sweat caused the chemicals to run and sting before their effectiveness expired. Men generally thought it better to urinate on a spare sock rather than use the helmets. Indeed Rees observed his sergeant-major, who throughout the war believed that so long as he kept smoking his pipe he was safe from gas. Only in 1917 did the definitive article appear, invented by a man who had joined the Sportsman's battalion at the age of forty-seven – the box respirator. The chemicals neutralized all gases while the cheese-cloth filter dealt with the arsenic particles of the sternutators in their blue-crossed shells. Protection was complete but never comfortable. As Hanbury-Sparrow noted, 'We gaze at one another like goggle-eyed, imbecile frogs. The mask makes you feel only half a man. You can't think. The air you breathe has been filtered of all save a few chemical substances. A man doesn't live on what passes through the filter – he merely exists. He gets the mentality of a wide-awake vegetable. You yourself were always miserable when you couldn't breathe through your nose. The clip on the gas mask prevents that.'

Counter-measures were not limited to masks alone. Notice boards twelve miles from the front reminded, at five miles they cautioned, and at two miles they alerted. All along the front were empty shellcases serving as gongs if there was a suspicion of a gas attack – the French 75 half a tone higher than the eighteen-pounder. The compressed-air-fired strombus horns, which warned siege gunners, could be heard for nine miles, distributed at twenty-eight to the mile and were alerted by twenty-four-hour weather reports.

Men were trained in gas schools with one week on theory, one hour immersed in cloud gas, and exposed to raw tear gas for thirty seconds, with just six seconds allowed for getting the mask on. It was a brisk business, which sent men back to the front with an aggrieved feeling of the unfairness of gas and with tarnished green buttons.

The BEF thus came a long way fast from early 1915, when counter-measures seriously considered included the use of 100,000 fans, setting fire to a cloud of coal and carborundum dust, issuing divers' helmets to three men in every 10,000 and pumping air through a 100-foot line, so that these armed divers could stay in the front line and repel the enemy. By mid-1916 the new establishment at Porton was keeping pace with German developments and briefing the front line through divisional gas officers, those quiet, civilian-mannered specialists with their dark-green hat bands, trusted by the men.

The success of all counter-measures was indisputable. After 1916, when accurate figures began to be kept, it was found that just 3 per cent of gas casualties died, under 2 per cent were invalided, while 93 per cent returned to duty. Overall 70 per cent were deemed cured within six weeks. Nothing was said of the impaired efficiency of these men, or their fears. So long as they could move arms and legs without actually collapsing, the army deemed them fit for duty. Nevertheless the power of the gas mask is reflected in the lightness of the doses men got. The absolute numbers of those involved are equally impressive. The official figures are as follows:

casualties:		deaths:	
1915	12,792	1915	307
1916	6,698	1916	1,123
1917	52,452	1917	1,796
1918	113,764	1918	2,673

Infantry were not affected only by the enemy's gas; British counter-gas work involved the foot soldier in a way he might have expected – as a beast of burden. Cylinders holding 60 lb. of chlorine weighed 190 lb. and needed the shoulders of two men. When phosgene 'mice' replaced chlorine 'oojahs', the burden was slightly easier, for a 50 lb. 'mouse' could be managed by one man with a shoulder sling though both were regarded with equally profound distaste and suspicion. Nor was it not just a matter of weight in a long haul. Once in the parapet, waiting for a favourable wind, there was a constant feeling of danger. If a prisoner gave away the news, if alert sentries saw the exodus of rats from leaky cylinders, then a bombardment made mental balance the more difficult for those who slept next door to gas day and night.

Gas supremo Foulkes later pointed out that in the six months after June 1916 some 20,000 cylinders had been kept in the front line with only twenty-five burst by shells, and thirty-one men dying as a result; that in 110 cloud attacks there had been driftback only once, with just nineteen dead as a consequence. Even had this been publicized at the time, no doubt it would have been treated with the same suspicion reserved for all divisional news. When the chirruping sound of gas shells and the smell of an apple loft replaced the hiss of the cylinders, infantry felt a change for the better, one burden less. They couldn't see the danger, didn't need to carry it and noted retaliation coming down in back areas. That the gas in shells could be dropped on a sixpence regardless of wind and kill a man at a cost of sixteen shillings they would not be likely to notice. Unreasonable assumptions were, after all, almost as destructive in chemical warfare as the chemical itself. In this it was not far removed from shell warfare. Moran wrote: 'After July 1917 gas partly usurped the role of high explosive in bringing to a head a natural unfitness for war. The gassed men were an expression of trench fatigue, a menace when the manhood of the nation had been picked over.'

There were weapons apart from artillery shells and gas, weapons which had not been used in earlier wars. Since men could not fit them into any frame of reference, they tended to draw the worst possible conclusions.

The flame-thrower had been invented in 1900. Nitrogen and carbon dioxide threw oil twenty-five yards which had been ignited at the nozzle. Huge noise and vast black clouds hid a jet which swelled to an oily rose six feet in diameter at its burning end. Though men lying flat usually escaped, they were terrified nonetheless. The inflammable mixture would soon give out even if it were not hit by a sniper, but this was scant comfort to men near the receiving end.

Where chalk lay beneath the front, mining would be constant. In 1916 alone, the British had 25,000 men digging towards the German line to blow 1,500 mines. Listening posts warned trench reliefs of enemy counter-measures. When sounds of mining ceased, it was sure sign that the explosive was in place, tamped with sandbags and ready to be detonated electrically when the storm troops were ready to seize the crater lip. No threat could give the men a greater feeling of helplessness. When the explosion came, all the sound would be absorbed underground. Men would just feel the vibration rushing towards them and through the soles of their feet, then a great pressure on the chest if they escaped fast enough. If not, they would die without trace. It was the impression of vast power, greater than any shell, combined with the lack of warning which men could not accept.

No weapon was newer than the aeroplane. The first demonstration to the War Office had been in 1910, when a 5 lb. bag of flour had been dropped within a thirty-yard circle. Only when Grierson in the manœuvres of 1912 captured Haig's army by means of aerial observation was progress considered sufficient for the BEF to be able to take seventy planes to France – including Blériot's venerable channel flier. Most generals regarded planes like machine-guns, as weapons which would have little place in the coming war. Field-Marshal French told his men that 'should it appear inevitable that an aeroplane flying low must strike any individuals, they should lie down in order to avoid being struck by the propeller'. By the end of the war it was clear that the aeroplane could kill men without necessarily hitting them with its propeller. By then the British had 22,000 planes, including bombers capable of flying at 25,000 feet to Berlin and back with bombs as large as most of those used in the Second World War. As Grierson had whimsically and perceptively observed to George V before the war; 'I think, sir, that those aeroplanes are going to spoil the war. When they come over, I can only tell my men to cover their heads and make a noise like a mushroom.' Here was the novelty – a new dimension had been added to war within which little could be kept secret and even less kept from aerial attack.

The impact of planes on the infantryman came in three ways. He was not at first aware of the aeroplane's potential. Cloete found all planes terrifying and wanted to run away, bewildered by the noise and the inhuman, goggled figures at the wheel just forty feet up. In addition to terrifying men, the planes could also kill. Though crudely dropped over the side of the plane, the aerial bomb was as dangerous as the shell and more likely to be dropped over a specific area. The *British Medical Journal* in August 1916 remarked that a typical missile was 20 lb. of explosive in quarter-inch steel dropped from 4,000 feet. Its noise was a hissing shriek, it had a danger zone of fifty yards radius and fragments up to two feet square. Symons, an eyewitness, wrote: 'Bombs dropped from aeroplanes do great damage. One was dropped thirty yards from our HQ. Two fellows near by saw the plane coming and one said to the other, "Wouldn't it be a bugger if they dropped the bomb here." Drop it they did and he had his leg blown off. I saw it hanging across his chest like a leg of beef. All he said was "Dear me. Dear me," about a hundred times and said the Lord's Prayer over and over. He died in the night. It then dawned on me what war was.'

Least sensational and most dangerous of the aeroplane's uses was in making up maps for artillery largely from aerial photos. No machine-gun bay, no latrine avoided detection. Trenches were over-printed on 1/10,000 maps with news imposed when only thirty minutes old; just so long did it take to bring the plane down, develop and dry the plates with burning meths. A gun cast a shadow, the gunpit broke surrounding lines with tracks leading to it or with blast marks etched more lightly. Newly dug earth, reflecting white light, glinted. Early in 1917 a camouflage officer was sent to each corps, but the plane supplied an all-seeing eye.

This full arsenal of weapons, which was orchestrated on a Great War battlefield, reflected the two most magnificent centuries of social development in European history. No other continent except North America could have supplied and gathered so many men at such a distance from their homes in so confined an area. No other continent could then have killed and broken so many in so many ways. The engineering required to encapsulate poison gas securely in a metal case, the mathematics required to propel that case a precise distance, the chemistry needed to produce both gas and propellant, the organization required to bring all the components together, the medicine needed to mend the man who was in the path of the gas shell represent the highest achievement of modern man. Later wars could only scatter the destruction more fairly between those on the battlefield and those left behind. The front-line soldier of the Great War saw little of this progress, for intensity of feeling precludes that state of calm leisure in which there is detachment to discuss and compare. Survival within the arsenal became a full-time occupation, so that experience regressed to a state of heightened awareness, non-verbal emotion. In this way the artefacts of the twentieth century commingled with the thought processes of prehistoric man. Infantry became merely hunters and hunted, while technologists in khaki manipulated the primitive cutting edge of their sophisticated back-up tools.

8

THE STRAIN OF TRENCH WARFARE

Writing in the *British Medical Journal* during November 1914, Dr Albert Wilson gave his opinion that 'I do not think that the psychologists will get many cases'. Any wear and tear would soon be rectified by alcohol, he added. As a source of quickly absorbed calories, alcohol might be poison to the office worker but was, in Wilson's professional opinion, manna to the hill gillies who grew so old in Scotland. What, after all, was the soldier but another type of peasant plying his trade in the open air.

Visitors to the front line may well have agreed with the *BMJ*. The matter-of-fact response of soldiers to the dangers round about them was most striking. A strict convention laid down that all reference to fear was to be avoided except perhaps obliquely and in jest: 'Cheer up, cockie. It's your turn next'; 'three to a loaf tomorrow lads'. Such wounded men as would be encountered were still in a state of initial shock and appeared to accept their condition stoically. Moran described a typical case: 'Just now a man was brought to my dugout on a stretcher. Half his hand was gone and his leg below the knee was crushed and broken. While his wounds were being dressed he smoked, lighting each cigarette from the stump of the old one. His eyes were as steady as a child's. Only his lips were white. Afterwards he was carried away, with the men looking on in silence. But, when the groundsheet flapped down again over the entrance, my servant grinned. "You always know the old 'uns," he said.' The casual visitor might therefore conclude that the Kitchener soldier fitted into the same quietly heroic mould of which he had read so much in his Henty or Kipling or *Boy's Own* magazine.

This proved not to be the case. Though De Lisle always insisted that there was no fear in the 29th Division, and that his cure for men who showed the first symptoms was to tie them to front-line barbed wire for thirty seconds 'with most effective results', no amount of bravado could cover the facts. In 1914, 1,906 cases of behaviour disorder without physical cause were admitted to hospital. In 1915 the number grew to 20,327 or 9 per cent of battle casualties. Often the men had good war records – heroes like Owen or Sassoon – so the blanket tag of 'cowardice' could not be applied. By the end of the war 30,000 mental cases had been evacuated to England, and in 1922 some 50,000 men had been awarded war pensions on mental grounds alone. Though these figures were never publicized and are often forgotten today, the government acknowledged them discreetly. When planning for war in 1938, the authorities laid it down that in the next war mental to physical casualties would probably be in the ratio of three to one, while four million hospital beds should be laid aside for psychiatric cases during the first six months when Britain would be bombed from the air.

Just what the soldiers classified as mental cases were suffering from baffled most people at the time. Though shell bursts apparently triggered off most of the patients, only 3 per cent of those classified officially as 'shellshock' cases had actual brain lesions. In February 1915 the *Lancet* could only suggest molecular commotion in the brain as a result of high-frequency vibration. *John Bull*, Bottomley's sensational magazine widely read by the troops, advertised Dr Muller's Nerve Nutrient (guaranteed not German). 'The primary trouble in all phases of nerve exhaustion', ran the advertisement, 'is the semi-starvation of the nerve cells, the reason being that the sufferer fails to extract from his daily food the precious, concentrated nutrient that nerve cells live and thrive on.' As an opinion, it was no farther from the truth than official medical pronouncements of the time.

Today we understand better how severe physical symptoms may be generated by mental anxiety and we know in addition that, given the way Kitchener's armies were recruited, casualties of the mind were bound to be numerous. In the 1940s, the US army examined eighteen million men and rejected 29 per cent out of hand, one-third of these on mental grounds. Nevertheless one in seven became ineffective for mental reasons alone. In 1914 all men were swept into our army – the alcoholic, the subnormal, the mentally unbalanced. Very soon after the start the army's psychological consultant, Myers, submitted a written memorandum to Haig, stating his belief that such men would be better employed in the Pioneer corps, where with tact, firmness and understanding they could survive in a relatively low-stress environment. Having invited the memorandum, Haig turned it down, and these men were then bound to become a greater disability than the diseased, supplying a high proportion of the discontented, the inefficient, the absentees.

Even for those perfectly A1 in health and mental balance, the

Great War posed a greater test than any previous war. It was not just that a civilian had been taken from his family and friends and fitted into the Procrustean, disciplined army, where he found his individual will hamstrung, his diet and sleep subverted, his hands taught to kill and mutilate in a way which conflicted with his basic civilian standards; it was rather that he was hardly ever out of danger. In earlier wars battles had gone on for a day, and then with little noise and over so small an area that a general on horseback could control operations by eye and voice. High-explosive missiles in the Great War changed all this.

In France no man was safe. My father saw a man shot in the stomach miles from the front when a bullet ignited in the heat of a brazier burning waste material. Dearden observed a man whose stomach had been blown away while he was cutting down a tree. The axe had missed the tree and hit a buried grenade. Death could hit men in the same way in the relative safety of the reserve line. Few shells could reach at that distance, but Moran described an unnerving exception. 'The medical officer of the Durhams, who had been through the battle of Hooge in autumn 1915 without a scratch, was walking in the woods around Poperinghe. His head was taken off by a stray shell, the only one that dropped in those woods in our time.' Men expected heavy casualties in a battle or trench raid; what they could never adapt to was the constant haemorrhage in the front line. Plowman wrote of a mother's petition after two of her three sons had been killed. Colonel Rowley promised that the remaining son would be sent into the back area the next time out of the line. The man involved, Private Stream, was the only company fatality in that particular tour of duty. Another case concerned Hann of the 7th Somerset light infantry. He had come from the yeomanry and went up to the front wearing a bullet-proof waistcoat sent by his parents. He was shot through the forehead the first time up in the line.

Death on such a scale and in such unexpected places worried most men. Maze recaptures the unspoken fear beautifully in a story of two days before the attack of 3rd Ypres.

I rode slowly along the marching battalions. I heard the regular sound of an engine and saw puffs of smoke shooting up from a house on the road. A steam saw was cutting rhythmically through wood, working at high pressure with a tearing sound. Seeing the yard in front of the house piled high with wooden crosses and thinking to spare the men, I hurried in to have them removed. The Belgians engaged in the work threw up their hands in despair and pointed through the window to the back of the house and an ever bigger pile. Nothing could be done. I watched the men as they passed by. Some smiled, others passed a joke, some wouldn't look. But I knew that they all saw and understood.

The chief trigger of this deepest of all fears seems to have been the sight of a corpse. Seldom could front-line soldiers get away from these reminders of mortality for any length of time. Confronted with so many visible witnesses, the mind tried to defend itself by a stead-fast refusal to think beyond the concrete and immediate. 'There is no man so totally absorbed by the present as a soldier,' wrote Allen. 'It claims all his attention and he lives from moment to moment in time of danger with animal keenness that absorbs him utterly. This is a happy and saving thing.' Boy soldier Hope recaptured well the stock defence of the front line man attempting to distance himself from uncomfortable thoughts and pretend that death had no rela-tion to himself. 'Death lies about in all its forms. A limbless body here, the tunic fitting the swollen body like a glove. He may have wanted a tunic to fit him like that all his life – he gets it in death. A body without a head like a rumjar without a label. A form fast turning green, lying in a pool of grey-green gas vomit. Death in a thousand different masks. A youngster not much older than myself is bringing his inside up. Poor blighter. It's a pity. Heaven knows when our next rations will arrive.'

Nevertheless always at the back of the mind was the knowledge that the corpse was once a living man like oneself, in the same situation and therefore initially no more likely to meet death than oneself. Here Manning describes the deepest feelings of the fearful eye-witness:

The dead are quiet. Nothing in the world is more still than a dead man. One sees men living, living desperately and then sud-denly emptied of life. A man dies and stiffens into something like a wooden dummy at which one glances for a second with furtive curiosity. One sees such things and one suffers vicariously with the inalienable sympathy of man for man. One forgets quickly. The mind is averted as well as the eyes. It reassures itself after the first despairing cry: 'It is I – not it is not I. I shall not be like that.' And one moves on, leaving the mauled and bloody thing, gambling on the implicit assurance each one has in his own immortality.

Corpses newly dead or in a lifelike position broke right through morale no matter who the observer. Gladden wrote:

The dead man lay amidst earth and broken timber. It seemed like a sacrilege to step over him but there was no evading the issue. Never before had I seen a man who had just been killed. A glance was enough. His face and body were terribly gashed as though some terrific force had pressed him down, and blood flowed from a dozen fearful wounds. The smell of blood mixed with the fumes of the shell filled me with nausea. Only a great effort saved my limbs from giving way beneath me. I could see from the sick grey faces of the file that these feelings were generally shared. A voice seemed to whisper with unchallengeable logic, 'Why shouldn't you be the next?'

There are references without number to the depths of fear soldiers felt when confronted with death in its most tangible form. Ewart after Loos saw a whole company, one by one, turn to look at a dead man who seemed almost to be asleep. They did not find the clue they were looking for. Reid once emptied three Lewis gun drums into a German platoon 'with fierce satisfaction at doing frightful execution' at Morval, but afterwards he and his whole section stood for a few moments silently watching a heavily bandaged, dead German holding a rosary in his sole remaining hand. Reid thought that most of the men were visibly shaken. They had not expected an enemy to die like themselves.

The effects of these thoughts and the situations which triggered them was cumulative, reinforced by shellbursts, illness, lice, mud and constant uncertainty. Perceptive men saw that at the time. Sassoon observed that the effect of war could be traced in weeks and months, though differences of age and rank affected the precise timing. Graves pinned the thing down more precisely. He thought three weeks sufficient to learn the rules of safety and degrees of danger, with peak efficiency reached in three months. Thereafter there would be rapid decline. Aldington concluded that after six months most line troops were off their heads, horribly afraid of seeming afraid. It is interesting that Second World War studies agreed with these subjective opinions and timings.

Rest could not save a man. Indeed the constant stop–start pattern of the war routine might add to the problem. Priestley found himself more apprehensive every time he went up the line. Burrage once remarked that the longer he was away from the trenches, the more he disliked going in. Some recent animal experiments support this in a curious way by suggesting that development of stomach ulcers is related not to the degree of stress nor to its intensity but to its repetition at unpredictable intervals.

At the time little was known of the physical nature of fear or of the stresses which progressively wore a man out, though acute observers plotted clearly the physical symptoms – as the sharpest of them, Lord Moran, put it: 'men wear out in battle like their clothes. In battle the soldier's senses are dulled but, even if he comes out unscathed, the ordeal will shorten his life in the line ... it is the long-drawn-out exercise of control which is three parts of courage that causes wear and tear.' Most men did not realize what was happening, but in their diaries many plotted the stages of the decline. Private Wear joined the RAMC at the age of seventeen. His diary reads progressively:

> ... a story book come true ... extraordinary luck ... not dismayed by the sick or wounded ... applied for a commission since I felt the war eluding me ... one evening, just after supper, a 4·2-inch shell came through the wall into the room, bursting at once. We were thrown to the ground but marvellously no one was hurt. It was from this time that I began to experience what fear was. This sudden shock (I trembled for an hour afterwards) gave me a completely new outlook on life, life and war being of course synonymous terms ... found myself on quiet nights in the trenches shivering with horror at what might happen ... changed mentally and morally by leave on 31 December 1917 ... going up the line a horrible necessity ... no sustaining feeling of the slaughter leading anywhere ... nightmares even now ... bitterly unwilling to go back ... prompt rations and whisky the only concern ... depression increased by new drafts ... feeling that I had outlived my time ... trying to grow young ever since.

The unpublished letters of the Eton schoolmaster, Christie, who founded the Glyndebourne opera are as moving. Despite bad eyesight and crippled limbs, he had volunteered. By October 1915 he was writing back to Eton: 'Yes. I should not refuse a job at home. Should like a home battalion to train. Think I could do this rather well. Doubt whether I can pull this before I am wounded. Might develop rheumatism in my ankle.'

The most vulnerable men could stand very little extra stress. Enid Bagnold describes a typical case of a man who in civilian life and in a well-protected job might have been able to cope but broke under the greater demands of Flanders, demands in his case which did not even reach the test of high explosive.

'Me 'ead's that queer, nurse. It seems to get queerer every day. I can't 'elp worrying. I keep thinking of them 'orses.' I said to the charge nurse, 'Is number twenty-four really ill?' 'There's a chance of him being mental,' she replied. 'He is being watched.' Was he mental before the war took him, before the sergeant used to whip the horses as they got to the jumps, before the sergeant cried out, 'Cross the stirrups'? There are strong and feeble men. A dairyman's job is a gentle job. He could have scraped through life alright. Now he sleeps in the afternoons and murmurs, 'Drop the reins. Them 'orses, sergeant. I'm coming, sergeant. Don't touch 'im this time,' and then he shouts in a shriller voice, 'Don't touch 'im,' and he wakes. He nods and smiles every time one looks at him, frantic to please. He will sit in a chair for hours, raising and lowering his eyebrows and fitting imaginary gloves to his fingers. An inspecting general, pausing at his bed this morning, said, 'A dairyman are you? Afraid of horses are you? Then what do you do about cows?' He was pleased with his own joke and the dairyman smiled too, his eyebrows shooting up and down like swallow's wings. Such jokes meant nothing to him. He is where no jokes but his own will ever please him any more.

More often men reached the front line, stood it for a period, then cracked suddenly. Moran described such a case.

At Armentières there was a big curly-headed sergeant with a red face and an open smile, who appeared quite indifferent to the war. He really commanded the company in those days. He was so imperturbable on patrol that men liked to go out with him. He was deaf and could not hear the bullets or any of those sounds which set men's brains working to their undoing. Then at Vimy something happened all at once. It was not the shelling – only mortars which made a big crater but did little harm. The sergeant got into the habit of watching them. He seemed fascinated by them. Soon I discovered to my astonishment that they were doing him no good. As he stood with his eyes glued to the little dark objects still high in the air, he began to think. It occurred to him that he had been a long time with the battalion. He began to go over in his mind what had happened to those who had come over with him. A fortnight after we left Vimy, he came to me to report sick. He got back to England.

When men did crack, they often showed the most diverse responses to identical pressures. Myers noted one incident in which a shell had hit a dugout. Only two men survived. One wandered in the open with his clothes off, believing that he was going to bed. After just four days at a field ambulance station he was back in service. The other man was in a coma for a fortnight with rigid limbs. On the seventeenth day he sat up and said, 'Did you see that one, Jim?' then relapsed, remaining deaf and mute. In a final hysterical seizure he shouted battlefield orders, then came round to his normal condition. Another man who came under Myers was a soldier who had seen his closest friend killed at his side. He went into a tearful semi-stupor, showed no reflexes and took no notice of pinpricks. After two days, however, he got out of bed and talked to his orderly quietly about his old civilian life but retained no memory whatsoever of anything in his war hitherto.

For all the varied nature of their symptoms and their probable background – a sample of shellshocked men between November 1916 and May 1917 found that 80 per cent had a previous psychiatric record – the prognosis for such men was good. Indeed 87 per cent would be back again in front-line service within a month of being incapacitated. This was due to the prompt response of the Army Council. Myers, made 'specialist in nerve shock' in May 1915, had by the end of 1916 created four special centres with forward sorting centres. The four centres provided a picturesque view, the expectation of recovery and a reassuring medical officer, who made no examination, so suggesting that the original diagnosis was infallible. On the other hand, just fifteen miles from the front line, the guns could be heard. The soldier could not be under the impression that he had escaped while PE was regular and men were marched about by patients who were NCOs. Malingerers were picked out fast. The 'deaf' were caught by lip reading: the 'blind' by having their heads plunged into water; the 'severe headaches' by lumbar punctures and the 'blackouts' by sodium amytal injections. With so bracing and 'normal' a regime, sedation and rest and the avoidance of the words 'shellshock' and 'neurasthenia', most men were reparable. After all, to an old hand like Myers, shellshock symptoms were not new. They were just like the symptoms shown by the survivors of industrial accidents or natural disasters.

Many soldiers under such severe stress staved off the breakdown of 'shellshock', though very few could do so easily. Trembling eyelids or reflex shivering under shellfire showed with what effort soldierly bearing was maintained. 'The men usually cast off a bad day as they would have dismissed a nightmare,' wrote Partridge. 'Human nature's elasticity and power of recovery is never more helpful than in wartime. Yet there always remains a residue of impaired courage, destroyed enthusiasm. The driving force had gone. For instance, the shelling of brigade HQ in August 1917 when the men had been out of the line for two months brought back the old haunted look and restless hands.' The drain of reserves could suddenly show itself when there was no immediate trigger, in one of those panics so well known to our men of the two world wars.

Carrington recalled:

> We were well below the skyline and a mile from the nearest section of front when we encountered a large party of men from a strange division without an officer. They were carrying water up the line unarmed. A stretcher party converged on us and fifty yards of trench was jammed with about a hundred men going different ways. Suddenly shelling broke out about a furlong from us. It was near enough for some over-strained stretcher bearer. In a hysterical voice he suddenly shouted, 'Look. They're coming over the top.' In a flash of time the whole trench was in confusion. My little party of stalwarts was swept away. The whole hundred men vanished in all directions. Looking back, to my joy, I saw Yates and my other men lying on the parapet loading their rifles and looking for an aim at imaginary foes.

For men who did not crack suddenly but slowly wound down, there was little official help that could be given. The men could only shelter behind such supports as could be found.

The chief prop was mates. Moran explained why. 'There is no answer to fear. It shakes the foundations of the mind. Physical contact is the one thing that helps.' Proximity allowed the dispersal of free-floating fear in conversation, while songs expressed indirectly all the shared fears. Private Kenway trembled during working parties in no-man's-land throughout his three years' service but never if he was out with the imperturbable Bob Lawrence, a slow and easy-going butcher in civilian life with his hairless body part disguised with a ginger wig. Lucy's nerve broke and he wept profusely on the death of his closest friend, Ryan. Lucy's colonel, thought to be a ferocious killer, confided to Lucy that he had never been the same since the death of his inseparable friend, Collins. His hand shook every night at dinner so that he had to lead every night patrol just to reassure himself.

Responsibility provided another prop. If a man felt the need to uphold the reputation of a crack regiment, had a special job to do like running a message or being the senior soldier of a section, then he would go on longer. The officer in particular, looking after the comfort of his men, strolling round the trenches rather than stuck on sentry, spreading a feeling of purpose, was kept going by the awareness that in a tight corner men looked to the officer for guidance and example. Macmillan remarked once how much easier it was to lead his men into battle, since custom laid down the role; how lost he was when alone and wounded in a shellhole, reading his own pocket edition of Aeschylus. At the end of the day officers were just half as likely to break down as their men.

Other props might be more durable, but these were more personal. Highly neurotic men seem to have survived best and even gone on fighting to the end. Failure to adapt to a changing environment could be beneficial in war as it had been a handicap in civilian life. In an environment where danger was so constant that it could not be predicted and where no regular pattern of behaviour fitted, those who responded in only a limited or maladaptive way to the present were fortunate.

Moran gives us a beautiful picture of such a man.

He was a soldier of the old style because his father had been in the service and his grandfather. His mental processes were not easily followed. When a man came before him on a charge, he was convicted *pour encourager les autres*. A trench to him was but another billet to be inspected for empty tins and stray equipment. In his mind it stirred no tactical problems. That was the problem he could deal with. For him, the people who emptied tea leaves in odd corners were the real problem. Maps were his pet aversion, especially trench maps. They conveyed very little to him. He loathed all paper. One morning a gunner came into the mess and asked the colonel if he would mind marking the line which the battalion held. He stood gazing at the map, his broad, flat face a little sulky and quite without intelligence. Presently he placed his fat, hairy paw with mere stumps for fingers where it covered the greater part of north France then with a rude and impatient gesture he moved away and rapidly began to describe the ground as he must often have seen it in his travels overland, for he had the horseman's eye for the country. No man could ever remember that he was sick or sorry. When anyone fell ill, the colonel plainly could not understand it, though at bottom he was good-natured. He got up before anyone else to turn out the servants. He got into his trench kit and set off alone by some overland track that he had discovered was mostly dead ground. He had an old balaclava drawn over his head. Across his shoulders he threw an old waterproof sheet, which he secured below his chin with a bit of string, and in his hand he carried a long pole. When he came to a particularly exposed place, he stopped and pulled out a knife to remove great lumps of mud from his shoes, which he wore with stockings in all weathers, holding that gumboots made him slow. The men grinned as he jumped into the trench, though he had never been known to praise anyone and mostly went about finding fault. After dinner he spread out the *Morning Post*, which made up his literature.

Better even than the neurotic were the schizoid, men cold, aloof, unable to express hostility or fear, men noted as eccentric or secluded introverts in civilian life. Preoccupied with an inner reality, these men could not sustain personal relationships and tended to face all complex situations with a withdrawal response. In the Second World War such men were more likely to join the air force, where there was little interpersonal contact in combat; during the first war, of necessity, most stayed on the ground. With their quixotic judgement and unpredictable behaviour, they won a disproportionate number of decorations. The Cheyenne Indians had called them 'the contraries', the Crow Indians 'crazy dogs wishing to die'. General Seeley noted with surprise how the most lasting and violent soldiers, as during the Boer war in his experience, 'were in every instance the quiet, gently, dreamy type' – in other words, men outside the group, detached, driven by an inner daemon in a dangerous situation.

Some endured, more broke entirely, the majority ceased to fight except in a shadow-boxing way after a few months in the front line. This seems the gist of stress pressure in the Great War. The fact of the taboo on expressing fear, in France and later, cannot eliminate the 65,000 soldiers in mental hospitals when pensions were finalized in 1929. These were the tip of a vast iceberg. Each week I see in Leavesden mental hospital, the largest in England, a man whose memory is perfect, within the limits of his great age, to 1917. Thereafter he can remember nothing. An explosion had wiped the recording mechanism from his life and hospitalized him from that day to this. Nor can the taboo eliminate those broken men whose lives were needlessly taken. If a man accused and convicted of cowardice or desertion pleaded shellshock, he was kept under observation. Dr Macpherson checked about seventy such men, observed them for about four weeks, talked with them twice daily and examined their dossiers three or four times. These men were therefore only shot after some scrutiny. The official figures stated that 11 per cent of court-martial death-sentences were carried out. Macpherson thought the proportion about right from his own experience. Nevertheless it is hard to believe that mistakes were not made – or from the sample of memoirs that I have taken that the official figures are correct. Most fighting soldiers would have backed Evans at the time:

A man was shot for cowardice. The volley failed to kill. The officer in charge lost his nerve, turned to the assistant provost-marshal and said, 'Do your own bloody work, I cannot.' We understood that the sequel was that he was arrested. Officially this butchery has to be applauded but I have changed my ideas. There are no two ways. A man either can or cannot stand up to his environment. With some, the limit for breaking is reached sooner. The human frame can only stand so much. Surely, when a man becomes afflicted, it is more a case for the medicals than the APM. How easy for the generals living in luxury well back in their châteaux to enforce the death penalty and with the stroke of a pen sign some poor wretch's death warrant. Maybe of some poor, half-witted farm yokel, who once came forward of his own free will without being fetched. It makes one sick.

9

INTO REST

Men returning from the front into rest were often profoundly tired. C. E. Montague recalled:

> If a company's strength was low and sentry posts abounded, more than usual in its sector, a man might for eight days running get no more than an hour off duty at any one time, day or night. If the enemy guns were active, many of these off-duty hours would have to be spent on trench repair. After one of these bad times in the trenches, a company would sometimes come out onto the road behind the communication trench like a flock of overdriven sheep. The weakest ones would fall out and drop here and there along the road. Men would come out light-headed with fatigue and ramble away to the man next door to them about some great time they meant to have at home; or a man would march straight on into the ditch in his sleep. Upon a greasy road with a heavy camber I have seen a used-up man get the illusion on a night march back to the billets that he was walking on a round, smooth, horizontal pole above a fearful gulf. He would struggle hard to recover imaginary losses of footing.

Perhaps a senior NCO or part of the band would come to meet the men, but the mental collapse after the tension of the front would invariably wipe from all faces that façade of wary dignity which the fighting soldier usually put on.

Without exception men were transformed by rest. Read wrote of 'the total reversal of mood' compared with up the line. Sassoon called it 'the usual miracle' within twenty-four hours of coming into rest. 'It is marvellous to be out of the trenches. It is like being born again. We are free to say "in an hour's time". When freedom to anticipate is being permanently challenged, one understands as never before how much a man lives by hope. To be deprived of reasonable expectation is the strain. It is the perpetual uncertainty that makes life in the trenches endurance all the time. Certainty, even of violent death, would come as a relief. But here we are again, like men redeemed from the grave . . . we gave death the chance. Death did not take it and we escaped alive.'

The march from the zone of destruction was the first part of the cure. Men came into an area of trees with branches and turf without shellholes. There was no need to strain the ears for shell sounds nor was stooping a condition of survival. The hushed wariness of the trenches merged into bustle, which became noisier all the time, with blacksmiths' shops, horse lines, supply depots and motor repair shops roaring with sound. All this hit the tired men hard. They were like blind men recovering their sight, normalcy growing by degrees, and feeling coming in gradually from extremities of sensation. It was just like a man on night sentry slowly thawing out after sunrise.

Men prayed fervently for domestic billets. Contact with women, children and animals reassured the soldiers of their continuing existence as civilians temporarily in khaki. If the men were fortunate, billets would be in a village. Then the billeting officers would go round, bargaining hard with the local people and registering the deal with a chalk mark on each door – 'three officers and six batmen', 'mess for four officers', 'barn for one and a half platoons'. With officers at five francs and other ranks at just one franc each, competition would be fierce among the more acquisitive women.

More often the men would be put up in one of those scattered farms which litter northern France, each one remote as if there were no other settlements within a week's journey. The buildings were always of one storey and of brick, built round a midden. The house was on one side, a barn for livestock on the other, with two barns for straw completing the square. The floor in the house would be of beaten earth, with shutters instead of glass over the windows and a dog turning a wheel on the outside connected to a churn within. The centre of the farm was a stove with its boxflue leading to the wall yards away. Women wearing sabots and smoking pipes would add a pinch of coffee periodically to a pot standing always on the stove, to replenish the powerful, bitter liquid, drunk without milk. In the evening men would gather quietly and gratefully around this stove, but with about 200 billeted per farm, room was scarce. The others would sit in the barn, its straw sour from earlier tenants.

Relations with French civilians when out of the war zone had not begun easily. To the regular soldiers of the early days all foreigners were 'niggers'. Frank Richards's mate Billy had told him that the only way to treat foreigners from Hong Kong to Paris was to knock hell out of them. Even if later soldiers paid less attention to these stereotypes, they were likely to be offended by the differentness of the people, with their dog carts and their wayside shrines. Ellison observed that 'they spoke a little broken English, but they had their own dirty language with the manners, habits and morals of tame monkeys'. The farmyard dirt in particular offended him. Surely even the Welsh were cleaner. 'But what can you expect from a people who pin their faith to sloppy, slippery sabots? Give me neat Lancashire clogs every time.' The soldier moreover came across civilians mostly in a mercenary capacity. When Abraham bought a bar of chocolate, he was charged 2s. 6d. for a one-franc bar. When he protested, the girl just said, 'Garn, you fucking long bastard,' and ran off. Smith remembered the French at Meaulte near Albert charging very high prices and saying that they would have preferred the Germans in occupation. Bradley recalled the shacks run by refugees offering eggs and chips to the soldiers, refugees usually 'smelly, pregnant and sordid' with prices to match.

On his side, the Frenchman tended to look on the British soldier with equal dislike. As Mottram pointed out, if three million Frenchmen squatted down in an area the size of Cumberland and Lancashire with the purpose of driving the Irish from Scotland, 1 per cent of them speaking English and all of them blasting shortcuts through hedges, climbing walls, scrounging wood, draining wells and banging rickety gates, then no doubt feeling would have run high among the natives of the area. The list might be continued: mud would be trampled in houses, lice spread, virgins deflowered and cows milked before the farmer got up. Subaltern Gillespie noted in his diary an occasion when in exasperation he set two of his platoons digging and harvesting for these sort of offences. Much damage would be made good by colonels, inheritors of that gentlemanly tradition of the Master of the Hunt going round with a purse of sovereigns to compensate farmers whose fields had been trampled. There was too a special commission in Boulogne early in 1915 to deal officially with complaints. But irritation remained. Wrote Smith: 'I had a wordy argument today with a Frenchman who tried to hit my horse because he imagined he was being forced into the mud beside the road. I also had trouble with a fat old wench who swore at me. One of her fowls flew through the mud and sprayed my face with splosh. As I was in a bad temper I gave vent to my wrath by chasing the offending chicken up the road. The owner happened to see the chase and ran after me, jabbering away nineteen to the dozen and shaking her fist, which led to retorts in equally strong language but conveying nothing to her unreceptive mind.'

The Frenchman too regarded English soldiers on his soil with a more abstract suspicion. Seeing all the new railways, Decauville tracks and cindered aeroplane runways, it was easily believed that the British intended to stay. Had the English not always coveted the north of France? Was not Crécy within gunshot of the front line? Moreover what did the English know of the war? How could an army which spent its spare time hunting or playing football have more than a dilettante involvement? France had lost 50 per cent of her coalfields, 64 per cent of her iron. To recover her property, France had called up a quarter of her male population immediately. Four million were to follow, with five million summoned to the public service, women as well as men. In 1914 alone, the French lost nearly a million men; in 1915 nearly one and a half million and in 1916 nearly a million. Until that time, the first year in which the British committed themselves in significant numbers, with the Kitchener armies beginning to percolate over to France, De Gaulle estimated that each French division had been engaged from ten to seventeen times and not relieved each time until it had lost one-third of its effectives. It was not just that the French suffered more than the English at every point of the war; they regarded the war as an inevitable and honourable burden worthy of sacrifice – a sacred cause. When Gibbons went back to his former billets in Andruicq after the war, he was shown the family album. There were soldiers in the uniforms of 1815, 1850, 1870 and from the colonial wars of the eighties as well as from the Great War. In France there were therefore fewer illusions about the war away from the front line.

But when all is said about the suspicions and the incomprehensions and the irritations, the balance is pleasing. The Kitchener men had not willingly surrendered their civilian behaviour like the old professionals. Glimpses of human relationships in which gentleness brought no shame and the recognition of individuality no punishment conjured up painful memories. Burrage wrote of being invited into the home of three middle-aged refugees from Ypres, who spoke perfect English and treated the lousy soldiers like gentlemen. What would have been homelike three months earlier felt then terribly

1. The recruits are kitted out. Few of them would ever manage to fit their own puttees as well as the sergeant who measures them.

2. Platoon training in the harsh atmosphere of a 'bull ring' in France. Dress is battle order, and scene, Etaples. By the car stands a 'Canary' – one of the much-hated yellow-banded instructors.

3. Marching men in column of fours put on a show as they pass through a typical French village. With luck, the old ladies' daughters may appear. Gas masks round the necks of the soldiers suggest the later stages of the war, and shrapnel helmets, that the front is not so far away or that enemy planes are active.

4. The ten-minute rest after fifty minutes' marching. Men sleep on their packs after the complicated little routine of piling arms.

5. A study in headgear as a group of Lewis gunners comes out of the line with their handcart.

6. A study of a road near the front line with munitions moving towards the line and replaced men moving into Rest. Such intense and organized use of roads had been learnt from the French at Verdun.

7. These trenches in a back-area show the ideal. From right to left: parapet, revetted side, firestep, duckboards on the trench floor, revetted parados at the rear. Firebays are dog-toothed to minimize the effects of shell blast and enfilade fire.

8. A typical dugout in the support trench line. A gas curtain hangs in readiness by the door with a duty-roster pinned to the doorpost. The rum jar and petrol tin are for water, while food is hung in a sandbag from the roof to deter rats. A candle is the only light, and home-made gramophone the only luxury.

9. A 9.2 in. howitzer worked by the RGA and observéd by a French officer. The house and lack of camouflage suggest the early days of 1915 before the active days of aeroplanes. The gun is being laid with the aid of a dial sight.

10. A shellstore in Britain showing a minute proportion of the four million tons of shells fired by the British army during the war. The lifting ring on the nose will be replaced with a fuse just before firing. Only once did one of these stores blow up – at Silvertown in East London – with appalling effect.

11. Communion before the battle.

12. A still from the film of the Somme battle. A stretcher-bearer carries a wounded man to the rear. He has been too badly wounded even to dump his kit – the wounded man's privilege.

13. Many shell victims were even worse mutilated than this man, but our photo archives were carefully vetted so that very few pictures of dead Englishmen remain.

14. A marvellous study of men just from the line. Puttees and surplus ammunition have been thrown away. Rifles, on the other hand, are carefully covered to protect from moisture. Layers of clothing and comforters fight the cold, since greatcoats were not allowed in the front line. The sandbags probably contain enemy equipment which will be sold to non-combatant soldiers.

15. The Maxim machine-gun, the most successful weapon of the Great War. To conserve water and prevent a column of steam giving away the gun's position, a condenser bag is fitted. Periscope sight and steel plate safeguard the firer's head.

16. Men in a back area watch an 8 in. gun being towed by its tractor. The tank was a direct descendant of such tractors. Though cavalry played a minimal part in the war, the horses in the background remind one that throughout the war they were the chief means of moving army supplies.

17. Battle fatigue.

18. A rest camp improvised in the devastated war zone. Groundsheets, stolen tarpaulins and barbed-wire picquets have all been brought into use. The roughness of the army-issue shirt can almost be felt.

19. A flimsy structure of wire-netting and timber packs as many resting men into a barn as possible. Many received Blighty wounds from the collapse of such constructions.

20. Battalion sports. The intensity of the activity suggests a barrel of beer is at stake.

21. Cooks with their field kitchen and mascots.

22. The field kitchens in use. Men must balance the comfort of a seat against a standing position close to the cookers and nearest when cooks serve seconds with a shout of 'gyp–o'.

23. Fatigue for the RGA as resting men are brought in to move shells by light railway to the dump. Rations in sandbags wait by the line, suggesting the relatively independent lives led by the heavy artillerymen.

24. Shovels and boots suggest digging fatigue for the Sappers, while breadth of smile hints that the job will be done well away from enemy fire. The shortness of the Lee Enfield shows in the photo: the loss of muzzle velocity compared with French and German weapons was sacrificed so that the rifle might be used by cavalry.

25. The trophies of 'Wild Eye', the Australian souvenir king, are better kept than his puttees and uniform.

26. Estimates were made before each battle of just how many mass graves would need to be dug. Identity discs would be cut from the corpses and all details punched in metal and put onto the waiting crosses. Note the stretcher-bearer among the dead here.

27. Probably the luckiest men after the battle were the prisoners. Here an 'Old Bill' type ASC man serves water from a rum jar to Germans. One of the prisoners has been given a cigarette which he carefully files behind an ear.

28. The wounded are gathered from the battle area, helped by German prisoners. Men tilt their shrapnel helmets towards any shell explosion and use duckboards wherever they can.

29. Men temporarily blinded by mustard gas wait for treatment.

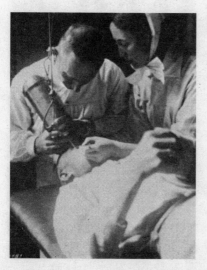

30. A magnet is used to extract shell fragments from the eye. This type of treatment was pioneered by American surgeons during the war.

31. Men wait for their new limbs to be adjusted.

32. A soldier with extensive plastic surgery to his face exercises a mutilated hand. His uniform is the standard one worn by wounded men under treatment in Britain during the war.

alien to Burrage. The effect was indescribable – like a magic carpet.
Later, he was billeted in an unspoilt village near Arras. The men
linked arms and danced round Madame, singing, '*Est-ce que vous
avez des œufs, Madame?*' to the tune of 'Here we Go Gathering
Nuts in May'. She laughed at their clumsy gambols and sold her
omelettes at a reasonable price. When the men went to an old mill
near the village which offered coffee and meals at any time, they
were almost ashamed to visit the place and never swore. This was
the clue. In a hard war, in an institution which took from men
many of the inhibitions of what they would once have regarded as
decent behaviour, the soldiers never became wholly cut off. Confronted with good, gentle people, men recognized themselves, felt
ashamed of crudities of speech and manner which war and male
society feed. They yearned for their old life, where they could be
their real selves. This was the precious experience which French
civilian life allowed – easy domesticity. 'Don't let's 'ave no fuss.'
'Alf, 'ow's this? Madamaselly, avey voo dee pang?' 'Wot der yer si
for gimme a tuppeny packet o' Nosegay?' In the end soldiers paid
three times the right price for eggs, not knowing or caring for their
value. What estaminet and cottage offered men was beyond price.
If there were small children or animals about, the temporary psychic
transfusion would be complete.

Individual soldiers treasured more intimate memories of their
French hosts. Drake wrote of a billet with a woman who looked like
one of the witches in Macbeth. She refused an officer permission
to sleep in her son's bed and nursed Drake through his pneumonia
in that bed with bowls of milk. For payment all she would take was
four sous-worth of snuff. '*Bon pour la tête.*' When questioned on her
kindness, she replied, 'You are like the son I had who God thought
fit to take from me. You have his form and almost his face; his age
too. Sometimes I have prayed that the Blessed Virgin might send
him back to me, but you know that is impossible. She sent you to
me when you had most need of a mother and for these last days I
have been with my son again.' Wrote Drake, her heart was as big as
a drum. More usually the norm was more formal, more ceremoni-
ously courteous – like the Scottish reserve of the people of the *nord*
today. Village curés in their heavy boots and vast soutanes would
take off their broad-brimmed hats and stand with bowed heads as
our soldiers went by. Brian wrote that one only had to ask for anything of the French and one would get it. He hoped that the French

would have been as well treated in England if the circumstances had been reversed.

Soldiers might not be lucky enough to be rested in a populated area. If they were in a remote spot or in a zone previously fought over, then there would be bell tents. Twelve would be shoe-horned into each tent, feet pointing to the centre and boots used as chamber pots to be later emptied under the tent flaps. Nissen huts were an improvement, invented for the war. With twenty-four to a hut, all men shared the stifling fumes of the central stove, which glowed red hot. Like wearing army boots, keeping tobacco and matches dry and secreting valuables on the body, living in bell tents and Nissen huts was a wartime art barely sweetened by necessity. With duck-boards, stale sweat and stinking incinerators, mud everywhere, these rest camps carried the army stamp on them like the mark of Cain.

Once encamped, the men looked forward to a bath and change of clothing. However coarse a man, whatever his social origins, personal cleanliness was always the highest priority. Perhaps it was because uncleanliness symbolized everything that was undignified in a way of life where all dignity became irrelevant to the constant and huge strain of preserving life. It might even be based on memories of earliest childhood, when dirt meant faeces, which shamed the men by infantilizing them. But, whatever the cause, bath was sheer pleasure. Drinkwater's memoirs noted that he still heard the singing of the bathed men as they marched briskly and happily back to their billets, for 'though roughly done, it was well done'.

In a typical bath house the men would soak in a combination of bleaching vats and half beer barrels. Parties of fifty would be marched in in alphabetical order. They would leave outside their underclothes to be soaked for four hours in creosol, and their uniforms wrapped in their identity discs and handled by nubile young refugee girls from Belgium. The vigorous nudity of an unending cavalcade of young men gave great and noisy pleasure to both sides. A cold hosepipe would serve the dual purpose of driving out the men and washing off the suds ready for the fresh uniforms, theoretically de-loused.

With baths working from 7 to 7 and dealing with 1,000 men daily, there was always a margin of error. The limited capabilities of the C3 classification men who worked the boilers often produced cold baths and showers. The water might even run out, certainly if too many men were allotted. New underwear was always irritating after the heat of the bath and was pretty sure to be the wrong size. Men would emerge with giant pants, bagging at the buttocks, together with babies' socks. Clean shirts might be issued with dirty pants. The only beneficiary would be the louse, who was beaten only if new clothes were issued – which never happened.

Good food came second only to good bathing. Away from the cold tack of the trenches, the soldier in rest re-joined his company cooker. Like a Victorian cooking-range on wheels, it provided coffee before noon, stew after and tea at 4 pm. In addition a mixture of bacon grease, hot water and dust would be served to first-comers when the cooks shouted 'gyp-oh'. Though there was often the flavour of tea in the stew and tea leaves in the coffee, many working-class men had seldom eaten better than during the war. Bread and tea in the morning and afternoon with just one cooked meal was the manual worker's norm at the time, just as it had been the pattern of the old regular army. Now, according to a report of June 1916, soldiers got 4,300 calories at a time when civilians averaged 3,859, and a passable daily average was 3,400. According to the records, a soldier should have received daily $1\frac{1}{4}$ lb. of meat, $1\frac{1}{4}$ lb. of bread, $\frac{1}{4}$ lb. of bacon, 3 oz. cheese, $\frac{1}{2}$ lb. fresh vegetables and small quantities of tea, jam, salt, butter, mustard, pepper, condensed milk and pickles.

Four thousand three hundred calories was a good statistic on a Whitehall desk; what appeared in a man's mess tin was another matter. Trains might be misplaced or limbers hit by shellfire, while butter and milk never reached the ranks under any circumstances. For the rest, the ASC took the best and the officers' batmen the pick after that. The result was that few men got more than half a loaf a day, and jam might arrive one day in four. The 22 oz. Maconochie tin was a real meal, a mixture of 1 lb. of unboned beef with carrots, onions, haricots, and potatoes. The trouble was that, if the order was two men to a tin meant for one, the men thought themselves lucky. The pork and beans tin was regarded more darkly. Authority held one-third of such a tin to be the equivalent of a meat ration, though as the official medical report pointed out 'troops must not be misled by the name pork and beans and expect to find a full ration of pork. As a matter of fact, the pork is practically all absorbed into the beans.' Taking these into consideration, along with the rind of the bacon, the bones in the meat and the biscuits which could shatter dentures and served better as kindling, then it is clear that army rations were like an assault course. The effects of bad administration, inferior materials and poor cooking could hit the stomach of the most honest soldier.

Food in rest was a reasonably safe fixture. It needed to be to make up for rations elsewhere. Gladden commented that hard labour in the open air made food amounts seldom adequate. Bombardier Pressey was hungry for four years. Parker thought that the teenagers in khaki were always hungry too. Since the food supplies were too little, erratic, dull and unbalanced, the wonder is that the men endured as well as they did with what amounted to full board in a bad transport café.

Good sleep, good baths and warm food were the basics. Pay on the first day out of the line was a bonus. The company would be stood easy in front of the pay table. The table would be covered with a grey army blanket and presided over by an officer with the quartermaster and his sergeant as witnesses. NCOs were paid first then the men in alphabetical order. Each man stepped up when his name was called, saluted and removed cap. If hair was too long, then pay would be credited. What the man got would depend on his job. Infantry got a bob a day at the start while the ASC got six bob. When these amounts were inscribed in the paybook, they tended to follow a man round for his army career. Thus a driver in the front line would get his specialist's pay though doing the same job as a man getting one-sixth the amount. One of the men I talked to in Chelsea hospital still remembers this as his chief grievance in the war.

The pay came in five-franc notes. Few women would accept such notes easily, since a cup of coffee was just ten centimes. The best method was to eat or drink before paying then face the *patron* with a *fait accompli*. Change would then arrive as notes the size of tram tickets only valid locally. What could you get on a bob a day? To see it in perspective; one could stay at the Faulkener Hotel by Charing Cross station for 8s. 6d., which included room and bath, a four-course lunch and six-course dinner. Houses at Leicester could be rented at 3s. 6d. a week and 4½d. bought one pint of beer, a potato pie, cheese and pickle and a twist of tobacco back in England in 1914. One must remember too that few received just the bob. With various payments for service and proficiency, 1s. 9d. was a more normal figure. Yet, when all allowance is made, the amount must have been inadequate. Poverty to Coppard was the saddest memory of the war. The officers with their cars could spend their money in Abbeville, Amiens, Rouen or St Omer. The limit for Other Ranks – then just for one day – would be lorry hopping into Béthune, Armentières, Albert, Lillers or Arras. In these simpler country towns close to the front there were cheap pleasures to be had. Cheap they certainly needed to be on 1s. 9d. a day, from which part would have already been mailed to families in England.

Tobacco was the first thing bought. Brett-James noted that even Wellington's soldiers regarded tobacco as their greatest luxury, using green leaves and herbs if the genuine article was not available. A hundred years later the need was greater. The period before the war had seen a great expansion in the smoking habit. Between 1900 and 1913 tobacco consumption in the UK had increased fourfold. Thus the soldier received a weekly issue of up to thirty cigarettes. These were Trumpeter, Red Hussars, Oros, Ruby Queen or Arf a Mo's, but the men always hoped for Player's or Woodbines, which were thought to be better. In the canteens seventy Woodbines could be bought for a shilling, the same price as six panatellas. In addition many men got extra from relatives, so that at any time pockets and haversacks would be filled with cigarettes. These countered the smell of decay and explosion, but they did so much more. Noakes wondered how non-smokers could survive, for to light up was the first reaction to any dangerous situation. A night alert would produce countless pinpoints of light, shielded in cupped hands. Better to be short of rations than short of cigarettes, Noakes thought, for a cigarette gave a man a better hold on himself. Gladden once saw two men killed by machine-gun fire at Jackson's Dump in the Ypres salient, because one man could not refrain from lighting up and drawing fire.

Old soldiers found smoking more like eating. The effect seemed so distinct as to be felt in the pit of the stomach. A sleepy feeling of contentment countered cold, damp and fatigue. After a few puffs a man could endure more – or thought he could. Perhaps, since tobacco was the only indulgence a man could take with him in the front line to assure himself of his individuality, it tranquillized the more. Perhaps it was the most complex alternative focus of attention and thus allowed overwhelming danger to be atomized most satisfactorily. Soldiers without cigarettes in this century are the difference between Hollywood films and newsreel actuality.

Second only to tobacco came women as a commodity and comfort to be bought. It may be that fight-flight conduct, as psychologists would term battlefield behaviour, inhibits sexual desire. Even coarse references to women, the staple of any conversation in France, were muted within gunsound. That Homeric epic, 'I love my wife, I love her dearly', which ran through every part of the anatomy in every billet in France, expired when the communication trenches began to fall below ground level past the heavy artillery. Manning was aware of this at the time:

> The girl moved him a little. She had awakened in him that sense of privation which affected, more or less consciously, all those segregated males so that they swung between the extremes of sticky sentimentalism or rank obscenity. In the shuddering revulsion from death, one turns instinctively to love as an act which seems to affirm the completeness of being . . . in the actual agony of battle, these cupidities have no place at all and women cease to exist so completely that they are not even irrelevant. Afterwards, yes.

Added to this deeper motive was the fact that the infantry were largely working men and it was part of the working-class ethic that good health required a regular lay. By convention, much sexual experience was available at home to lads between the ages of thirteen and eighteen. Now, in some areas of France, there was wider opportunity than even in England. In the base area were many refugee girls as well as prostitutes who invested themselves in this deprived community of homeless young males. Even on leave a change in established moral codes eased relationships between the sexes. The slogan 'There's a girl for every soldier' was welcomed by many soldiers, while main-line stations acted as a magnet for women who had never had so constant a supply of unattached, disoriented young men.

The flesh trade can be exaggerated. For most front-line men the biggest town they ever knew was a semi-deserted village with a few cellars and perhaps a wrecked cottage producing eggs and chips for the men. Gibbons complained loudly that there was little chance for vice. Nevertheless 27 per cent of all diseases for which men were hospitalized were venereal of various types. By the end of the war some 416,891 men had been treated for VD.

The Official History reckons that about one-third of the cases were contracted on leave. Certainly Cloete describes being accosted sixteen times between Piccadilly and Berkeley Street, while the promenade of the Empire theatre – a notorious rendezvous for the highest class of prostitute – had to be closed after many complaints about the quality of the 'fairies'. No occupation, it seems, was safe from the dilution of labour in wartime. Back in France each base had its semi-institutionalized brothel open from 6 pm to 8 pm. The men would queue up patiently with military police ordering the line. Madame serving behind the bar would take the money, which seems to have been about two francs but might go up over ten and up to thirty if the more highly paid colonials were about. Drinks anyway would be about five times normal price. The girls involved were reputed to make up to 6,000 francs a week, but, with a working life of one month at most and the division of 6,000 by two, this suggests the myth of disappointed men. With so few francs in his pocket and the long queue behind, the relationship was of the most fleeting, hence the bitterness.

As far as the army was concerned, syphilis meant the loss of a man for thirty-seven days and gonorrhoea for twenty-nine days. In the old days the army had been better prepared, with Indian brothels checked twice weekly by doctors for towel, vaseline and Condy's fluid. In France the problem was greater and the time shorter to establish a system. The official line was that 'efforts to attract officers and men to pleasing and health-giving recreation huts, fields of sport and places of healthy amusement during their off-duty hours or during leave in a town should be re-doubled'. In private the army pursued a more negative line with 'sick through negligence' the verdict. It involved stoppage of pay and no leave for twelve months. In order to enforce this, men were subjected to random short-arm inspections, standing with their trousers and pants round their ankles until ordered to 'lift the curtain'. It was unlikely that a subaltern would have much idea what he was supposed to be looking for, but the idea perhaps was to surround VD with an aura of humiliation. VD nevertheless kept pace with the civilian rate of the time despite the practical difficulties the soldier faced if he was looking for vice. By 1916 there were eight hospitals in operation in France offering 9,000 beds for men suffering from VD. In the UK there were twenty more with 11,000 beds and 15,000 other beds in fourteen other hospitals.

Two other approaches might have been tried apart from the punitive, which clearly failed. The simplest would have been to issue contraceptives, as the colonials did. Cloete thought that knowledge of them was not widespread among soldiers, but the Webbs in 1906 reckoned that 50 per cent of the people they interviewed randomly used them. The other idea was the French one. Announcing in 1915 that VD weakened men for the march and increased fatigue, Gallieni ordered that brothels be licensed and all men be inspected twice monthly, women driven from the war area, and rail and barrack areas rigorously watched. The British army tentatively followed suit when it set up *maisons de tolérance*, with success. The one at Rouen was visited by 171,000 men in its first year, with just 243 infection cases, but public opinion at home forced closure.

Third to tobacco and women came the estaminet as an outlet for money. Fed on a diet of greasy stew, dry bully beef and hard tack biscuit, men needed fried food and crisp bread rolls to restore both self-respect and digestion. The estaminet where they got all this might be the kitchen of a farmhouse, a village cottage or a tin hut with newspapers lining the walls and selling lace as a sideline at two and a half francs the yard, but to the infantryman it gave pleasure out of proportion to its appearance. Voigt wrote:

> We entered the estaminet. Soldiers were standing round the walls waiting for vacant seats. An oil lamp was hanging from the ceiling. In the middle there was a long table and soldiers were seated around it, squeezed tightly together, eating eggs and chips and drinking wine and coffee. The air was hot and moist and smelt of tobacco, burning fat and steaming clothes. There was a glowing stove at one end of the room. It looked like a red-hot spherical urn on a low, black pedestal. A big bowl of hot fat was seething on it. A woman with flaming cheeks was throwing handfuls of sliced potatoes into it while she held the saucepan in which the eggs were spluttering. Now more men came in until there was no more standing room left. The conversation was boisterous and vulgar, much of it at the expense of the woman, who laughed frequently and pretended to be shocked and called the soldiers 'naughty boysss'.

The social side noted here was almost as important as the culinary. Eating in a crowd brought back domestic friendships more strongly than almost any other activity, for a man eating food of his choice at his own time was close to home. Against this, the limitations were slight. 'Light and warmth and a chair to sit on conspired to make a sauce that would have rendered chopped hay palatable to us. I remember with gratitude many a stumpy little cottage where we gathered under an oil lamp, sitting as near as we could to the monumental stove while huge shadows clambered over the ceiling.' The price at the end of the session would probably be about one franc or 10*d.* for the egg and chips, roll and coffee; small enough, but for men on soldiers' pay, a pleasure rationed perhaps to once a week. To wash the meal down, stout at twelve sous a glass compared with French lager at two, though both tended to the same watery, dandelion colour. Vin blanc was cheaper and, mixed with grenadine syrup to give the sweetness men craved, almost drinkable. Spirits of course were for officers only.

Before going up the line, men would spend their last centime in the last estaminet. It was truly a little piece of England even down to the opening hours, for no British soldier was served before 1 pm and at 8.30 pm all estaminets shut down.

If a man had more money to spend or was imaginative, he might try to hitch a lift if there was a town of any size near. Smith recalled once being near La Gorgue, whose facilities included a YMCA selling cheap cocoa, two cinemas, many estaminets, a canteen, a theatre with the 'Bow Bells' resident and a divisional reading room. Further north Armentières had a similar life geared to the army, enjoying the same immunity as Lille just behind the German line at the same point until mid-1917. For the salient, the Mecca of our troops was Poperinghe, a town bustling with mess presidents shopping, leave men returning, divisionally billeted men and men on a day out. Omelettes, brothels and silk-embroidered postcards, in that order, were the chief objects of search.

If a man's money ran out, he could try and recover his fortunes by gambling. As with Wellington's infantry, who played cards while they besieged Badajoz as well as on the march, gambling filled many gaps in the army's timetable. The simplest game was Pitch and Toss, much played by northern miners. Pennies were thrown at a line, with the man whose coin was nearest taking the stake or Hoy as it was called. A similar simple game was Under and Over. Played with a dice and three squares, the aim was for a man to throw seven whereupon he was paid at odds of three to one. The most complex game tolerated by the authorities was House. Twenty-four cards were issued at 2*s.* 6*d.* a time. Each card had three lines with five numbers on. One man handled the cash and cards while the other called out the numbers. Ninety pips were drawn out of a bag and each number had its epithet – Kelly's eye for one, doctor's shop for nine, ten and twenty were blind, legs eleven, twenty-two dunky doo, thirty-three Gerty Lee, ninety-nine top of the bleeding bungalow, and so on. The game was universal enough for these numbers to be taken into everyday speech – 'What time is it?' 'Legs eleven.' Men would cover the called numbers with pieces of bread, and the first to cover his lines shouted 'Housee' and won the stake. The first game would be free, and the prize at the end of five minutes' play would usually be about 1s. 6d.

The only game for the gambling hard core was Crown and Anchor. Illegal at the time, it is hard today to find out the rules, though a pub near the Elephant and Castle in South London keeps the name alive. The board for the game was divided into six sections – spades, diamonds, clubs, hearts, crown and anchor. There were three dice with a symbol of the game on each facet. The participant placed his money on one of the board symbols. If that figure came up on all three dice, the man got three times his stake back, if on two dice, double, and so on. In the parlance of the game, the crown was the sergeant-major, the spade the shovel, the diamond the curse and the anchor the meathook. The game might be known as Bumble and Buck, and the symbols as the dart (heart), shamrock (club), gravedigger (spade) and Kimberley (diamond). The chat, recalled by Graham, was part of the game.

Here we are again. The sweaty socks. Cox and Co. the army bankers. Badly bent but never broke. Safe as the Bank of England. Undefeated because they never fought. The rough and the tough, the old and the bold. Where ye lay, we pay. Come and put your money with the lucky old man. I touch the money but I never touch the dice. Any more for the lucky old heart? Make it evens on the lucky old heart. If you don't speculate, you won't accumulate. Are you all done, gentlemen? The diamond, the meathook and the lucky old sergeant-major [shakes dice]. Now then, will anyone down on his luck put a little bit of snow on the old hook? Has no one thought of the pioneer's tool? Are you all done, gentlemen? Cocked dice are no man's dice. Change your bets or double them. Now then, up she comes again. The mandrake, the shamrock and the lucky old heart [rattles dice]. Now, who tries his luck on the name of the game . . .

and so on interminably. The third man involved kept a close watch for approaching authority while, as the worn notes accumulated in an old cigar box, the worst-looking ones might be sent off periodically for vin blanc to be shared round and keep the group spirit going. With army pay so low and the future so uncertain, the old working-class custom of lashing out money unwisely at holiday-time could only be financed by such unofficial methods of gambling. But no doubt, as with the One-Armed Bandits of today whose principals and symbols – and odds – so closely resemble the old crown and anchor, few were the fortunate.

There was only one other way to increase worldly possessions apart from gambling and that was by the sale of war-zone debris brought back in sandbags. Smith bought a German forage cap for two francs and sold it to a quartermaster's batman at Fricourt for ten francs. With their higher rates of pay the auxiliary services could always afford to pay well for trophies from whose origins their higher rate of pay kept them well clear. There were more unofficial ways of making a fast buck, recalled by Mottram.

Wangling was the art of obtaining one's just due by unfair means. Men wangled from NCOs the better sort of jam and extra turns off duty. Scrounging was a morally simpler activity. You walked about whistling with your hands in your pockets and a cigarette in your mouth until you saw what you wanted, then took it. The armies were provided with coal and coke and presumably intended to light it by holding a match to it. Thus no great percentage of wood ever reached its correct destination whether shelving, benches, ladders or hop poles. A dumb, putty-faced sentry would be produced who had heard, seen and knew nothing. NCOs scrounged rum by keeping a thumb in the dipper while doling out. Officers scrounged the best horse lines from other units. Colonials scrounged telephone wire to snare rabbits and so on.

Tarpaulins inevitably ended their lives with one end tied to fences and the other supported by sticks to make excellent waterproof bivouacs, or they left cash in the hand if flogged to the exigent.

There were other ways of spending rest than in handling money. The greatest spellbinder was always soccer. Even in Wellington's time it had been a common pastime of the troops. By Edwardian times it had become almost the manual workers' religion. In 1906 the first £1,000 transfer had taken place and 110,802 attended the cup final of that year, just thirteen years after the founding of the FA. 'However tired the rascals may be for parades, they always have enough energy for football,' observed General Jack. Haig naturally could not understand the psychology involved. When he remarked that no troops travelled without a football, he thought the time would have been better spent in sleeping or relaxing than in running about in search of the ball. But even he blessed the game in the bitter winter of 1917 when it was made compulsory, with every platoon issued with a regulation ball. Games of a hundred a side were played, with officers joining in if 'go as you please' was the order.

Now and again there might be mule races, swimming galas or battalion athletic events, with competition fierce if crates of stout were at issue, but generally diversity of sporting activity was available only to officers with their greater freedom of movement. Hunting, shooting and fishing were their preserve. Pigs supplied the biggest game in Hesdin, driven from the Vosges and Ardennes by war and in search of potatoes. Foxes and hares, however, provided the most certain 'sport'. Bodger tells us that the Northants yeomanry kept a foxhound pack throughout the year, with the first and second whips of the Pytchley hunt serving as officers' batmen. The tradition was an old one. Wellington himself had once been a patron of hounds on active service, breaking military routine instantly when the 'view-hallo' was sounded during inspection at Talavera. The dogs involved could also double as ratters, and what better status symbol could there be than a large dog. The Earl of Feversham's deerhound was a well-known sight on the salient, urinating on table tops and following his master to that isolated grave on the Somme where he still lies today.

Shooting was mostly of partridges. Buxton recalled galloping them over fenceless country in early autumn. Since the bird had only two bursts of flight in its fat body, proceedings could be terminated with a polo stick, which saved ammunition and gave the horse exercise which it enjoyed, or so Buxton thought. Another method of slaughter was to station guns about 200 yards in front of the long grass of a barbed-wire area, which was the birds' chief cover. Old shell craters served as butts, so that in the late afternoon, when the partridges flew low and straight for the oats of the horse lines, a good afternoon would bring in twenty brace. Cartridges of course were brought back from leave; fishing rods as well. Buxton remembered with pleasure seventy trout hooked at Blangy as 'the best moment in my war service' but wondered what the English would have thought of poilus fishing with cheese bait in the Itchen – or galloping birds on the Holkham estate. Their reaction to the Australian custom of fishing with hand grenades would have been clear.

The battalion concert epitomized all that was best in the leisure of rest – relaxation proportionate to the release of tension after front-line duty, magnificent companionship and the reassertion of civilian habits. Noakes recalled an order in the Household battalion early in 1917: 'officers to present for the entertainment of Other Ranks in the battalion . . .' With less than one week to prepare, the show that was finally produced was so popular that it had to be repeated on four successive nights. 'Colonel Portal gave a realistic impression of George Robey and brought the house down with a spirited rendering of "The flowers that bloom in the spring, tra-la" with dance accompaniment. One man remarked to me with surprise, "Who'd have thought that the old man was such a decent old bugger?" The star of the show was the company officer, Captain Hazlitt, made up as a fetching young lady. Several satirical sketches poked fun at military regulations, brass hats, politicians, including one which depicted a draper's shop run on military lines after the war.' The general formula of the concert was to move from comedy, through satire to sentiment with a dash of patriotism at some point. But, if the concert was turned open to Other Ranks, the unaccountable would always appear. Burrage was staggered to hear a countryman in rich brogue sing a version of 'Lillibullero' mentioned by Smollett 150 years earlier, while the natural leaders among the Other Ranks of the army could often get the men with them, with a rousing chorus and chance to bang the tables, singing:

> 'Cassidy, Private Michael Cassidy
> he's of the Irish nationality,
> he's a lad of wonderful audacity,
> Private Michael Cassidy [crash] VC.'

The concert gave the chance for a group of ordinary men to show what remarkable talents in communication lie dormant in normal civilian life, so that most old soldiers today look with contempt at television entertainers after their memories of more talented entertainers among the amateur ranks 'somewhere in France'.

Listing all these activities, one might think of rest as a time of unmitigated bliss. Knowledge of the army should arouse one's suspicions. 'Oh-ah-Perks. Can't you find these men something to do?' How colonels and brigadiers hated resting men. Sword scabbards which had been painted for going up the line would have to be burnished, together with the backs of buttons and bullets in bandoliers. There would be kit inspections, foot inspections, gas mask inspections. Parties of men would be sent out to cut brushwood for no clear reason. The men would be fitted to a Procrustean routine – 6 am reveille, 7 am roll call, 8 am breakfast, 9 am to 1 pm inspections, drill, training, then two hours of training after dinner, taking the men to 4 pm followed by tea with supper at 7 pm. Only then would the men be finally free, just for two hours.

Liddell Hart defended this ceaseless round: 'the way of endurance lay through deadening reflection with action and where action was restricted, trivialities came to the rescue. A hindrance to the development of military intelligence in training yet in the rest camp it had a healing virtue.' Perhaps there was also the need to integrate new drafts and re-build the regiment; perhaps moral and intellectual 'trench feet' were best dealt with in this manner. But one suspects that suspicion and distrust were the chief motives. 'Some of you 'ave been to the front and you've got a bit 'eavy. 'Eavy some of you 'ave got. I knows you. You takes on sullen. We know the men that comes on sullen that means to get through with as little work as possible.'

Liddell Hart need not have worried. The crippling weight of fatigues deadened reflection even more effectively than drill. The French used territorials for these jobs and Maxse, in charge of training after 3rd Ypres, pressed for special companies so that men in rest from battle could actually rest. Nothing was done. Men were therefore impressed for all the carrying which needed to be done. Pit props, duckboards, coils of barbed wire, two petrol tins of water per man linked with belts, dixies of stew and boxes of bombs all went up by hand. These articles gathered weight progressively on the way, while no sagging telephone wire, no uncovered sump, no worn duckboard, no unexpected projection would be missed. Falling into shellholes and losing the way all added to the length of the fatigue. Wiring fatigues were particularly feared. Puttees and hands would be torn; men would tie themselves in their own wire; starshell flares might expose a whole group to aimed machine-gun fire.

This burden was not evenly shared. Old hands boasted that they had done their share so pushed more onto the new men. Bombers, snipers, observers, machine-gunners kept relatively clear. With inefficiency added to all this skiving, grievous burdens might fall on some men. On the Arras front in 1916 Drinkwater recalled a 6.30 am breakfast for parade at 8 am. There followed a five-mile march ending with manual labour for engineers in a mineshaft until 4 pm without food then back to billets by 5. Parade was called at 8.30 that evening and the fatigue of bringing rations to the support line was imposed, so that Drinkwater only got to bed at half-past midnight. He wrote of three men dumping girders when the rain started and being put under 'open arrest' till they finished the job next night. Lane saw two men drop an ammunition box in an open section of a communication trench and begin fighting, to release the cumulative grievances of their labours.

True there were some compensations. Quartermaster's fatigue meant a ride on a lorry to the railhead and plenty of time to work. At the end of it there was usually something to be scrounged from sacks of bread, carrots and meat. Cookhouse fatigue was warm work in winter and cooks fed well. In the cookhouse, parades and inspections could be ignored and food stuffed in trouser pockets. Gladden recalled a fatigue for the RAMC which meant pushing stretchers on a light railway all day. Time was easy, and half a loaf and a tin of Maconochie rewarded at the end of the day. Yet still today men remember the unfairness of using rest for hard manual labour, back-breaking labour with doses of that crippling fear in burial fatigues and wiring parties, which men thought they had been rested from for the time.

The last night in rest would come inevitably. Swinton described the scene.

It was one of the many last evenings before going again up the line. The sergeant-major came to say that a piano had been found and that for a small fee the owner was willing to let us take it to the orchard for the evening provided we kept a tarpaulin over it to keep out the damp. Would the officer come and would the adjutant play the piano? We assembled in the orchard in the dusk, 150 men lying about on the trodden grass, talking and smoking. A thin haze of tobacco smoke hung as a pale blue shadow against the darkening sky, and two candles in the piano sconces gave a round blur of yellow light. The air was still and in the distance the rumble of far-off shellfire served as an echo to the thunder of the limber waggons passing along the road. We sang a chorus or two somewhat untidily to weld us into a unity of mood. Some forms had been lashed together to make a precarious platform and on this the sergeant-major, by virtue of his office the president, stood to announce that Corporal Jackson would oblige with a song. Jackson walked across to the piano. 'Music?' asked the adjutant with a smile. 'No, sir, got no music.' 'What are you going to sing?' 'Don't stop me, sir.' 'I won't, but what's the tune?' Jackson bent down and hummed into the adjutant's ear. 'Right you are, Corporal. Carry on.' Jackson walked to the centre of the stage and gave an expert shuffle with his feet to test its stability. 'Mind them boots, Corporal. The quarter's looking,' shouted someone. The words and the tune were old even in those days. 'Don't stop me. Don't stop me. I've a job to do. T'was advertised in ninety-eight. If I'm not there I'll be too late.' Then Private Walton hunched his shoulders and adjusted the weight of his body carefully from one leg to the other until he found a position of equilibrium. From his pocket he pulled out a mouth-organ, wiped it carefully on the underside of his sleeve, shook it, knocked it gently against his palm to remove any crumbs or tobacco or biscuit then suddenly burst into harmony. He blew and tapped his foot and swayed until he made his audience sing to his tune. And then another tune forced itself onto the surface of his mind, breaking through the years and silence to remind me that Sig-naller Downes also stood up to sing. It was the long-drawn-out sequence of Gertie Gitana's 'Nev-vah-mind', a song which declined in speed as it grew in sentiment. The moon rose in the blue sky, grey now, mellowing the darkness and deepening the shadows under the trees. Over the subdued chatter of many voices and the noise of the occasional lighting of a match came the silvery spray of notes from the piano. The adjutant was play-ing quietly to himself, meditating in music. The talk ceased and men turned away from their comrades to listen until there was dead silence under the trees to make a background for the ripple of the piano. The silence broke in upon the player and he removed his hands from the keyboard for an instant. The world plunged into a deep pool of stillness, rising again to hear a supple cascade of showering notes as he played one of Debussy's arabesques. When he had finished, there was a pause for a second or two before the applause began – enough of a gap to show that the listeners had been travelling with him into a foreign land.

Then the men would go back to their barns. Since candles were not issued, darkness brought its own curfew unless improvised fires could be lit around which men might gather. Talk would be of friends, the war's duration, the fighting merit of cockneys as against Welsh, of the contribution of the French and battalion losses since coming to France; finally, of the coming stunt. Then to bed, perhaps for a smoke, with dire consequences always possible in a straw barn. 'Good excitement today,' wrote Drinkwater. 'Great sport killing rats then burnt down the barn. £120 damages and the order "No smoking in barns". Personally I am not taking any notice. I imagine the brigadier in his room at HQ in front of a good fire whilst we in this wretched place cannot keep warm. Have nothing to do at night except write letters and slowly sink into the straw and sleep. Lights out at 8.30 pm.'

When next day dawned and it was time once more to go into danger, there was some resentment. 'It is surprising how one's tautened nerves relax as a result of a few days' rest and quiet – and how, once more in the danger zone, the strain on sorely tried nerves begins again after the painful process which makes one feel conditions more acutely and which take time to acclimatize one to the previous level one had attained. Do not believe that soldiers get used to war and danger. They never do.' Worden expressed the minds of most soldiers.

10

HOME LEAVE

During the Napoleonic wars Private Wheeler recalled men shedding tears as they spoke of friends and relatives. He noted, too, 'much talk of home'. So it was in the Great War. Nearly all the men carried with them photos of parents, friends and sweethearts or wives, and such photos turn up today among dead men's effects. The sepia tone and stilted poses strike an immediate note of remoteness and poignancy. Less carefully protected, in side pockets and haversacks, were letters from home or inscriptions on the flyleaf of bibles and hidden in the memoranda section of – illegal – diaries. These strike with the immediacy of the photos:

> God send me back to you
> over the sea.
> Dearest, I want you near.
> God dwells above you;
> knows how I love you.
> He will bring me back to you.
> Though we are parted, love lives for ever
> where hearts are fond and true.
> So till our meeting, let us remember,
> ever I pray to you.

The writer of these lines, Harry Ingham, did indeed return.

The most vocal reminder of the longing for the old life and the friends within it were the songs of the march. There were songs which made a mockery of fear, songs which followed the course of men going to mow and of officers jumping over grasshoppers' backs, but the largest number came from the music halls and shows remembered from the past or brought back from leave. In 1914 came 'Tipperary', 'Marching through Georgia' and Mark Sheridan's

> 'Ere we are, 'ere we are, 'ere we are again
> Pat and Mac and Tommy and Jack and Joe.
> Never mind the weather. Now then all together
> are we downhearted? NO ('ave a banana)
> 'ere we are, 'ere we are, etc. etc.

Then came George Robey's 'There's a Long, Long Trail' in 1915 followed by 'Pack Up your Troubles in your Old Kitbag' and 'If You Were the Only Girl in the World' in 1916. The haunting 'Roses are Blooming in Picardy' was a product of 1917, and 'Goodbyeee' of 1918. Lines and fleeting melodies of these still survive over two generations. Though they could be squeezed into the march, it was only at the cost of butchery, since the rhythm of the boards was hardly the rhythm of army boots, while some, like 'Roses of Picardy', were too highly treasured to be exposed in that way. At a concert or in a darkened hall they would be quietly sung as men wept silently for what they had lost. Even today Priestley finds that some of the lines of these fragile songs tell him more and bring back more than whole anthologies – songs like:

> Where are the lads of the village tonight?
> Where are the nuts we knew?
> In Piccadilly or Leicester Square?
> No, not there
> [*more quietly*] No, not there.
> They're taking a trip to the continong . . .'

These were not the most popular. In estaminets and billets men liked best to sing those songs which brought them even closer to the mean streets and terraced homes of Britain. These were the songs which made Kipling and educated men like him cough and blow their noses with embarrassment. They had such titles as 'The Roses round the Door Make me Love Mother More' and 'The Sweetest Blossom on the Tree Cannot Compare with Ma . . . aaa . . . ry'. Lyrics might run:

> When you're a long, long way from home
> your mother's voice rings in your ears.
> It's hard to find a girl that's true
> that you can tell your troubles to
> and then you write a letter home
> when you're a long, long way from home.

Another favourite was:

> Hullo, my dearie, I want you tonight.
> I shall meet you tonight, dear,
> in my beautiful dreamland

and your eyes will be bright, dear,
with the love light that shines for me.

It was songs like these that were sung everlastingly, as Wilfred Owen
rather sourly remarked, for as men huddled in groups out of the line
just as they tended to do under shellfire in battle, so they saw that
only the end of war could bring a beginning of hope. Home for these
bewildered men was the memory of a time when there was no explosive remorselessly to probe maturity; it was too the hope for a time
which they hardly dared formulate to themselves when lice, cordite
fumes and the parched throat of fear would be taken away by a
maternal figure and in a home where similar nightmares of childhood had been soothed and eased away.

The most practical way of getting in touch with home was by
letter. Rest was the chief time for writing home. Free franking was
allowed on two letters a week, while a special green envelope, which
the soldier could himself seal once a month (in theory), allowed
uncensored communication provided a man guaranteed to give no
tactical information away.

A good knowledge of what was in these letters survives, since
many green letters were opened at base to check on morale, while
company officers had the job of reading all other letters and acting
as censor. This embarrassed them, but Macmillan among many
remembered it as the most valuable experience of his war because
of the 'knowledge of the poorer classes' which it gave. He recalled
the simplicity, humour, steadfastness and sentimentality which gave
him a new sense of confidence – and of humility. 'Some of them
write so nicely, it tells what they are really like under an unpromising
surface,' wrote Gillespie. Cloete too recalled the crude but moving
cries from the heart. A typical letter might recall in detail the last
time writer and recipient were in bed together, then go on to regret
the absence of beer and steak-and-kidney pudding before the con-
ventional assurance that the writer was in the pink, hoping that the
condition was mutual, promising battle souvenirs and requesting
practical things like socks, lighters, lavatory paper or jam.

Letters and parcels from home were received with equal regu-
larity. Nothing ever took longer than four days, even though name
and regiment were the only permitted addresses. The army had
accordingly to handle 7,000 mail sacks and 60,000 parcels daily.
Notwithstanding, mail was delivered punctually even in the very

front line, where it would come up on top of the ration sandbag.

These letters were welcomed quite apart from their practical contents. 'You say the news from home must seem trivial compared with my experience out here,' wrote Noakes. 'Please don't get that impression. Out here news of home is like food and drink to us, however trivial. Indeed, this life is like a dream and the old life is the only reality. We live on memories. Our constant thought is – what are they doing at home.' The parcels would give more tangible backing. Contents might range from the over-ripe partridge and a bunch of violets, which Ellis once got, through to the homemade cakes, Oxo cubes, chocolate bars and cigarettes which were the more common staple. The contents of all parcels naturally were shared out equally among mates. The thought was the private and valuable part. In addition might come unsolicited parcels from various sources backing the war anonymously. For 5s. any civilian could donate a gift via Queen Alexandra's Field Force Fund Despatches. It would contain Bovril, bull's-eyes 'the soldiers' favourite', Keating's powder with its slogan of 'Kill that insect, Tommy', coal tar soap, twelve boxes of matches, Black Cat cigarettes, a French–English dictionary (toilet paper?), Thermogene against rheumatism, Kephaldol against headaches and Spagnol for the feet – food indeed for body and soul. Some parcels might be even more rewarding. 'Dear soldier,' wrote the children of a St Alban's primary school sending a parcel to the Hertfordshire regiment: 'We are sorry that you are cold at night so we are sending you a blanket. We mean to send one every week because you are so brave and taking care of us and our dear country. We send you our love and pray to God to end the war soon and bring you safe home. Your loving little friends, Garden Fields School(girls). PS we are not going to buy sweets till the war is over but save our money for blankets and tobacco.' It is not hard here to see the ideas of the teacher and those of the children but, with such a message, there was a very special blanket for a Herts. man. Several of the memoirs I have read expressed gratitude for parcels from the many organizations at home backing the troops.

Better than letters was the direct contact of leave. The problem was that it came very seldom. Ellison had a typical ration of three leaves in two years, one of four days, another two of ten days each. By way of extenuation one might point out the difficulties of organization. With two million men to be organized, just one week's leave in the year required the movement of 40,000 men daily. Only by the middle stages of the war had an administration been developed capable of moving such a mass of men. Carrington in 1916 was able to find many men who had had no leave for twenty months.

After 1916 leave became as well administered as most of the other admin. matters in our war. Lists were kept and a strict rota followed. Soldiers would not be pre-warned, so that the good news came only on the day they had to start back for home. Waugh recalled 'few more thrilling memories'. Men would dash from the front as fast as they could, knowing that a chance shell or bullet, a raid or a battle planned might steal the prized leave. Compassion certainly had no part in the process. Fairness and the rota were the only criteria. Thus Feilding wrote of a man in tears bringing him a letter which told of the death of the eldest of his two daughters in a car crash. This was in July 1916 and the man's last leave had been in August 1915. Feilding doubted correctly whether the army would deal with the matter with any understanding. Commonsense equally had no part in leave proceedings. Seven days' leave was little use to a Highlander, since it took fifty hours to reach Aberdeen, meaning that the man would have to return almost as soon as he arrived.

Leave trains were specially designated, for leave men were in a disciplinary limbo so far as practical regulations were concerned. Doors were missing, windows broken and areas of flooring were often torn up to feed braziers hung outside the train to get a good blaze going in cold weather. In between the status of soldiers and civilians, the nerves of most leave men were strained. Even officers would come to blows over the distribution of seat cushions in their specially reserved compartments. The Official History terms the transport 'Noah's Ark trains'.

Better organized was food. Society women ran canteens at the larger stations, otherwise men would go hungry on a journey of up to fifteen hours to the coast. At the port came new kit and new underwear. Vermin-free certificates were a necessity. Then would come the 'electrical sensation' of passing through Kent after the mad dash for seats on the Victoria train at Folkestone. At Victoria there would be cigarettes and chocolate freely given by waiting crowds and buffet fare from various religious organizations.

Leave seemed hardly credible to most men, even when it was going on. That war which had plunged men abruptly into extremes of fear and hardship ended with equal abruptness at Boulogne.

Anyway most men were too tired to think straight. Some would use the leave just for rest. Laurie Lee remembered his uncles sleeping like the dead all day. Others found it difficult to rest. Lucy had to sleep on his bare bedroom floor, so used had he become to sleeping rough. While Lucy could not adjust to rich civilian food, Andrews went out of his way to guzzle fried eggs, sausages, fried tomatoes, and went in and out of the local dairy for the most richly creamed milk available. Some slept; Beale lived his fourteen days' leave by the hour, resenting any sleep.

Though it was valued beyond the power of words leave was not an entirely easy experience. Above all, soldiers were disconcerted to find how their outlook had drifted away from that of those who had stayed behind. Hutchison, like many soldiers, just wanted to forget everything to do with the hateful war when he was back home. Nevertheless he could not help noticing just how little civilians knew what was going on and how bizarre was their approach to the whole thing. To the home front, 'cheerful Tommies with the glint of battle in their eyes' were the norm, slowly but surely wearing down 'the square-headed Huns'. Burrage could not decide which was more offensive, to be regarded as a splendid fellow or to be treated as a lucky lad on a picnic. He resented also the patronizing attitude of older men who had 'given' their sons. Returning early in 1915 with a kitten inside his shirt, Lane found civilians reluctant to sit next to him and was later asked if he was not tired of killing Germans all day long. Fitzclarence, leader of the Worcesters in their crucial bayonet charge at Gheluvelt during 1st Ypres, was presented with a white feather on his next home leave while in civvies.

Soldiers had a more practical grievance than incomprehension; they believed that people back home were prospering from the war which was grinding the men of the front. A soldier might well compare his bob a day with the wages of munition workers – people like Rosina Whyatt, who had earned 16s. a week as a farm labourer and got 70s. as a shell operative. The soldier also noted all the humbug. Middlesbrough was typical here. It offered 'patriotic shopping weeks' as 'competitive operations' and donated £828 to its war heroes' fund while putting £7,121,926 in war loans bearing a good rate of interest. If the soldier read *John Bull*, a favourite source of literary grousing for the front-line man, his attention would have been drawn to the excellent profits being made by shipping lines and meat companies. Horatio Bottomley was correct in this hunch.

The *Economist* in 1919 published war dividend figures. Iron and steel had risen from 1·4 per cent to 6·3 per cent; motor dividends from 5·2 per cent to 16·5 per cent; shipping from 4·3 per cent to 17·9 per cent. Anglo–Persian petrol profits rose from £26,700 to £1,090,200. It is hard to resist the conclusion that the soldiers' impression of profiteering on their own predicament was a correct one. The Great War in this area was indeed a war to save freedom.

On their side, civilians too could argue a degree of provocation. Men conscious of risking their lives for their country often demanded a degree of licence on leave hard to bear by civilians, who did not realize the degree of privation and danger which was the justification. An impressive list of incidents emerges from the pages of local papers and memoirs.

Kingsbury observed that in Blackmoor Vale, Somerset, soldiers were allowed to poach rabbits during 1915 but were pointedly asked when they were going back. Blythe discovered the same attitude in Suffolk.

Drink was a constant stumbling block. Two gunners in April 1915 were fined 2s. 6d. for feloniously receiving eighteen eggs, which were discovered under their army caps. Originally there had been some trouble in establishing their identity, since with alcoholic indistinctness they had told PC Kemp, 'We don't know whether you are a policeman or a German spy.' On the same day in the same court Private Williams of the 3rd Battalion the Argylls was fined for breaking a beer bottle over PC French's head. Being on leave, he had wished to see his injured mate in hospital but had been refused admission since he had been in civvies. Drawing a bottle, he had told the constable that he would serve him in the same way as he had served the Germans. Fined 5s. for being drunk and 15s for assaulting the constable, he was given the chance of only paying half if he would go back to the front at once. Privates were not the only drinkers. Second Lieutenant Johnson knocked down three men in a recruiting procession in his car and had to be chased for 200 yards. When his car was examined, it was found to have brakes worked by string, no bell, no licence and no registration number. He was duly fined £27 5s. and had his non-existent licence suspended for a year.

The chief problems, however, seem to have been sexual. The number of cases coming before courts in this area were truly legion. On 7 May 1915 Katherine Laverty, aged thirty, threw carbolic acid into the eyes of ASC John Macdowell of Grove Park, South London.

'He has ruined me,' she said. 'I have pawned and sold everything to keep him. He deserves what he got.' Macdowell lost his right eye, but perhaps saved his life since he was unable to return to France. Winifred Penrose of Truro stood at the other end in terms of righteousness. 'Shocking revelations' were headlined in the Cornwall *County News*. Her husband was in the naval reserve and had been sent to Gallipoli in 1915. Thereafter the lonely wife had been under constant police supervision. Her 'conduct nevertheless had been most unsatisfactory'. Three or four soldiers visited her regularly 'in spite of everything the chief constable could do'. At weekends she went to Newquay 'no doubt for purposes of immorality'. Constables visited her house on several occasions, even the chief constable himself. She promised reformation. But then Private Cocks and Mrs Penrose were one morning discovered together under the bed, Cocks having been absent without leave for three weeks. Winifred's husband requested the court to stop the separation allowance and take the two children of the marriage into care, sending an illegitimate child to the workhouse. Winifred herself went to prison for two months with her youngest child of a year and a half, and the bench considered it 'a very bad case'. The local press thus revealed constantly how great an irritant of customary relationships was war and how great a revealer of indiscretion.

All soldiers were bitterly depressed when the time came to return to France. On drunks at Victoria station military police would turn a blind eye, since six weeks in the glasshouse at Aldershot was a poor exchange for a man who might be back on Vimy Ridge within forty-eight hours. Dressed like arctic explorers, Miles thought that all men looked 'dreadfully tired'. They would stand very still, holding young ladies close for a moment, then drawing away they would both immediately make the effort to seem gay and unconcerned. 'Oh, the second partings. There seems to be a new look in their eyes as if they were looking into the eternal. Somehow one felt as if one must talk in a whisper to them.' Leave was thus an experience which began and ended with overwhelming suddenness and emotion, and was so different from what came before and after that men were left as baffled and unsatisfied as if they had been in battle.

11

BATTLE

At the end of the war, Field-Marshal Sir Douglas Haig attempted to sum it all up in a final despatch. Overall he considered the war 'one great and continual engagement . . . a steady and continuous fight which had gone on day and night, above ground and below it'. This is how it had seemed to civilians as well. In most homes during the war there had been a *Daily Mail* map of the war zone, scoured with lines and stuck with pins. Artillery duels, raids, battles, combined operations noted in newspapers had been transferred to it, with pride for country and fear for a son 'somewhere in France'. Coloured lines would show successive advances, dates written on would mark phases of the war. In retrospect it seemed almost like a soccer match between the Corinthians and the Wanderers, counter-attack following attack without break, each kick of the ball purposeful and forceful.

The old soldier rejects all this. The word 'battle' hardly appears in memoirs. The word, after all, implies a precise location in time and place as well as a clear-cut purpose. Since soldiers were for-bidden to keep diaries, seldom saw maps and knew only as much as they found out from heavily censored newspapers and the risible divisional newsflashes, they were absolutely unable to establish any outlines for their activities. Watch the veteran read a book on 'his' war today. His face registers pleasure. The concern of scholars gives greater importance to an event which he assumed was of importance only to himself. He is happy too that he can fit places which stuck in his mind into some sort of order. Yet, at the end, there is a half-smile on his lips. What the scholar sees today as a single event, the participant was aware of only as a rapid succession of brilliant cameos, suffused with tension and fear. The civilian overview bears no relation to the participant's experience. It is the measurement of pain to the experience of pain. Instead of '2nd Ypres' or 'Cambrai' the veteran thinks of particular faces and unique actions. He remem-bers too an intensely personal journey etched in his memory like the stations of the cross.

The first of these stations of the cross was a rumour. There had probably been a longer period in rest than usual, perhaps with oranges and chestnuts in the rations to arouse the suspicions of the men. They might notice an increased coming and going of red-tabbed staff officers. Then would come the order to muster, a company on each limb of a three-sided square. With the men standing at ease, the colonel would appear on horseback and announce the fact of battle. 'I rather think it is, ahem, incumbent on me. Yes, that is to say, my duty to inform you fellahs that an action with the enemy is imminent. Yes, rather. I mean to say and naturally, yes, let me see, quite naturally you will be expected to conduct yourselves with valour, by gad, I mean to say courage. I might add that you are bound to be successful but do not forget when blooding your bayonets, do not on any account bury them deeply. Damn' nuisance, you know, endeavouring to withdraw an unnecessarily deep bayonet. Awkward, you know, and rather a waste of time.' Read recalls how profoundly moved he and his mates were when their colonel went on to give them the history of the 17th of the line, told them that the Leicesters did not know the meaning of the word 'retreat' and that the eyes of all were on the deeds of the New Army, finally requesting that a new honour be added to the colours. Invariably came the addition of base metal. Once the colonel had gone, his adjutant or the sergeant-major would follow with the assurance that the severest military law would apply. Coppard writes of his stupefaction at listening to a long list of executed men read out, with their names, ranks, units and offences carefully itemized and the date and hour of execution of each carefully appended.

The men had been told of their future at the last possible moment. There remained but one night of safety. But, as the square of men broke, thoughts would not be on present safety. Many veterans write of a feeling of profound depression on being told of imminent action. Fears of hand-to-hand fighting or of lying wounded in no-man's-land overwhelmed. Manning tells us:

There was a glassy quiet. Many of the men seemed oblivious of each other as they sat about with pondering brows. One might pass a group of two or three hastening on their business, talking quietly together, and one caught a hint of something desperate in their faces. One only caught glimpses of the tension momentarily, beneath the surface and at unawares. And, while it was more or less apparent in each individual, the temper of the men was quiet and grave. The simplicity of their outlook gave them a certain dignity. They had been brought to the last extremity of hope and yet they put their hands on each other's shoulders and said with passionate conviction that it would be alright, though they had faith in nothing but themselves and in each other.

Added to the support of friends was that of religion. The voluntary communion service before battle was a more sincere and more intense affair than compulsory church parade. There might be an altar of stretchers, the music of a broken-down piano, with men kneeling on the mud floor of a barn. Photos today show the men with head bowed, face covered by a hand. Behind the closed eyes, one senses a profound sense of isolation, of disconnection with time, which only those about to die can feel.

After making his peace with God, the soldier's thoughts turned to home. With the last letter home even more than with the signed will in his paybook, the soldier finalized his worldly business. Some of these last letters have come down to us, for example, these two quoted by Grant:

Dear Mother and Auntie Lill, as we are about to go into work that must be done, if anything should happen to me, not to worry. I have been over the top once already this week. I feel a sort of sickening dread of the horrors which I knew we should have to go through. Auntie, I know you will think more of me if I tell you that I went into action with the absolute certainty of death. Others felt emotions not far different from mine.

This is written on the eve of our going over the top in a big attack. It will only be seen in the event of my being killed in action. You I know, my dear Dad, will bear the shock as bravely as you have always borne the strain of my being out here. I believe I have told you before that I do not fear death itself. The beyond has no terrors for me. I am quite content to die for the cause for which I have given up nearly three years of my life and I only hope that I will meet death with as brave a front as I have seen other men do before. Well, Dad, please carry on with a good heart, then I shall be quite content. Good-bye, dearest of fathers.

Then the last night would fall on the men. There would be subdued, earnest talk in the barn. Cash would be pooled to be divided amongst survivors after the battle and thus saved from the hawks of the battlefield. Addresses would be exchanged so that

news of death might reach families more personally than through
the official War Office telegram. Finally talk would cease as men lay
back on the straw, though few remember sleeping much on the
night before a major engagement. Ball wrote:

All through that night I never slept a wink of sleep. My
stomach would insist on rising to my throat to choke me each
time I thought of some lurid possibility. I would find myself
calculating the chances of survival. Surely a quarter of our number
would remain unscathed? And the other chances – what are they?
Maybe one in three against being killed. One chance in four of
being wounded which means a respite and one in four of being
taken prisoner – as good as escaping scotfree. At times I would
nod off to sleep. Our emotions come and go like clouds in the sky.

With dawn came the action which cut short such courage-sapping
thoughts. Surely there was safety in the old routines? God would
not allow men to be hurt with army tasks uncompleted. Packs
were dumped by companies and blankets stacked in bundles of
twelve. Dress this morning was battle order. From its usual place
on the left side, the haversack was moved to the back below the
shoulder blade. Beneath it, in the small of the back, was the rolled
groundsheet. A hundred and eighty rounds of extra rifle ammunition would be carried in a spare bandolier over the right shoulder.
A Mills grenade fitted into each tunic sidepocket – at 5 lb. each no
slight addition. Finally came the waterbottle on the right side, together with the white linen bag containing the iron ration. All these
preparations would be completed, with barking NCOs hustling like
sheepdogs to get the men through their breakfasts and onto the
road. Lord Moran described one viewpoint of these preparations:

At noon today our car pulled up by the road and we got off for
lunch by the roadside. The chauffeur had pulled the cork out of
a bottle of white wine and M. had handed round the sandwich
basket when the curious crawling music of a flute band floated up
to us from somewhere over the hillcrest behind us. I walked up
to the crest to see who was coming and saw below the rolling
wave of a line of infantry on the march. Soon the heads, then the
bodies, then the horses of the leading officers rose over the crest
of the hill and hard behind came the troops. The flute band was
playing something lugubrious and the feet of the marchers were

beating on the wet pavé a rhythmical 'trudge, trudge' in accompaniment. Why are the lower notes of the flute so doleful in the open air? Every man was loaded heavy. Rifles were being carried anyhow as it was 'marching easy'. Pipes and cigarettes sent up a thin blue film of smoke that writhed and hung like a pale spirit for a moment over the undulating head of the marching column and then wafted away to the east in long curves. The boys were talking quietly and naturally as they passed. The sound of their voices made a faint, many toned hum in the quiet country road. Then a sudden booming roar from the west brings an equally sudden stillness in the ranks. Just here and there is a forced and weak laugh but the majority just 'carry on'. The booming continues. A sudden lapse in the wind seems to have brought it closer. These are fine, serious, thoughtful faces, leaning to the weight of their load. They will be in battle tomorrow. They know this as they march along the road. They are thinking their first thoughts about it. The marching line ends. The stretcher bearers with their little, wheeled ambulances come along; the baggage column with its long-eared mules; then the field kitchens – black, oily-looking boilers on wheels. The column halts further along the road. Packs are unloosed at once, one man taking off another's. You see men stretching their shoulders with a sigh of relief. Dinner is served. The men lie on the grass bank by the roadside. Then an order and they form up at once. But now the khaki caps have been changed for iron shrapnel helmets of dull green. The change is significant. The flutes begin their crawling whimper once more and the men are off – to the front.

The marching men entered the battle area progressively. Everywhere they saw newly built roads, metalled for guns and coarse for men. Between the road veins ran the capillaries of Decauville light railways and the deep slits for telephone cables. Strings of marching men, pack mules and horsed waggons dovetailed like a symphony on these lines of communication, passing dumps of material beyond number – planks, sandbags, shells, wire, cable. It was like a vast, fissured ants' nest of khaki, dust and power. No doubt men moving towards the front line plotted danger more systematically amongst the apparent chaos of movement and activity. First came the observation balloons, then the heavy guns as their path changed from road to communication trench, sinking deeper into the ground until they found their vision totally obscured by the time they reached the light field guns, by which time their security had been increased by nightfall.

The final point might be the front line; it might be one of those ten-foot-deep, wired-over labyrinths specially dug for the second wave. Either way men waited uncomfortably for the dawn. Most old soldiers considered 'going over the top' the greatest test a man would face in his life. Hopes, however irrational, of a magical removal or last-minute intervention could no longer be sustained. The hand-to-hand fight with cold steel filled a man's mind with the more vigour for having been put off so long. In their long wait through the coldest hours of the night, death permeated the slouching men. Maze tells us:

> The rushing past of the shells seemed completely detached for the time being from that peculiar stillness into which nature sinks after the sun has set. But the momentary peace was tinged with apprehension. As time went past, it crept into my mind and became acute as I weighed my chances of surviving the attack. No. I could not so easily give up life, so alluring and precious at that moment. For the first time, I was facing a conflict. The grip of life on me was tightening and more than ever I wanted to live. None of the men spoke except to ask for more room to move to their fate. I heard something within me say, 'You'll get through,' and I clung to that as I slipt into the trench, shuffling my way along.

The only check to these thoughts was the weight of the final barrage. If wind and humidity were right, the sound could be heard in London from the furthest part of the British front. In the front-line trench it was all but overwhelming, as Griffith discovered: 'The sound was different from anything known to me. It was not a succession of explosions or a continuous roar. I never heard a gun or a bursting shell. It was not a noise; it was a symphony. It did not move; it hung over us. It seemed as though the air were full of a vast and agonized passion, bursting now with groans and sighs, shuddering beneath terrible blows. And the tumult did not pass in this direction or that. It did not begin, intensify, decline and end. It was poised in the air, a stationary panorama of sound, not the creation of men.' Lieutenant Carver wrote that he would never forget the roar of the final barrage, so like enormous waves breaking against a beach, the breakers of the sea of death. Livering remembered looking for comfort at the face of a stolid old corporal, a veteran of Gallipoli, 'but he was shaking all over with a face white as parchment'.

As the moment of attack approached, men's thoughts branched out away from the apprehension of the night. Heath recalled the radiance of Captain Neville one hour before his death in the great first attack on the Somme. Maze writes of the slightly hysterical jokes. Carrington was astonished by Corporal Weller, invariably coarse of speech, singing a hymn to the Virgin in Latin. More often all would stand silent, dry lips twisting, furtive glances at photos and letters. Grant wrote:

> I gave the men a good look. They seemed more or less in a trance. Their eyes were glassy and their faces white as chalk. But the way their mouths were set gave me confidence. One or two shook hands. An old private, lying down by a very young corporal, suddenly kissed him on the cheek and then lay down again flat. My orderly behind me tugged at my ankle. I could see he had something to say but the din was terrific. He looked very excited. I noticed the beads of sweat all over his face. Putting his mouth to my ear, he yelled, 'Till the very last, Lieutenant.' I remember patting him on the shoulder.

At ten minutes to zero the rum issue might be brought round – one sixty-fourth of a gallon, a small coffee-cup full of overproofed, treacly forgetfulness; then the men would be ordered to fix bayonets. An officer would check equipment – picks and shovels, Verey lights, sandbags to consolidate the captured position, Lewis-gun ammunition, barbed wire. Winter tells us that the check would be personal as well: 'Wally, take care of them new boots you got on. Mind you don't slip. Arthur, feeling alright? You're looking a bit, you know what I mean, like?' 'Don't bother 'bout me, Sergeant. It's waiting about, like. Once we get going, I'll be OK.' And so the men stood by the ladders or pegs driven into the trench-side, two to a ladder, with the man on the right going up first. 'Not a word spoken. The officer has the whistle in his mouth and keeps his eyes fixed on the synchronized watch. All eyes are on him. For a moment or two longer you are safe in the land of the living.' Thus the men took comfort from their imperturbable officer. What was the officer thinking? Grant: 'What did I think about? Nothing very much

except that I was thirsty and the leg of my breeches was torn.'
Cloete: 'Funny to live by a watch minute by minute as if I were
going to catch a train.' Probably their faces were as white as their
men's.

The shrill of a whistle or the drop of a cap and the men went
over the top. No man could know if instant death might not meet
him. A split second's lack of care in the weeks and months before
the attack, the most fleeting glance over the parapet of the trench
and a sniper's bullet was likely to punish on the instant. Now the
whole body was exposed to machine-guns set to sweep along the
brim of the trench. Lane later distinctly recalled the feeling of
physical nakedness as well as mental numbness blurring all impressions. An anonymous writer in the Catford *Journal* wrote of
feeling demented after leaving the security of the trenches, out of
breath too, just like the first sensation on plunging into a cold bath.
'A man who stepped out of the trenches at that moment and lived
through has never in all the ensuing years faced such a climax,'
wrote Winter.

Along the line as far as the eye could grasp, a single line of men
climbed out, rifles at the port, bayonets glinting in the dawn, with
a man every two yards, two platoons abreast every 200 yards, the
second wave some twenty yards back. Then slowly they would go
forward, the barrage lifting a hundred yards every three minutes.
A slower advance would allow the Germans to get their machine-
guns operational; a quicker advance would touch the curtain of the
barrage. The mechanical nature of the initial advance came almost
as a relief to the attacking force, for any movement served to displace
the initial feeling of total vulnerability even if only to replace it with
a feeling of the most total confusion. Wrote Manning:

They seemed so toy-like, so trivial and ineffective when opposed
to that overwhelming wrath of shells and yet they moved forward
mechanically as though they were hypnotized by some superior
will. That had been one of his most vivid impressions in action, a
man close to him moving forward with the jerky motion a clock-
work toy has when it is running down. It had been vivid to him
because of the relief with which he had turned to it and away
from the confusion and tumult of his own mind. It had seemed
impossible to relate that petty, commonplace, unheroic figure in
ill-fitting khaki and a helmet like the barber's basin with which

Don Quixote had made shift on his adventures to the moral and spiritual conflict, almost superhuman in its agony, within him.

As they advanced, so officers and NCOs would chivy the men – 'Keep the line straight,' 'Not so fast on the left,' 'Steady on the right.' The example of an officer with his pipe and shooting stick was crucial. Wedgwood wrote: 'If you look inside a uniform, a battle is a pathetic business. They all carry rifles and are helpless. They are highly strung and nervous and have never done it before. It is so novel. You look and see what the fellow next to you is doing. The more helpless you are, the more you crave for someone to follow. An example in battle means more than in any other crisis of life. One man may with his eyes turn a thousand into heroes or rabbits.' Bultitude's colonel gave the classic example: 'My old colonel walked in front of our ragged line and gave the signals by a wave of his cane. We had no cover and advanced in open order under terrific fire – a few paces forward, then flat on the ground and, on each upward wave of the colonel's cane, forward. I had the foolish notion that if I had an umbrella I should feel safer. The man on my left was fast asleep immediately on throwing himself to the ground and I had to prod him with the butt of my rifle each time.' All signals naturally had to be visual, since the noise tore away from the mouth any words.

Initially the line could be maintained by example and occasionally by such orders as penetrated the demonic volume of noise – 'Keep your extension.' 'Don't bunch.' 'Keep up on the left.' But shell-bursts and broken ground would soon turn order into crowd and confusion. Maze recalled: 'The ground seemed to quake under me and everything appeared to be moving along with me, figures popping up and down on every side over the convulsing ground and I felt the rush of others coming on behind. The waves in front were merged in smoke, moving like animated figures projected on a glaring screen. Flashes made everything wobble and vacillate. I felt stunned and hardly conscious of anything. I caught stray words of company commanders urging their men forward. Down in a hollow, a barrage of shrapnel shook us like leaves. Many went down and remained. The noise was deafening.' This appalling noise seemed to come anonymously, for the enemy was hardly to be seen. Attacking 10,000 Germans, a soldier might perhaps see ten. Shells represented the enemy by proxy, bursting with a vast upward rush of black smoke, lit from underneath by a red flame. As treble to the bass of the shells were the machine-guns, engines letting off steam, and sniper fire sounding like twigs crackling underfoot.

If enemy fire confused the attackers with its noise and sense of danger, the ground did so by its unexpectedness. Grassless and honeycombed by intersecting shellholes, it was littered with tentacles of barbed wire attached to smashed picquets, cans, bodies, smashed limbers, stains of cordite, fissures of old trenches. The scenario was brown as the veld, powdered to the subsoil by high explosive like crumbled peat. An Australian might see in it the likeness of an Australian creek bed in the dry season; to an Englishman it was not a country at all but a stinking, smoking apparition. The distinctiveness which existed on HQ maps, where space was bounded by a grid, divided by coloured objective lines, had no place on the battlefield. There all identifications looked alike, all directions equally hard to establish without a compass. Thus Chaband on the Somme saw the Glosters and Camerons charge each other, with casualties resulting, before a captain shouted, 'Stand fast Glosters,' while MacGill at Loos saw kilted Highlanders noisily charging parallel to a trench in which his men thought themselves facing the enemy.

Confronted by so much appalling confusion and danger, why did the line try to advance at all? There may have been a fraction of self-preservation, because the men knew that military police might well be following up behind. Thus Chandos recalled being nearly bayoneted by a sergeant of the Coldstreams while taking shelter in a shellhole – 'Oh, I beg pardon, sir, but oughtn't we to be going THERE?' A more significant aim driving the men was to keep with the group. Isolated men in the battlefield always became fearful. In the same way soldiers facing unexpected danger at any time tended to bunch, and later in the war they were trained to resist the herding instinct. The chief impulsive force, however, appears more unexpected. The impression left by memoirs suggests that, after the initial moments when men advanced head down, wincing and blinking in dread of a bullet and in a spirit of dogged hopelessness, they were often affected by two moods successively.

The first of these moods was one of complete abstraction. Gladden talks of 'a peculiar, dreamlike illusion . . . for a moment I was detached from the awful present', feeling as if his feet were rooted while his surroundings moved past him. While Edwards spoke of 'an elevated state of mind with a sense of dual personality'. And Noakes commented on 'an extraordinary sensation that I was no longer responsible for my own safety'. The rational basis of this release from anxiety is supplied by Professor Tawney, reflecting on his feelings on the first day of the Somme; 'I hadn't gone ten yards before I felt a load fall from me. I knew it was alright. . . . I knew I was in no danger. I knew I shouldn't be hurt – knew it positively, much more positively than things I'm paid for knowing.' Men were so certain that they would be hit when they got out of the trench that, when after a moment they found themselves safe, relief became euphoric.

There followed logically the second mood, one of positive enjoyment. Bowra hated war but, during the attack of 8 August 1918, he recalled advancing with jokes and fits of laughter into 'the terrible fascination of battle'. This mood, he thought, fitted in with his attitude neither before nor after the engagement. Glyde reflected in bewilderment on the invigoration of battle. 'The difficulty lies in curbing ridiculous impulses and in forcing the brain to work slowly. The smallest nature rises to the greatest heights. An ordinary, self-centred creature performs acts of dazzling generosity towards fellows he does not even know. He will rescue a wounded man under heavy fire to whom an hour before he would have refused to lend sixpence.'

A vignette of 3rd Ypres, by Quigley, both describes the joy of battle and gives a possible explanation of it.

Our division had the task of attacking Passchendaele. None of us knew where to go when the barrage began, whether half left or half right. A vague memory of following the shellbursts as long as the smoke was black, and halting when it changed to white came to me. The whole affair appeared rather good fun. You know how excited one becomes in the midst of danger. I forgot absolutely that shells are meant to kill and not to provide elaborate lighting effects. I looked at the barrage as something provided for our entertainment – a mood of madness if you like. A fat builder loaded with 500 rounds acted the brave man, ran on ahead, signalled back to us as if on a quiet parade. The last I saw of him was two arms straining madly at the ground, blood pouring from his mouth while legs and body sank into a shellhole filled with water. One Highlander, raving mad, shouted at us. 'Get on you cowards. Why don't you run at them?' . . . an aeroplane swooped down and treated us to a flood of bullets. I never enjoyed anything so much in my life – flames, smoke, SOSs, lights, drumming of guns, swishing of bullets all appeared stage properties to set off a majestic scene. From the pictorial view, nothing could be finer. It had a unity of colour and composition all of its own. The most delicate shades of grey and green and brown fused wonderfully in the opening light of the morning. I confess my first feelings of deadly fear only arose first when lying wounded on a stretcher. The first excitement was wearing off and my teeth were chattering with the cold. Shrapnel was drumming overhead down the line of the duckboard track. Nothing frightens one more than high shrapnel for the bullet strikes the head first. With high explosive one can lie down or side-slip . . .

It is the sudden coming of rationality in addition to the dreamlike state which suggests that men advanced and fought in a self-drugged state. The upset in body chemistry produced by a state of high fear long sustained gave strength to eliminate a calculating response for a limited time. This would explain too the difficulty in recalling battle details afterwards, even of comprehending the elation of battle a day afterwards. Crozier wrote more truthfully than he knew when he observed that 'God is merciful and it almost seems as though he chloroforms us on these occasions'.

The one happening during the advance which seems to have had the power to break through a man's intense fixation on himself was the death of someone he knew close by. Many memoirs, like Mac-Gill's, can give only the most general account of an attack until they fix on a particular death:

I came across Flannery lying close to a barbed wire support, one arm round it as if in embrace. He was a clumsily built fellow with queer, bushy eyebrows and a short, squat nose. His bearing was never soldierly but on the march he could bear any burden and stick to the job when more alert men fell out. He never made friends and led a solitary life, a being apart. Now there was something savage in the expression on his face as he looked slowly round, like an ox under a yoke, on my approach. I knelt down beside him and cut his tunic with my scissors where a burnt hole clotted with blood showed under the kidney. A splinter of shell had torn part of his side away. All hope was lost for the poor soul. 'In much pain, chummy?' I asked. 'Ah, Christ, yes, Pat. Wife and two kiddies too. Are we getting the best of it?' 'Winning all along.' 'That's good. Any hope for me?' 'Of course there is,' I lied. 'You have two morphia tablets and lie quietly. You'll be back in England in two or three days' time.' I placed the morphia under his tongue and he closed his eyes as if going to sleep. Then with an effort he tried to get up and gripped the wire. His legs shot out from under him and, muttering something about rations being fit for pigs and not for men, he fell back and died.

If the wire had been cut and the enemy was where the staff had expected him to be, engagement with the enemy followed the advance. A generation before, that great French soldier Du Picq had laid it down as a rule of combat that, if two sides were on a relatively even footing, one or the other would give way according to which side appeared the more confident. This was often the case in the Great War. 'Fritz in mass formation was one thing but on even terms he dearly loved to become a prisoner of war and eat white bread,' wrote McKee. But on the large and confused battle-fields of 1914–18 the relative strengths were seldom so clear, and neither were the escape routes. In any age trapped soldiers fight with desperation. Cloete saw his own men fighting to the end with Prussian guards, bayonet to bayonet, two men running each other through simultaneously. The fortunes of war might swing to the other side. At Béthune in 1918 Cooper last saw his CSM, Bathy of the Royal Lancasters, fighting with his fists and boots, surrounded by Germans until a Prussian officer shot him with a revolver at point blank range. The most moving account I know can be read between the lines of Berthelot's Order of the Day to the French 5th Army:

On 27 May 1918, at a time when the British trenches were being subjected to a fierce attack, the second battalion repelled successive assaults with gallantry and determination and maintained an unbroken line to a late hour. Inspired by the *sang froid* of Lt.-Colonel Anderson-Morshead, DSO, in the face of a fierce bombardment, the few survivors of the battalion, though isolated and without hope of assistance, held their trenches and fought to the last man with unhesitating obedience to orders. Thus the whole battalion – colonel, twenty-eight officers, 550 NCOs and men responded with one accord and offered their lives in an ungrudging sacrifice to the sacred cause of the allies.

Similar British actions during the March 1918 retreat and German counterparts during their great retreat of August 1918, added to the names of Mametz Wood and Delville Wood, show that civilian soldiers often did fight to the last when *in extremis*.

Most men were not called upon to make such a decision, for the issues of their battle seldom reached such a clear definition. Often blundering was the cause. Evans described an occasion typical of many. His men had captured their first objective at Bazentin on the Somme field.

It was now ordered that we should make an attack. No preparation had been made. No one knew an inch of the ground ahead or where the Germans were entrenched. The scheme was wantonly conceived by some idiot far back who consulted the map as a chess board. We were the pieces moved at whim. So we prepared as best we could. We never got there, for halfway someone cancelled this sortie. I was bringing up the rear and was disinterested. Nothing mattered. Fatalism had set in. On another night we were sent out in front to dig out a hastily pegged site. The men, expert with spade and pick, seemed to have trouble in getting started. Their tools would not respond. A Verey light went up and we went down on our hands and found them touching cold, jelly-like swollen faces. We slithered and rocked and lost our balance on wobbling, bloated bellies. It was a jerry graveyard. The stench was indescribable . . . up there we lost all sense of time. For half an hour, we argued as to whether it was Sunday. Two of us thought it was. We were a day out. We had our clothes on for ten days with never a wash or a shave. Thirst always assailed . . .

More often than blundering, it was the fog of war which provided unexpected inertia on the battlefield. A lag in the reception of orders, a strategic withdrawal by the enemy, the falling of night and both sides would quickly disengage and blunder about like blind men. Alec Waugh at 3rd Ypres spent three days in Van Diemen's 'farm' (a pillbox). He had no idea where the Germans were and his runners could get no information. Contacting his flanks by night, he was passive by day. Men souvenired for watches, pens and cigarettes, while Waugh himself strolled about during the night, watching the Vereys on the horizon. If anything, veterans remember Waugh's experience as being the most typical in battle. Indeed most were very happy to live a shellhole existence if only HQ would leave them alone. At night they would keep vigilant for enemy patrols and refrain from smoking. By day they would live on stale bread, cheese and cold bully beef, getting water from shellholes or dead men's water bottles, while the platoon sergeant crawled around to check the line.

Here was the unsolved problem of the Great War – to find out what was happening after Z hour. On the instant of advance and in the absence of practicable field radio, fighting men became detached from their order-giving roots with a cut as sharp as a geological fault. Visual signalling was suicidal on the battlefield, and any telephone wires laid down were likely to be severed by shellfire. Thus, when the barrage lifted, officers at any HQ could light their pipes, since reports brought by runners could be at least thirty minutes behind the action. At Bullecourt in 1917, for example, brigade HQ was one hour behind the action, during which time the Australians were cut to pieces. Such lags explain Swinton's typical experience during 3rd Ypres. 'During the height of the battle a runner from brigade HQ stumbled in. We were expecting to be relieved the same night. I tore open the envelope in full expectation of relief orders. In fact it was a rebuke from the area sanitary officer to the effect that the grease traps in the horse lines some twelve miles back were not in perfect condition.' In addition there was the human factor. When Cloete, during the Somme, was sent back for further instructions to divisional HQ, he found the sixty men there playing cricket, and the single captain on duty unable to read a map. To maintain continuity in the direction of a battle under such conditions was like a draughtsman working with a pencil tied to the end of a billiard cue.

It is fashionable today to emphasize this remoteness from the battle of the higher command as if it were due to human failings rather than to the deficiencies of communication. But incurious detachment was also the outlook of fighting soldiers not actually on the field of battle. Woodward, awaiting orders on the fringe of Loos battle, had no idea at all what the firing was about and got out of his trench with a subaltern to pick blackberries. In his diary for 15 July 1916, when the Australians were fighting ferociously a few miles away for Pozières, Richardson at Hedauville wrote: 'Rose at 8. Fine day. Nothing much doing.' Fraser-Tytler gave the typical gunner's attitude: 'In a battle there is usually plenty of time on one's hands. Nothing to do except sit in a shellhole where the telephone exchange is and wait for hours for some line to be made good. There is little to inspect. Waiting for something to happen, we watch the next battery being shelled or a waggon ricochetting down the road as it dodges salvoes of 5·9s. There are few returns to send in and no infantry to fuss over.'

Even eye-witnesses found it hard to feel involved. Watching the bloody struggle for Mametz Wood on the first day of the Somme, Williamson about a mile away saw no men, only 'a dust cloud with a mad drummer beating his drum within it'. Billy Bishop, flying at about 500 feet over the battlefield near Arras early in 1917 after a snowfall wrote:

No-man's-land, so often a filthy litter, was this morning clean and white. Suddenly over the top of our parapet a thin line of infantry crawled up and commenced to stroll casually towards the enemy. To me it seemed they must soon wake up and run; that they could not realize the danger they were in. Here and there a shell would burst as the line advanced and halted for a minute. Three or four men near the burst would topple over like so many tin soldiers. Two or three other men would then come running up to the spot from the rear carrying stretchers, pick up the wounded or dying and slowly walk back with them. I could not get the idea out of my head that it was just a game they were playing at. It all seemed so unreal. Nor could I believe that the little brown figures moving about below me were really men going to the glory of victory or death. I could not make myself realize the full truth or meaning of it. It seemed that I was in an entirely different world looking down from another sphere on this strange, uncanny puppet show.

Battle was thus an experience which only those involved could understand, a madness and a terror and an elation, which qualified men for the world's most exclusive club. Then and today total strangers speaking English, French or German can meet and within minutes be talking with a passion and warmth which no other common experience can provide.

12

AFTER BATTLE

Roll-call was a fixed point immediately after coming out of battle. The fortunes of war might produce startling figures. Regimental lists today on west front memorials show some battalions almost wiped out, others surviving almost intact. For the attack on Crucifix Corner, on the first day of the Somme, the 2nd Middlesex started with twenty-four officers and 650 men. At roll-call a single officer and fifty men answered to their names.

Manning re-creates the scene for us:

'Redmain' was the name called out and at first there was no reply. It was repeated. 'Has anyone seen anything of Redmain?' 'Yes, sir,' cried Pike with sullen anger in his voice. 'The poor bastard's dead, sir.' 'Are you sure of that, Pike?' Captain Malet asked quietly, ignoring everything but the question of fact. 'Are you sure that the man you saw was Redmain?' 'I saw him, sir. 'e was just blown to blazes. e' was a chum o' mine sir, an' I seen 'im just blown to blazes.' Then, with a temporary roll established, the men returned to camp. From the tents camp details, cooks, snobs and a few unfit men gathered to watch them with sympathy genuine enough but tactfully aloof, for there is a gulf between men just returned from action and those who have not been in the show as unbridgeable as that between sober and drunk. Captain Malet halted his men by the orderly room tent. There was even a pretence to dress ranks. 'Dismiss.' His voice was still pitched low but they turned almost with the precision of troops on the square. Each rifle was struck smartly, the officers saluting. And then the will which bound them together dissolved. The enervated muscles relaxed and they lurched off to their tents as silent and dispirited as beaten men. One of Taylor's men took his pipe out of his mouth and spat on the ground. 'They can say what they like,' he said appreciatively, 'but we're a bloody fine mob.'

The tiredness and lassitude indicated by Manning was characteristic and it represented more than lack of sleep. One writer suggested that, in five minutes of battle, the physical organs performed the work of twenty-four hours. Certainly the innumerable physical defence mechanisms so grossly overworked now took their price. Bean, Australia's official historian, observed that 'the survivors, even after a day's rest, looked like men who had been in hell. Almost without exception, each man looked drawn and haggard and so dazed that the men appeared to be walking in a dream and their eyes looked glassy and starey. Quite a few were silly and they were the only noisy ones in the crowd. They were like boys emerging from a long illness.' Even humble soldiers, immersed in their own affairs, couldn't help noticing the cost of battle. Read recalled meeting about eighty men of the South Staffordshires coming from the Somme battle front. 'Every now and then their step broke and they seemed to march anyhow, with heads bent, either looking straight before them or at the ground. Impossible to tell if there were any officers among them. "How d'you get on, mates?" But no one took the slightest notice save a corporal carrying three rifles bringing up the rear. He half turned and half shrugged expressively. "General Fanshaw in command again. Back where they bloody well started again. Beribboned toy dogs!" '

Added to tiredness was great sadness. Boyd Orr with the Sherwood Foresters (his company reduced from eighteen officers and 800 men down to five and 200) burnt his blood-soaked kit then wrote in his diary: 'I have never in my life been so unutterably sad. My friends and comrades were nearly all gone.' In war conditions mates and comrades were forgotten with great speed against the urgent necessity of daily survival – but not immediately and not possibly during the temporary security of rest after battle. Circumstances could emphasize the loss, as Griffith observed.

After the Somme, marching in column of fours, there was no ring of feet and no swing of shoulder. There were slackness and frequent hitching of packs, a rise and fall of heads, much leaning forward. Men were marching abreast who had never before stood in the same file. There are no gaps in a battalion on the march though many have fallen. The closing up that follows losses tells its own tale. The faces of many silent and hard-eyed men showed that they were not half-aware of their neighbours – newcomers who jostled the ghosts of old companions, usurpers who were themselves struggling against the same griefs and losses and longings, marching forward with minds that looked backwards in time and space.

Tiredness and sadness one might expect, but the bad temper usually associated with battle-worn men surprises us today. Manning thought it due to the sudden removal of enemy danger and of the full rigours of army discipline for the time. Perhaps there was an addition of physical strain as well. 'Surreptitiously jettisoning any remaining grenades and much surplus ammunition,' wrote Noakes, 'it might be supposed by those who know only the soldiers of Bairnsfather or the novelist that we were tired but happy, enlivening the road with cheerful songs and jokes. We had broken the Hindenburg Line. We were tired to the point of exhaustion and limp for lack of food. Our mouths and throats were as dry as lime kilns. Nerves were on edge and tempers frayed after the intense strain of going over the top and small disagreements were liable to flare into a quarrel.'

All the strands which made up post-battle depression were remarkably soon dispelled. General Jack observed that 'healthy young soldiers recover with remarkable rapidity from the most gruelling experiences when they had a good sleep and a square meal'. As so often, it is Manning who gives us the closest description of the recovery.

It was late when they awoke but they were reluctant to move. Their tent gave them the only privilege they knew and they wanted to lie hidden until they had recovered their nerve. Among themselves they were unselfish, even gentle, instinctively helping each other, for having shared the same experience there was a tacit understanding among them . . . they kept their feelings very much to themselves. There was something insolent in the way they tightened their belts, hawked and spat into the dust. They had been through it and lapsed a little lower than savages. Life for them held nothing new in the way of humiliation. Men of the new draft wondered foolishly at their haggard and filthy appearance. Perhaps there was something in their sad, pitiless faces to evoke in others a kind of primitive awe. Gradually their apathy lifted as first their bodily functions and then their habits of life asserted themselves. One after another, they started shaving.

As men recovered, they began to look back on the battle. Most of them thought it a happening of indefinable but vast personal significance. Looking back almost sixty years, Gladden recently wrote of himself on the Somme: 'Thus I had endured my first battle and there was little in it that matched my expectations. I had wandered in an unreal world – a damp, muddy, stinking world more horrible than anything I had visualized . . . yet nothing much had happened. There was a sense of anti-climax. To suffer so much for so little seemed the final indignity . . . but I had been in battle and was henceforth a different being. For the first time I felt myself a man, indefinably changed . . .' Voigt talked of 'a great cut in my life and personality', while Allen, who listened to a fiery battle story, wrote of the teller: 'He was a different man. Something had come to him which had not yet come to us. It was the trial of battle and no one who passes through it is ever quite the same again.'

But, if a battle left a feeling of importance, it seldom left anything of detail. Kipling remarked at the time that 'men could give hideous, isolated experiences of their own, but no man could recall any connected order of events'. Andrews carried a reporter's notebook into Neuve Chapelle battle. He had been a journalist in civilian life. When he came later to look at his battle impressions, he saw that his sweat had smeared the pencil and he found it impossible to remember what had happened. In his own words, he had gone through the battle 'like a sleepwalker'. All that remained, as for most combatants, were the brilliantly limelighted vignettes set in a confused, timeless, grey sea of fear. Most of these episodes seem mainly concerned with the deaths of particular men. Belhaven recalled a German with a pork-pie hat jumping up with a stick grenade then throwing up his left arm and collapsing like a pole-axed ox, a distinct hole in his throat above the collar. Advancing in a ragged line on another battlefield, Bultitude writes with the characteristic intricate detail of fighting soldiers: 'a bullet pierced the exact centre of the helmet of the man on my right as he walked forward with head down. He spun round as he fell with a stream of blood spurting out of a circular hole in the top of his head and he scrambled back for about ten yards then rolled over. A short, white-haired lad rushed screaming, right along our line with an eye shot away. Another near neighbour was hit in the groin and lay in the ditch at the foot of the slope screaming.'

The only tangible memento which might come to a survivor after battle was a decoration of some sort. Its very tangibility made it highly valued. As Feilding observed: 'I have known good men eat their hearts out through want of recognition. How petty this sounds. Yet a ribbon is the only prize in war for the ordinary soldier. It is the outward visible proof to bring home to his people that he has done his job well. And, say what you may, a man's prowess will be assessed by the number of his ribbons.' Old soldiers then and now could pick out a man's record with startling rapidity from his service dress. Reverse blue chevrons four inches up the left sleeve told the number of years' service; gold wound stripes above them suggested the number of actions the man had seen. Medal ribbons would confirm this. Thus a 1914 star showed that the man had been under fire from the start of the war to the end of 1st Ypres. A 1914–15 star indicated service in the Neuve Chapelle–Loos period. Then would come the different-coloured ribbons for the Military Medal, Distinguished Conduct Medal and so on.

The experience of one old soldier indicates the kudos which went with an award. The citation was read in front of the whole battalion – 'The Military Medal has been awarded for coolness under heavy shellfire and devotion to duty. On 23 September, on the Ypres front during a severe bombardment, Sergeant Winter maintained visual communication continually, though in a position where no cover was available. When the station was blown up by a shell, he at once installed another lamp and re-opened communication.' There followed a note from the major-general of the 58th Division in his own hand – 'Your gallant conduct has been brought to my notice and I take this opportunity of congratulating you on the good service you have rendered to your country.' Nor was this the end of the matter. On first leave, the local council would hold a widely publicized special meeting of the council, to which the public would be invited to witness the presentation of a special scroll with a £5 note enclosed. Such an accumulation of public recognition, official notice and cash moved the most hardened front-liner. The fighting soldier would certainly receive no other acknowledgement of his service apart from the medal and its appurtenances.

A recently published memoir suggests just how important this acknowledgement was to many. 'I was recommended for a medal five times,' Ernest Atkins complained. 'The grievance about it all exists in my mind to this day and is the main reason for writing.' I came across another such wounded man amongst the unpublished records in the Imperial War Museum. He is Private Gerrard. His account is in pencil, untidy and ungrammatic. Most of his war memories concentrate around an incident at Potsdam Farm on the

Ypres salient. The reward for its capture went to a second lieutenant
– a VC; Gerrard, to whom the credit should have gone, got a
Military Medal. 'A damned shame,' said the captain who had seen
the incident through his field glasses. When the general gave him
his medal, 'I could not speak to him unless he asked me and I were
never asked. I were afraid he would just think I were spinning a
yarn. That is the reason I have kept this to myself but now I am an
old man, I don't care what they think.'

Fighting soldiers collectively, however, were more cynical in
public about decorations. If the circumstances were known, there
would be a quiet respect, but generally too many brave deeds were
known to go unrecognized. Feilding recalled one such deed typical
of tens of thousands:

> A few minutes before 4 am the enemy tried to raid one of my
> Lewis gun posts, necessarily in an isolated position about 150
> yards in front of our fire trench in a sunken road. They were
> camouflaged in white overalls. Hesitating to shoot, our men
> challenged. The immediate reply was a volley of hand grenades.
> Mayne, in charge of our Lewis gun, was hit in many parts includ-
> ing the stomach. His left arm was reduced to pulp. Nevertheless
> he struggled up the parapet and with his uninjured arm dis-
> charged a full magazine into the enemy, who broke, not reaching
> our trench. Then he collapsed and fell insensible across his gun.
> The second sentry's foot was so badly shattered that it had to be
> amputated in the trench. Chloroform was unnecessary owing to
> the man's numbed condition. He looked on, smoking a cigarette
> and with true Irish courtesy thanked him for his kindness when
> it was over. Words cannot express my admiration for Mayne's
> magnificent act of gallantry which I consider worthy of a VC.

Feilding then gives us the follow-up. 'The Divisional Memorandum
stated that "another instance has occurred of an enemy patrol reaching within bombing distance of our line. This must not occur
again. Our patrols must meet the enemy's patrols boldly in no-
man's-land." How simple and grand it sounds. In the meantime
Mayne has died. I can only say God rest his soul.'

The basis of this injustice would seem to have been largely the
way in which the award was made, not by officers on the spot but
by the higher command remote from the action. Thus medals only
followed successful actions and tended to follow traditional social

channels. Three hundred and fifty-seven boys from Kelly's College, Tavistock, served in the Great War, receiving seventy-four medals, while the 150 veterans of Princeton Council School in Tavistock managed only three between them. Boyd Orr tells us of more blatant favouritism; his friend Ellis, an officer's batman, received no award, because of his socialist political views which led to his colonel refusing to forward Orr's recommendation.

Counter-measures, applied in order to short-circuit this obtuseness in communication, might produce odd results. Feilding again gives a fine example.

Some time ago I was told to put forward the name of an NCO or man for a certain foreign decoration. It so happened that at that moment there was no specific act outstanding. However, I decided to give a chance to the Lewis gunners. The Lewis gun officer either did not take sufficient interest in the matter or did not feel himself equal to writing up the necessary story. At any rate he said he had no one to recommend. Immediately one of the company commanders who happened to be in the room, more alert, said to me, 'Why not put forward Sergeant R. He has done excellent work since the battalion came over to France and has got nothing.' He got the Military Medal not long afterwards, a better decoration than that for which he had been recommended. Clearly the company commander's word picture of the 'specific act' had been well thought of by the powers that decide these things. Weeks later the general came while Sergeant R's company was at exercise . . . made a speech . . . glowing language . . . one night the enemy demolished part of our breastworks . . . R. collected six bombers and without orders . . . the look of modest surprise mounted in the face of Sergeant R. as he heard his specific act recounted. He stood like a solid block, his eyebrows rising higher and higher while the company gazed in amazement at their hero. I fancy that the general, who is very wide awake, saw through it. But he was far too wise to show the fact.

The wounded in battle are known to us most clearly, as statistics for the record survive in astonishing detail, composed first by units, taken over by the War Office in 1917 then handed to the Ministry of Pensions in 1920.

The first impression is of the high number of casualties. In relation to the total number of men serving on the west front, battle casualties are 56 per cent, of which 12 per cent are deaths. Bearing in mind the official estimate that the ratio of fighting soldiers to support men was one to three, few front-line men could have escaped wounding though their wounds would vary greatly in degree of severity. This bloodiness contrasts markedly with other theatres of war. Compared with this 56 per cent, Gallipoli comes closest with 23 per cent, followed by Mesopotamia with 16 per cent and East Africa/Salonika with 8 per cent.

That officers suffered relatively more severely than other ranks is implied by the figure of 27 per cent deaths as against 12 per cent. The figures for missing, however – 20 per cent as against 28 per cent – suggest that documentation for officers may have been more thorough and easier, given the officer's different uniform and the greater likelihood that he would have his identity disc round the neck rather than in puttees or hitched to his braces, or mislaid. This impression is supported by battle-wound casualty figures – 47 per cent for officers and 56 per cent for other ranks, since missiles do not differentiate between ranks and the brave and foolhardy are no more vulnerable to high explosive than the windy, shivering in their shellholes.

The area of wounding was duly recorded in a sample of 48,000 admissions to casualty clearing-stations, with just 21 per cent in the body, 51 per cent in arms and legs and 17 per cent in the head. The expectation of life depended on the area of the wound, regardless of the wounding implement or amount of tissue damage. Of a sample of 12,000 field deaths, head wounds provided 47 per cent of the total. Wounds which might today have been operable were marginal in a period in which brain surgery was in its infancy. Cushing, the American pioneer in this area, was actually developing his skills in the war zone at this time. Even more dangerous than head wounds were those in the abdomen. An English sample of 1,000 cases found 510 dying on the battlefield, 460 in the ambulance, twenty-two after the operation, thus leaving only eight survivors. Chest wounds had a more favourable prognosis, with only 28 per cent likely to die. For other parts of the body, only German figures survive – 12 per cent of leg wounds died, and 23 per cent of those with arm wounds. Infection here seems to have been the crucial factor.

The first impression a wounded man received was that of being hit violently. Wedgwood called it the 'cart-horse kick'. Arthur felt as if he had been hit by half a house when he got a dose of shrapnel in his leg. Reith thought it more like being hit by a cricket ball on the temple from a straight drive in the nets.

If the wound was in head, foot or hand, where a large number of ligaments and nerve ends would be ruptured, there would be immediate pain. Harold Macmillan thus found his first hand wound more painful than the machine-gun bullet in his pelvis later. Wounds elsewhere often gave little sensation after the initial shock. A curious numbness was produced by the rapid closing of capillaries severed by metal at high velocity or because the soldier was so intent on the matter in hand. Bell during 1st Ypres felt as if he had been knocked on the head, and only a few minutes later looked down to see why he could not run properly. His right foot had been blown off. With the shock of that observation, he lost the power of speech. 'Amateur officer' recalled a man with three fingers and half a palm shot off. 'He came towards us with the pleasant, smiling face, happy but with a trace of bashfulness as though he were screwing up courage for one of the minor ordeals of life such as a wedding or christening.'

As soon as a man found himself wounded, he would immediately cease to think further about the battle. He would indeed usually lose all sense of present time and place. Often he would feel profoundly tired. Buried by a shell he had not heard, Kingsbury saw things hazily as if waking from a sleep. He asked himself without reaching a decision whether he was alive or not and wanted only to sleep.

Many old soldiers have written of their experience of being wounded. Once they reached the mental state of indifference and somnolence, their thinking seems to have taken one of two directions. One group went over their earlier lives. Thus balloonist Lewis, whose parachute had failed to open when he jumped from his observation balloon, saw all his friends' faces and scenes from his life before landing on top of his mate's parachute and safety. Chaband saw his mother's face and her grey hair. Zweig, commenting on his dreamlike state, conscious but not of the world, looked at flashes of childhood experiences and heard his mother's voice distinctly. The other group of wounded survivors, more numerous than the first, drifted gently. Reith asked:

What could it be? Blast it, I've been hit. I wonder by what? Couldn't have been a shell as there wasn't an explosion. Damnation. Look at the blood pouring on my new tunic. I've been hit in the head. Has it gone through and smashed my teeth? No.

They are all there. Was the bullet in my head? If so, this was the end. Meanwhile I had better lie down. Apart from anything else, I was standing on exposed ground and if hit once, could be hit again and there was no point in that. It would be nice to have a few minutes to collect oneself. I suppose, in all, this had occupied four seconds but the processes of thought were definite and sequential. I got out my fountain pen and in a very shaky hand wrote my mother's name and address and then, 'I'm alright.' Then I thought I might write in Latin the message I really wanted to send, but I let it go. I was tired and I wanted to look up at the sky again. The opening lines of a children's hymn came into my mind: 'Above the Clear Blue Sky, in Heaven's Abode.' Well, very soon now the supreme mystery will be solved. I was completely content and at peace.

Realization that a man was just wounded and would not die brought a more practical frame of mind. Kipling once remarked on the urgent curiosity of the wounded with their condition. Sewn inside the lower right flap of the tunic was a field dressing, with which men could do running repairs. Tapes pulled apart the white linen bag and arrows pointed to the uncemented corner of the waterproof cover. A phial of iodine would be first emptied into the wound then the two-and-a-half-yard bandage would cover the wound, its gauze pad stitched eighteen inches from one end. Many men would have often rehearsed the use of their white linen bag in their minds.

The less afflicted would become 'walking wounded'. Men going forward to the battle front would greet them with the ritual, 'Good luck, chum. Don't worry. You'll be in Blighty soon,' in this way warding off a similar fate from themselves, like spitting to avert the evil eye. The wounded did not feel the relief which on reflection afterwards they realized would have been appropriate. They were, after all, out of the battle. But, at the time, mind was detached and body weak. Cloete wrote:

I remember thinking how untidy the battlefield was. There were hundreds of bodies. There were torn and bloody bandages, burst haversacks, abandoned rifles driven muzzle first into the churned-up soil to mark a body, a wounded man perhaps who had died before he could get help. And paper – there was masses of torn paper, letters, postcards, wrappings from parcels . . . by now I was through the area we had fought through this morning, still green between the shellholes, and back in the trenches we had attacked from. There was no grass here; only mud and duckboard tracks winding their way between the craters, many of them ten feet deep and filled with water. If I slipped, I should drown. I still felt no pain but I was tired. At this point I became two men. My mind left my body and went on ahead. From there I watched quite objectively and with some amusement the struggles of this body of mine staggering over the duckboards and wading through the mud where the boards were smashed. I watched it duck when a salvo of German shells came over. I saw it converse with gunners who were stripped to the waist, too busy to talk but a corporal gave my body some rum . . . I then rejoined my body. The rum may have done it.

Those more badly wounded lay on the field where they had been hit. Most would shout for assistance or scream in delirium. Others with more control of their faculties waited stoically, marking their position for searching stretcher-bearers. Macmillan lay for twelve hours in a shellhole at Loos reading Aeschylus, just as rifleman Green had done a century earlier in Spain, recalling 'agony beyond description' as he lay for three days, his arm alive with maggots.

The searching was done by regimental stretcher-bearers, all volunteers. Only the SB brassard and an absence of weapons distinguished these men on the battlefield. Humane considerations apart, they had volunteered as bearers for a more varied life. They were excused fatigues, were seldom checked on by authority and could easily acquire the comforts of dugout life outside of action. In action the price of these comforts was fully paid. General Birdwood once remarked that if he had thousands of VCs to distribute, all would go to stretcher-bearers. In terms of numbers, there were thirty-two bearers per 1,000 men, whose task was to deal with the 60 per cent of the fighting force estimated likely to become casualties during any battle. Usually about 30 per cent of these would be walking wounded. The rest would lie, pinioned by the weight of their equipment. Their orders were to take the less badly wounded. In the same spirit, priority of movement in the trenches went first to ammunition, second to reinforcements, third to the wounded. In battle all had to be sacrificed to the immediate purpose of winning.

The first call was the regimental aid post, the battalion medical officer presiding. The post would be in a reserve trench dugout or shellhole, since shellfire so close to action precluded a tent or hut. Field dressings would be removed wherever possible for something more substantial. For the most severe cases, amputations would be performed and the piles of amputated limbs would probably be the only objects in the post apart from the trestle table of the MO, since military law permitted wounded men to dump their kit on being wounded. All would receive a morphia injection with the cross of an indelible pencil on the forehead to warn the next treatment centre. Before departure the wounded man's paybook would be used for record purposes and a luggage label attached to a tunic button to describe the case and give regimental particulars. These stubs from the aid post records, daily taken to the orderly room, supply the basis of the remarkably complete statistics of battle which survive from the Great War.

The only tools of the medical officer were knife, bandages and morphia. With the journey to the casualty clearing-station, the wounded man entered the region of surgery administered by the Royal Army Medical Corps, the RAMC. Numbering under 20,000 at the start of the war, by the end the corps numbered about 150,000 administering well over half a million beds. In the course of their war duties they dealt with nine million cases and administered 1,088 million doses of drugs, over one and a half million splints, 108 million bandages, 7,250 tons of cotton wool and 22,386 artificial eyes. If the pain represented by these figures could be similarly quantified, then it would be beyond any man to comprehend such grief. By the grossest of measurements, the RAMC did an efficient job. Of their nine million cases two and quarter million were so severe as to require treatment in England. Nevertheless one and a half million of these cases were patched up sufficiently to be returned to France. The allowance that must be made for this measure is suggested by the case of Private Bell, whose foot we have noted blown off at Ypres. The RAMC sent him back to the front to serve in the Labour corps to the end of the war.

Most of the surgical work that had to be done during the war was performed at the casualty clearing station. The proliferation of these miniature hospitals was due to the discovery that, if all dead and injured tissue was removed within thirty hours of damage, much sepsis and gangrene could be successfully dealt with. During an offensive each division would have one forward and two back.

Ideally, they would be near road and rail but beyond artillery range (12,000 yards) and clear of towns, dumps, railheads – likely targets for enemy bombing or shelling. The CCS was a mobile unit, served by about a hundred assorted personnel, which provided six separate surgical teams, two always on duty.

Hayward, a surgeon, has left us his impression of the work.

On that evening the attack began with a continuous roar of heavy guns while the horizon was lit with the explosions of dumps going up, Verey lights and star shells . . . at about 1 am the ambulances began to arrive. It is impossible to convey an adequate picture of the scene. Into the tent are borne on stretchers or come wearily stumbling, figures in khaki wrapped in blankets or coats, bandaged or splinted. All of them are caked in mud or stiff with blood and dust and sweat. Labels of their injuries are attached. Many are white and cold and lie still. Those who make response are laconic or point to their label. I have never seen such dreadful wounds . . . it was an extraordinary thing that in this charnel tent of pain and misery, there was silence and no outward expression of complaint . . . even the badly wounded often asked for a smoke.

One must imagine a dark tent lit by acetylene flares, sister, orderly and anaesthetist standing by the surgeon, a figure dressed in an army-issue white smock drenched in blood. He operates on up to twenty cases at a time, surrounded by the silent, dirty, verminous brotherhood of silence and patience, men lying like run-over dogs in a ditch, quietly waiting for an attention gently given.

From the casualty clearing station, the path of the most severely wounded led to the base hospital or England. Barge and rail replaced the motor ambulance at this stage. Water was kept for the most serious cases in which any movement might be fatal – 'it was as if one had died and wakened in heaven. The peace, the silence were unbelievable. One had glimpses of lovely country and the scent of it drifted into the barge' – but train was the standard mover. They fitted into a complex timetable and could transport 1,000 men in thirty-six hours. Sassoon had direct experience: 'a train with 500 men and thirty-five officers conveyed me to the base hospital. My memories of that train are strange and rather terrible, for it carried a cargo of men whose minds were still vitalized and violent. Many of us still had the caked mud of the war zone on our boots and clothes, while every bandaged man was accompanied by his battle experience. Although many of them talked lightly and facetiously about it, there was an aggregation of enormities in the atmosphere of that train. The front line was behind us but it could lay its hand on our hearts though its reality diminished with every mile.'

For reasons of shortage of space or the need for specialized treatment, some of the wounded went straight to England. Issued with new socks and a linen bag for valuables, these men would be put in cots and stacked like baggage on the quays. Then cranes would swing them onto the decks of steamers in fours. The less fortunate would be received into the base hospital by a sergeant. His job was to make out the ward cards. He would ask the questions on his card in a loud, toneless voice to indicate his awareness of deceit: name, number then – quickly – 'Have you a jack knife with you?' Truly the army did not wish to be cheated of re-conditioned men, and most of the men were re-conditioned. Thirty-eight per cent of patients at base hospitals were out within a fortnight, 36 per cent stayed between one and three months, only 15 per cent stayed longer.

Such statistics do not delineate the feelings of the patients. Maze gives us this account:

The sun is out and there is an increasing glow inside the ward as the tent turns yellow and dries. But the dampness of the heat turns it into a hothouse. This change has brought a sensation of new life even into this ward where death is lurking round so many beds. All the men in the ward with the exception of myself are bad cases. They have been here some days and I have watched them with the eye of a man who observes but cannot feel – I can feel no more . . . there is now a routine as each case in the ward is dealt with. I see how nervous they become, those whom the nurses must prepare for the surgeon's visit. They have a horror of the pain which daily they have to endure as a long, sharp needle is inserted in their back and the fluid inside their lungs has to be drawn out by an instrument like a bicycle pump. They sit up one after another for their turn, supported by a nurse, and give that hopeless howl of a weak man who can resist no more. Some have to be anaesthetized to have their wounds dressed . . . there is a man with gangrene who has to be carried out every second day to have a bit more of his leg off. One boy has both his legs cut off and the nurses watch over him constantly – he smells terribly of decomposition, poor fellow, and infects the ward. I notice the nurse put a screen round his bed and attend him as if she were making him comfortable. I have not understood that he has died until I see a stretcher slip out of the side door, a blanket covering his pitiably short body . . . there comes a diversion. One young fellow, a very bad case, shouts, 'Nursie darling, don't leave me.' Throughout his delirium he makes love to her. She responds sweetly. He is so lively that I cannot believe that death is near him but he is shot in the head and there is no hope, so the nurse tells me. She has to leave him for a minute, an orderly watching him from the door. Several times he has attempted to get up. This time the orderly is too far off to catch him before he has nipped out of bed and slipped through an open flap of the tent where for a few seconds he sprawls and shouts, making diabolical gesticulations among the ropes and pegs. Like a truant child, he is carried gently back and with one last shout that rings in my ears for days afterwards, he dies. Every day there seems to be a critical period for bad cases to survive. Just as shipwrecked people clinging to the raft let go one after another, so sometimes a wounded man will die although his condition shows an improvement as if he were too tired to make the slightly greater voluntary effort required. A charming fellow in the bed next to mine seemed so much better. As he woke from his sleep so the doctor on duty, the Harrow school doctor, was waiting by his bed with a letter for him. 'Would you like me to read it to you?' I remember how gentle the voice sounded which read aloud to the young man the words of his mother who, with little bits of home news, tried to hide her anxiety. I saw the letter lying between two white hands as the doctor walked away to the other side of the ward—then suddenly two arms went up despairingly like a drowning man unable to shout for help. He never uttered a sound. His white face moved once or twice on the pillow and within a few minutes he was dressed for the last time and carried out.

Since patients were usually rigidly classified and filed into separate wards for gangrene, burns, meningitis, spine damage, fractured limbs and so on, Paul Maze was unusual in being able to give us such an insight into the moribund ward. It was possible for men to go through the entire war and not be aware of the cost of war except perhaps for the wooden crosses marking payment of final accounts.

Again and again one comes upon moving vignettes of hospital

suffering from the Great War. Doctors and nurses seemed to recall them more vividly not just because of the sheer quantity but because of the appalling tears made by iron and explosive in the bodies of a section of society normally the least likely to be found in hospitals.

> The arm of Rees does not get worse but his courage is ebbing. When he wakes, sobbing, he says, 'Don't go away, nurse', and holds my hand in a fierce clutch, then releases it to point in the air, crying, 'There's the pain,' as though it filled the air and rose to the rafters. As he wakes, it centralizes until at last he comes to the moment when he says, 'Me arm aches cruel,' and points to it. Then one can leave him. Walker isn't very clever but he is so brave. After his tenth operation, two days ago, there was a question as to whether he should have his pluggings changed under gas or not. The discussion went on between the doctors over his bed but the anaesthetist could not be found. He didn't take any part in the discussion but waited with interest showing on his bony face. From apertures six inches deep, the gauze stuck crackling under the pull of the forceps with blood and pus leaping from the cavities. There were five holes in all. He endured without even clutching his hands. I wiped the sweat reluctantly from his forehead as though one were being too exacting in drawing attention to so small a sign.

It always seemed to be in the evening that men felt their pain most, Millard tell us. Men would cry out for morphia long before they needed it. 'Night-time for the sufferers is easily the worst because the patient has nothing to distract him and it is so quiet that the throbbing of the wound seems to beat against the bed-clothes and to make as much noise as an oncoming regiment.' In such circumstances nurses would give injections of sterile water as a placebo.

Though sick people seem often to be most trying, they appear to have come in for much harsh treatment in RAMC hospitals. Memoirs, like Wedgwood's, complain uniformly of inhumanity, an inhumanity which seemed to have increased with distance from the battlefield. 'The wounded man is in a moment a little baby and all the rest become the tenderest of mothers. One holds his hand; another lights his cigarette. Before this, it is given to few to know the love of those who go together through the long valley of the shadow of death.' At the casualty clearing stations officers were in casual flannels or shorts and nurses gently personal. Thereafter RAMC personnel tended to treat each case as 'other ranks', while VAD nurses would look on them as heroic peasants, not as men with wife and children, a house and garden. West commented sourly in his lapidary way:

Brutal injections. Regulation quantity given to every man regardless of his condition. Eye wash for inspections. Dying men made to sit up and smile. Doctors looked on every man as a skrimshanker. Brutality in treatment of patients when they were unwilling to undergo a particular cure. Men wounded and minus an arm insisted on not being put on electric treatment. Was knocked down and held on the bed by two orderlies. Lack of men entailed suffering to those confined in bed. Couldn't relieve themselves without bed pans but no one to bring them. People nearly crying with pain. Gloomy buildings with bathroom taps all loose and tied to the wall with string. Case of a man who came from the front on a short leave to see his brother. Refused admission as he had no pass. Meals never hot, worse than ordinary camp food and only served at strictly regulated times. If men arrived at night, no meal until brekker at eight next morning.

Of the brutality after hospital and in convalescence there can be no doubt, for the wounded men made the cushy position of their non-fighting guardians a guilty one. The largest meal would be bully beef, biscuit and dates. Wilson remembered verminous blankets and having to place his faeces on a tin tray for inspection. When gassed men like Coppard were forced to run and drill at speed, their protests were quickly silenced – 'any bloody lip from any of yer and I'll whip him straight off to the guard room.' Duty back in the front line became almost a release from frustration.

Looking back today on the treatment received at the various stages of the process, one can only wonder at the high rate of success. The general level of medical knowledge was distinctly Victorian. At Charing Cross hospital during the war leeches were frequently used to bleed patients, mosquito bites were standard syphilis treatment and the unskilled use of chloroform was doing much liver damage. The professor of medicine at Glasgow University, Charteris, had just published a book for practitioners, in which he recommended, for typhus, a rhubarb purgative followed by the application of a cold lotion to the shaved head; for syphilis, the patient to be sat on a cane-bottomed chair while the fumes of calomel burnt on a spirit lamp underneath him were absorbed for twenty minutes; thereafter the patient was to drink wine but no spirits, wear flannel and go to bed early. It did not surprise me to find in a local paper during 1914 that the medical officer of Folkestone thought that scarlet fever was caused by sitting in dark cinemas.

Quite apart from these gaps in knowledge was a backwardness in medical technology. Since there were no practical X-rays for hospital use, battle hardware was likely to remain in the body with all its possibilities for septicaemia later. Haemorrhages were always likely to be fatal, since blood transfusion was in its infancy, although in 1917 Keynes was pioneering a transfusion apparatus which would remain standard for twenty years. Blood groups were discovered by trial and error, with donors sufficiently traumatized to merit fourteen days of Blighty leave in return. The lack of antibiotics was even more damaging. Nearly all field wounds went septic within six hours. The knife or packing with lime chloride were the only specifics and the wound had to be kept unstitched, filled with gauze and drained regularly to allow slow healing from the bottom up. If there was arterial damage and gangrene set in, washing with peroxide might be tried but the prognosis was gloomy. In the American expeditionary force (British figures don't survive) 44 per cent of those contracting gangrene died. Osburn remembers the smell of gangrene in the Boulogne hospital train lasting several days, even after disinfection, he and the nurses vomiting continuously.

What of the dead? Their number seemed to give to the Great War a bloodiness not to be rivalled again until the death camps of the Third Reich. Black Week during the Boer war had produced just 3,000 casualties. Compared with this were the 60,000 casualties on the first day of the Somme, the very first battle in which Britain was massively involved, to be followed by 13,000 in three days at Arras and nearly 25,000 in the seven days of Messines, these last two coming hard upon each other. When one moves from overall figures down to those of particular units, the loss of life is even more overwhelming. Tawney remembered 820 men in his battalion attacking on the Somme. Four hundred and fifty men died in the first attack, while after the second just fifty-four men answered the roll-call. Carrington's company at 3rd Ypres started with three officers, seventeen NCOs and ninety-two men; it ended with a single officer, two NCOs and forty-four men.

Nevertheless one must examine the figures with care. The vast lists of dead men whose bodies were never found, which can be seen today on memorials at Menin Gate, Tyne Cot and Thiepval, show clearly great variations in severity on different days or different sections of the front. Figures for the hardest-hit battalions cannot be projected onto the whole battlefield. Overall, too, army deaths are not markedly greater than in other modern wars. Though just 22,000 soldiers died in the Boer war, this was 5 per cent of the army fighting there. Four and a half per cent of fighting soldiers died in the Second World War, 10 per cent in the First – the discrepancy is less than commonly thought. Finally a modern study suggests that some thirty million civilians died in Europe as a result of war, from typhus, starvation, influenza and the like. The nine million soldiers, less than a million British, put the final figure into a different perspective.

When all allowances have been made, the Great War remains arguably different from any other war. For the first time young men from all areas and social classes died over a prolonged period, with speed of notification in the national press making the widespread nature of the sacrifice clear to everyone. The loss became national and, above all, the dead were civilians. However wrongly, the death of a professional soldier was put in a different category, an occupational risk, just as venereal disease was the risk of the prostitute. Despite Kipling's efforts before 1914, the two were still closely linked in the public mind. But after 1914 the soldiers were not soldiers whatever uniform they might wear. The public, their parents, saw them as civilians still. The speed with which the new recruits had themselves photographed in uniform at the local photographers showed that they too were aware of the theatrical-effects side of their new status. It was a game, just like dressing up as a child. Death was sudden, unfair. The rules of the new game had not been made clear. Men had had too little time to build such possibilities into their awareness of their role as a soldier – except in a pattern of words not really grasped. The men who died were therefore innocents, and if death became slaughter in the public mind, we must remember that the later generation which died in the second war had the memory of their fathers to fortify themselves against reality.

Tolstoy's last words were: 'But the peasants – how do the peasants die?' For the Great War, the answer is clear – mostly with great speed. About three-quarters of the deaths were from shells, and the massive explosive charges of these with the flying chunks of jagged iron they catapulted leave surviving veterans today still reluctant to talk about the results. General Crozier wrote: 'In the main communication trench we passed a man carrying a sandbag full of something. Thefts of rations and minor stores from the line are increasing. I therefore asked, "What have you in that bag?" "Rifleman Grundy, sir," came the unexpected reply.'

The bullet could be just as unpleasant for, if a man was sniped, it was usually in the head. Clapham remembered having tea with salmon, jam and biscuits in the front line when one man rose to get a better view of an observation balloon. Hit in the head, on the instant, the blood spurted three feet like a hose. The victim turned over the brazier when falling, then lay for three-quarters of an hour making inarticulate, moaning noises in his death agony. On the battlefield itself, the bullet was more clinical. There was a forward fall with a simultaneous bend at all joints, just like a man who had put his foot in a rabbit hole and tripped over.

If death came slower to a man, it seems to have been curiously painless for many. Dearden wrote:

> It was an awful job getting our fellows onto stretchers. One knew them all so well and under a bright sun it looked too horrible. The poor lad with his two feet off was quite unconscious and obviously dying. I patched him up and got him onto a stretcher, gave him a cigarette and left him, when he called me back. He said something I couldn't catch, for his lips were very cut about and bleeding. So I wiped his mouth and he said quietly and clearly, 'Shall I live, sir?' 'Live?' I said. 'Good lord yes. You'll be as right as rain when you're properly dressed and looked after.' 'Thank you, sir,' he said and went on smoking his cigarette. He died as they were getting him onto the ambulance.

Even on the battlefield such calm was common. Maze noted an incident on the first day of 3rd Ypres. 'Stopped a second with a wounded soldier who held out a hand from a shellhole while troops streamed past me. "It's alright, chum. I've got it in the chest," he said to me as I gave him my water bottle. He had cast off his equipment and laid his kit neatly by his side as though he had prepared for death.' One young medical officer who became the shrewdest observer of suffering in war this century, Lord Moran, wrote that he only ever came across one soldier, wounded and afraid to die. He noted how narcotically lives petered out with no terror, pain, apprehension or remorse. War, after all, is the business of youth and no young man thinks he can ever die.

Invariably before these slowly weakening men died, their minds went back to the warmest security they had known. General Seeley noted perceptively in his memoirs: 'It is strange and touching that, when men die of dangerous wounds, in almost every case "mother" is the last word that crosses their lips.' In many accounts of the battlefield one comes across this feature. It is almost one of the litmus tests of veracity. It even reached the greatest cartoonist of the war, Raemakers. In his albums there is only one cartoon which does not satirize the Germans or war in general. It is based on an incident in the early days of the war at Soissons which he came to hear of. It shows a German taking a dying English soldier in his arms. The caption reads, 'Is it you, Mother?' and startles us still with its immediacy.

Once a man had died, if his body had not been torn by high explosive, for a short time he might seem alive as if perhaps that narcotic slipping away of life had not reached an irreversible point. Bailey remembered asking a dead man the way at Fricourt on the Somme field, for the corpse's eyes were open and there was no sign of injury. Sassoon was more positive in his search for a clue to death: 'As I stepped over one of the Germans, an impulse made me lift him up from the ditch. Propped against the bank, his blond face was undisfigured except by the mud which I wiped from his eyes and tunic and mouth by my coat sleeve. He'd evidently been killed while digging, for his tunic was knotted loosely about his shoulders. He didn't look to be more than eighteen. Hoisting him a little higher, I thought what a gentle face he had . . . I hadn't expected the battle of the Somme to be quite like this.' For those whose interest was more clinical, the unmarked dead usually showed telltale blood drips on lips, in ears or lungs.

Once the dead were lying, they became fair prey for souvenir hunters. The further one moved from the battle line, the more cleanly they were picked, as Graham noted. 'Those nearest our encampment at Noreuil all lay with the whites of their pockets turned out and their tunics and shirts undone by souvenir hunters. Towards Quéant there lay a handsome six-foot-three-inch German very well clothed. Then his boots went. Then his tunic was taken off. A few days later he was lying in his pants.'

These new corpses had magnetic fascination for many apart

from looters, as they could visualize their own deaths in fleeting moments, however hard they tried to cauterize such few thoughts as strayed from the concrete, the everyday. Graham tells us:

> There was fascination in going from dead to dead, seeking and looking with great intensity in the heart. Blue bundles and green bundles were strewn far and wide. The story of each man's death was plainly written in the circumstances in which he lay. The brave machine-gunners with resolute look in their shoulders and face lay scarcely relaxed beside their oiled machine. They had been bayoneted at their post. Facing those machine-gunners one saw how men, rushing forward in extended formation, had fallen, one directly he had started forward, then the others in sequence. One poor wretch had got far but had got entangled in the wire, had pulled and pulled and at last been shot to rags. Another had been near enough to strike the foe and had been shot by revolver. Down at the bottom of the deep trenches many dead men lay flat in the mud alongside the duckboards or in the act of creeping cautiously out of the holes at the side. In other parts of the field one saw the balance of battle and the Germans evidently attacking, not extended but in groups and now in groups together. One saw Germans and British taking shelter in shellholes, fear in their faces. I remember two of our fellows in a shellhole. They were crouching unnaturally. One had evidently been saying to the other, 'Keep your head down.' Now in both men's heads there was a dent, the sort of dent that appears in the side of a rubber ball when not fully expanded by air.

The burial parties would soon be organized. Reasons of morale, hygiene and humanity imposed the unpleasant fatigue. Men would have on the nose and mouth pieces of their gas masks and probably sandbags on their hands. Breast pockets would be cut to extract pay-books. The red identity disc would be sent to the orderly room, the green one left on the body for identification. If explosive had shredded the body, flesh would adhere to the discs, and the smell was enclosed within the envelope. There would be little apart from paybook and discs to identify the corpse, for time levelled all men impartially. Cloete left a harrowing account of the work involved from an experience at Serre on the Somme field.

> As you lifted a body by its arms and legs, they detached themselves from the torso, and this was not the worst thing. Each

body was covered inches deep with a black fur of flies, which flew up into your face, into your mouth, eyes and nostrils as you approached. The bodies crawled with maggots. There had been a disaster here. An attack by green, badly led troops who had had too big a rum ration – some of them had not even fixed their bayonets – against a strong position where the wire was still uncut. They hung like washing on the barbs, like scarecrows who scared no crows since they were edible. The birds disputed the bodies with us. This was a job for all ranks. No one could expect the men to handle these bodies unless the officers did their share. We stopped every now and then to vomit . . . the bodies had the consistency of Camembert cheese. I once fell and put my hand through the belly of a man. It was days before I got the smell out of my hands. I remember wondering if I would get blood poisoning.

To a man versed in such fatigues, date of death could be established roughly by the colour of the corpses, as they changed from yellow to grey to red and to black until they subsided and dripped beneath the soil, ready perhaps to bring other men with them in their new form as spores of potential gas gangrene.

The attitude of survivors to these piles of human slime is deceptive. 'Life is a curious thing in war. Men who you like and with whom you have been close suddenly get struck down. You feel sorry for them and for a fleeting instant you feel their poignant loss. But presently vain regrets are cast aside and one plunges back into the activities of the present; new people take their place and life goes on. It is no matter of callousness. The exigencies of war demand all one's energies.' But death was never commonplace in the front line. Any burial party or impromptu service would be reverently attended. Rough grave-crosses would spring up. 'In loving memory of an unknown British soldier'; 'Sleep on, beloved brother. Take thy rest' would be untidily ciphered on the wood. Mourning would come later when time and lessening of danger allowed the expression of grief which might have interfered with battle tasks at the time. A new integration without dead mates as a prop would have to be worked on. The values of the dead man would be built into a unit if he had been a symbol of defiance. Then after the war would come the memory with photographic sharpness and an overwhelming sense of loss and anxiety.

13

ATTITUDES TO THE GERMANS

The official army attitude to the Germans was clear-cut. Men were to be always hostile and kill where they could. In order to foster this spirit, propaganda was carefully propagated through divisional HQs. These were the Intelligence broadsheets, known to subalterns as 'Comic Cuts', publishing such details as the letter supposedly found on the person of a Bavarian guardsman: 'Dear Greta Maier, in five minutes I bayoneted seven women and four young girls in the fighting at Batoville.' In an atmosphere of war's uncertainty and without evidence to the contrary, my uncle today reckons that most men at the time accepted what they were told about the enemy.

Certainly some men needed less convincing than others. Canadians and Australians refused to waive their hostility even after the war when on garrison duty on the Rhineland. With the Scots likewise there was no close season, so that even Australians would cheer the 51st or the Black Watch. New Zealanders, like men from southern England, were more placable. Cultural differences thus helped to determine the attitudes of war. If a man came from a male-oriented family circle with an emphasis on toughness in personal relations and a concentration on past glories in military history, he would be unlikely to see the Germans in any other role but the military one of 'enemy'.

Regimental factors might also play a part. The 9th Welch were keen to attack at the start of the Somme to avenge their carving up at Loos. Graham wrote of 'the immortal eighty' at Festubert. Early in 1915 a guardsman had been shot for cowardice, so his company took an oath to redeem their name at the next battle. Of the eighty, forty died. Coppard wrote of his B company in the East Surreys, who remembered an incident before the Somme when Germans pretending to surrender had thrown grenades. This memory was passed from mouth to mouth and to fresh drafts to the end of the war. Such memories would guarantee an irrational response potentially anywhere on the front line.

Even individuals might behave with greater anger than their comrades for private reasons. Evans wrote of shooting a giant, flaxen-haired raider who went limp and crumpled like a burst balloon. That was on 4 March 1917. He had been waiting since 1 July 1916. It was done in memory of 'my little scar-faced Collicot' and his mates Lee and Smith – 'we shall have no more long vigils or trudge weary miles together. Did they really think they could kill all these men and not pay for it?' Arnie Atkins likewise remembered killing with satisfaction after he had heard of his brother's death, killing otherwise only as part of the day's work and impersonally.

Regardless of these individual differences, all men behaved with bitter hatred in situations involving mortal fear and direct confrontation. There are incidents recalled beyond number in memoirs in which men wondered if it was really themselves who gouged, clawed, clubbed and bayoneted. How could they have behaved so wildly? 'I saw men fighting with spades. The way the Germans yelled was awful. Some made a good fight. Some would crawl on their knees holding a picture of a woman or child in their hands above their heads but everyone was killed. The excitement was gone. We killed in cold blood because it was our duty to kill as much as we could. I thought many a time of the *Lusitania*. I had actually prayed for that day and, when I got it, I killed just as much as I had hoped fate would allow me to kill.' Here the army would have noted with pleasure that their propaganda had sustained the killing wish even after the physical justification had gone.

Where there was no hatred, killing might still be a pleasure if it could be fitted into the framework of a game. Bean once watched the Australians ratting at captured Pozières. They looked for fugitives in the rubble heaps and chased the shrieking Germans with bayonets, or shot from the hip if outpaced. Sitting on doorsteps smoking, they waited for others to bolt. 'This grim sport of ratting, for as a sport it was regarded in the fury of war, was not without great risks to the hunters.' The 10th Londons wrote of a similar episode. A German machine-gun was hitting ration limbers at dusk. Sadleir-Jackson located the sniping nest and sent a man to fix three slabs of guncotton and a detonator to the sniper's wooden seat. 'At dusk a flash, a rumble of thunder, a dark object proceeding upwards, our CO in tears of laughter and our ration parties undisturbed.' The thought that the German proceeding upwards was a soldier like themselves appears not to have occurred to anyone. This same boyish irresponsibility and thoughtlessness comes out in another vignette.

One lovely morning I was in an isolated spot with six men [at Guillemont]. The sentry was looking over the top. Suddenly he exclaimed, 'Sir, there's a bosch carrying a bucket.' This aroused us to immediate action. 'Lend me your rifle,' I cried. 'What's the range?' 'Between 500 and 600 yards,' replied the corporal. I took careful aim and pulled the trigger. The man with the bucket took no notice. Once again I took careful aim, putting the sight at 600. He leaped into the air, dropped his bucket and ran for his life. This little episode amused the men and each morning they waited for him to re-appear.

All this was on par with Hyndson's memory of men calling out 'Waiter' at the start of the war and blowing off the heads that instinctively appeared above the enemy's trench to take orders.

Whether Germans were killed as an act of revenge, in self-defence or as part of a game, the overwhelming impression left by memoirs is that in most circumstances the enemy was disliked and feared. In part it must have been because, like Japanese in the Second World War, an enemy seldom seen would have projected into him all the fears and resentments of a soldier, himself in a situation of high stress. More tangibly, an enemy who had killed one's friends and would shoot any British head he saw without ceremony had to be disliked. Allen stated that it was this capacity for deadly destruction which was the basis of his own feelings.

The end product was dislike, a greyer emotion than hatred but a more constant one. When asked by a prisoner what he thought of the Germans, Dunham replied: 'We just looks on you like vomit.' Evans was surprised at his own feeling of revulsion when looking closely at Germans, comparing his own great fears with the smallness of the object – grimy, bearded and bespectacled. Allen felt the same loathing for Germans as for the rats wheezing under his bed at night. After a brief experience of fighting, all things German became associated with unpleasant experiences and organized fear. The warm, dry, flannelly smell of Germans lingering in their captured dugouts was for most men, as for Glyde, 'familiar to my dying day'. Evans was disconcerted to smell it again after the war in Cologne and experience again the dry throat of fear which it could still trigger.

Dislike did not preclude admiration. Originally the German army had been despised as amateurs dressed in baggy uniforms who were thought to be bad rifle shots. Lucy tells us just how soon the BEF found that the amateurs had a kick in them and that our professionals were not invincible in attack, as they had been trained to believe. In mid-1915 Jack wrote in his diary of 'the magnificent German army', while an officer during the Somme battle of 1916 told Gibbs of the German machine-gunners – 'topping fellows. Fight until they are killed. They gave us hell.' By 1918 Delisle was thankfully observing that the Germans were outnumbered and judged that the average German division was on par with the best British divisions. Few soldiers noted German trench systems or gun positions without grudging admiration for their superiority.

German bravery was noted with similar approval. Gladden described a single German dead on the lip of a crater at Messines. He had been killed in an advanced post. The file of passing men murmured in approbation. Colonel Cawston described an incident during the advance of 8 August 1918. 'The lone German soldier had carried on the war when the rest of the Sailly Laurette garrison had either surrendered or been killed. He chose as his fortress the old hut at the far end of the quarry. He took a pot shot at anyone who approached and refused to surrender. Our fellows, admiring his stubborn courage, were inclined to leave him alone.' Seeley recalled a similar incident later. 'As I rode through the wood with dismounted Strathconas, I saw a handsome young Bavarian twenty yards in front of me miss an approaching Strathcona and receive a bayonet thrust right through the neck. He sank down with his back against a tree. As I came close to him, I shouted out in German, "Lie still. A stretcher-bearer will look after you." His eyes in an ashen face seemed to blaze fire as he snatched up his rifle and fired his last shot at me, saying loudly, "*Nein. Nein. Ich will ungefangen sterben.*" Then he collapsed in a heap.' Both sides often came against this stalwart courage. 'Libels on Fritz's courage and efficiency were much resented by all trench soldiers of experience.'

This somewhat grudging respect which all experience imposed could sometimes turn into an even warmer feeling. Memoirs frequently mention fraternization, truces, the cessation of violence by mutual consent. Even today we are surprised that men who often hated and always disliked their opponent could come to terms with him in any way on some days, then start the killing again as if nothing had happened. The key to the situation would seem to have been the degree of danger. As danger lessened, so too did the hatred which geared a man up in response.

Considerations of broad strategy might be crucial here. Of necessity, activity in some regions would be less than in others. On the Ploegstraat to La Bassée section the marshy valley of the Lys made any movement difficult. From mid-1915 to 1918 therefore both sides declined to risk lives with so little to be gained. In the Cambrai area too the absence of worthwhile objectives cut down aggressive activity until late 1917. Dugdale at Villers Plouich found both sides using GS waggons for wiring in no-man's-land. The same considerations applied in the Somme area until the fatuous offensive of summer 1916. When the British took over, men could be paraded in the open just behind the front line. Even on active fronts, concreted positions with barbed wire and poised artillery made anything but carefully timetabled attacks unprofitable – a situation accepted by most front-line officers if not by HQs well to the rear. An impromptu clash would achieve little and certainly bring punitive counter-artillery fire for each side. Activity was therefore often of a ritual kind just to keep staff officers content. Lord Reith wrote of his soldier days: 'Funny business this. The enemy throws some shells at our trench. We've got your range accurately you see. No monkey tricks. Home battery replied. We've got yours; trench line and battery position – both. No more nonsense. Live and let live.' At the humblest level, this might be the case too. Belhaven saw patrols studiously avoiding each other and Tom Atkins wrote of a road in no-man's-land, the British patrolling one side and the Germans the other. Both sides waved helmets on the end of rifles and the invariable report back was that all was indeed quiet on the western front. At Blangy, where the trenches were just six feet apart, Tyndale-Biscoe described both sets of fighting soldiers creeping away whenever they sighted each other.

This stalemate in aggressive conditions might appear for short periods even on active fronts. So long as there was attack or resistance, war was sustained. When danger or a sense of purpose was removed, then men would revert to watchful but passive distrust.

Once a soldier removed his helmet and kit harness in battle, he might be killed if his captor was in the heat and anger of battle or had a personal grudge. Usually his life would be spared. The lowered head, the anxious face, the upheld bible or crucifix were sufficient. Seeing a man recognizably human and not that stereotype of inhumanity which the front-line soldier usually projected onto his foe, a civilian response subvened.

The surrender had to be immediate, however, and without any equivocation. 'Lying on his stomach, he turned his head and asked for mercy but his eyes said murder. I plunged my bayonet into the back of his heart and he slumped with a grunt. I turned him over. There was a revolver in his right hand under his left armpit. He had been trying to get a shot at me under his body. As I withdrew the bayonet, I pressed the trigger and shot him to make sure. I thought I may as well have a souvenir so I took his field glasses and watch. I still have them but the watch has had its day. It were really a pocket watch in a leather case with luminous spots.' One detects here perhaps a trace of guilt. Another instance, told by Allen, is more clear-cut:

In the early days of November 1918 our advance had been carried out according to schedule. Each division was given a line to which it must attain before nightfall and this meant that each battalion in a division had to reach a certain point by a certain time. On the late afternoon of 10 November we were still far from our objective. We were on the edge of a plantation with a wide open space of culti-vated land between us and the village at 500 yards, our objective. An officer was sent ahead with two men to reconnoitre. At the village entrance, propped up against a tree, they found a German officer severely wounded in the thigh. He was quite conscious and looked up calmly as Lieutenant S. approached him. He spoke English and, when he was questioned, intimated that the village had been evacuated by the Germans two hours before. It was nearly dusk. Our men gathered in the small square in front of the church. Then from the tower machine-guns opened fire to kill about a hundred men and five officers. The crews were mercilessly bayoneted. The corporal who had been with Lieutenant S. ran to the entrance of the village to settle with the wounded officer who had betrayed them. The German seemed to be expecting him and his face did not flinch as the bayonet descended.

This apparent charity in accepting surrender did not indicate the lifting of violent behaviour. If there was the slightest hint of resis-tance, even resistance against hopeless odds, then the highest pos-sible level of aggression would be maintained. Read wrote:

There was a small spring in a grove by the road where two Germans were lying. One was a big, brawny fellow with a brown beard. The other was a mere lad. He looked to be about fourteen with a pathetically childish chin. They had evidently stopped here to fill their canteens, both probably desperate with thirst, when they had been overtaken by a large body of our men. The young boy must have sheltered himself behind the man while the latter held our men back a little. There was a scorched place up the side of the ravine where a hand grenade had exploded, but the big German had been surrounded and killed by a bayonet thrust right through the chest. His hands were still clutching at the place where the bayonet had gone through. The boy was lying behind him. His back appeared to have been broken, probably by a blow from a rifle butt and he was contorted in a kind of arch, only his feet and shoulders resting on the ground. It was he that had probably thrown the grenade for he carried potato-masher type bombs.

Once the surrender had been accepted, however, the captive was safe. On his side, the prisoner was hugely relieved and wanted only to placate his masters. The masters, seeing a man like themselves, dropped into civilian behaviour which reassured them that battle had not de-humanized them beyond its immediate demands. Gibbs once watched two seventeen-year-old Germans being severely spoken to after the battle of Messines. 'You ought to be spanked and sent home to your mothers,' said a severe subaltern. 'Please, sir, that is what we would like, sir, if you please.' After such interrogation, prisoners would be taken to the cage. Bridges wrote of a cockney shouting: 'Cigrets, Chocluts,' during the Somme battle. Countered his NCO: 'Nah then. Enough of that coddlin'. Shove the bastards in the cage.' Even there Germans were likely to be treated more kindly than refugees. Each week they would get a tobacco allowance, Sunday afternoon off and a plot of land of their own. Eleven days after the 1 July disaster of the Somme, Feilding saw bully beef and cigarettes being passed through the barbed wire. 'Regular music 'all 'uns ain't they sir?' commented a man while the rest of the platoon grinned at them as men might smile at an unknown beast in the zoo. On his side, the German did not shed his military identity. He would stand to attention for the officers of both nationalities. He simply adopted the clear-cut role of non-combatant which blended with the equally defined behaviour of his captors. Thus Subaltern Jones wrote of Germans driving waggons and holding their guards' rifles, and De Lisle noted prisoners under their own officers repairing roads and clearing twice as much earth daily as their Labour corps counterparts. On one occasion De Lisle reported with relish the German officer asking to report regularly to his CO on the other side of the line.

During a battle, the extent of the action made most things unclear. Only if an enemy could actually be seen to surrender could his intentions be known for sure. In a limited trench raid, in contrast, it was much easier to see just when serious action began and when it ended. Once ended, non-violence would recommence on the instant. This account comes from Private Moodie:

> They made a night attack and we drove them off. At last a lull came in the fighting and we shouted to the Allemands to come and fetch their wounded. At first they seemed very dubious and would only show their helmets but we promised not to shoot and a man who wore the iron cross advanced boldly to our entanglements and proceeded to assist a wounded man. Another followed and, amidst our cheers, they carried him off. Before going, the first man saluted and said, 'Thank you, gentlemen, one and all. I thank you very much. Good day.' The incident quite upset me for a time and I wished that we might all be friends again. He was a handsome fellow and big.

Such incidents can often be found featuring in memoirs of either side.

That the degree of danger was the most crucial trigger of aggression and sustainer of it is best shown in engagements where men continued killing, since the enemy had not surrendered, but felt guilty in proportion as there was no danger. My uncle enjoyed blowing Uhlans with instant fuse in 1914 but recalled being worried by the sheer waste in futile attacks at Mons. A letter in the Whitby *Gazette* of December 1914 noted what a fine body of men the Prussian guards were at 1st Ypres – 'It pricked my conscience to mow them down.' On another occasion 'A German section were lying fully exposed to us on level ground where they had remained from the moment daylight caught them and they were shunning death like the masses about them, but small movements and their regular formation gave them away. We put bullets into the heads of the lying enemy. Two or three of them rose stiffly to their knees to escape but the bullets caught them and they flopped down again.

I felt disgusted. We had slaughtered too many already. I was miserable until the German line was still and I prayed for them as I killed them.'

Within this broad framework of strategic or tactical considerations suddenly curtailing violence and hatred, the peculiarities of trench warfare reinforced other tendencies reducing the number of violent clashes. When opposing armies are placed close to each other during long periods of relative inactivity, then communication is bound to take place which forces men to perceive that the enemy are human beings like themselves, civilians in uniform, men with families or hopes of families, men just as fanatically determined to live so long as a scrap of honour can be salvaged. During the Napoleonic wars, several days at close quarters without battle were sufficient to start fraternization in a wary way. Advanced pickets would converse, then limited contact would be established. Before the battle of Douro in the Peninsula, wood for building huts was sent over by the French. Drinking horses and swimming soldiers shared the river between the two armies – though only when no weapons were carried. At Pamplona in 1813 Lieutenant Wood noted men of both sides out after dark within eyesight of each other, digging for potatoes with their bayonets. During the siege of Sebastopol Anglesey noted in his diary the frequent fraternization between the opposing trench lines. The same was true of the Boer war. By mutual agreement shelling would stop for Sunday, while on one occasion a Major Pine-Coffin invited Botha to Christmas lunch.

The chief time for similar communication during the Great War was at morning stand-to or evening stand-down. Kingsbury wrote of the enemy singing 'Tipperary'. 'Good morning, Tommy. Do you see me?' a German would call out, waving a shovel from side to side, with English snipers replying, half seriously. Major-General Unruh scouted our front line just before an offensive in 1918 and was offered cigarettes by English sentries calling through the darkness. Occasionally trench communication might go beyond talking. Edmund Blunden at Givenchy described an officer and twenty men going over the top after a local engagement and calling out, 'Good morning, Tommy. Have you any biscuits?' There was an exchange of words followed by the arrest of our two subalterns involved. Visual communication might be more informal. Wrote Maze: 'I went to a spur where one of our forward observation posts had a plunging view onto a German trench. I had started sketching when

I saw the bald head of a German framed against a shirt laid out to dry on the parapet of the trench. In a hushed voice I called the sentry and pointed out the man. 'I know,' he said. 'He's been there all morning doing nothing but pick lice from his body. Lousy, that's what he is.' It hadn't occurred to anyone to shoot him. Evidently in their opinion being lousy was trouble enough for one man.' Even if the two sides could neither talk nor see, they could always hear. A detailed picture could be built up of the opponent by smells, sounds of wheels and feet on duckboards.

As a result of all this, it was often possible for either side to interpret any unusual situation rapidly and respond in the safest manner, firing bullets and throwing grenades on the minimum number of occasions. Thus when Canon Frederick Scott walked for a long period in no-man's-land during the Somme battle looking for his dead son, no German fired. Gillespie during April 1915 wrote of a German working party sent by daylight in front of the wire. Assuming the men to have been sent for punishment, no Englishman fired. Swinton reported an incident at Beaumont Hamel on 2nd July 1916 when the mist suddenly lifted. Taken by surprise at the suddenness, a solitary German soldier was allowed to reach his own trench. Barnett with the Leinsters saw two men carrying a sheet of corrugated iron first argue fiercely, then drop their load and climb on top of the trench and fight for a quarter of an hour. The Germans 350 yards away cheered and fired their rifles into the air.

On some occasions communication might produce even quite lengthy periods of unofficial truce. This would happen if either side found notoriously passive regiments opposite them. On the German side the Saxons were a byword. Herd at St Éloi in 1915 was told by the Northumberlands who were being relieved that there was no shooting while the Saxons were opposite. The Liverpool Scottish officers agreed to continue this truce. At night there would be a low whistle then both sides would send out men to the mine craters of no-man's-land (still visible today) and exchange food for ten or fifteen minutes. Prussians on the flanks disapproved and sniped but could do little else. 'Captain Davidson could hardly overlook the matter and he quietly reproved me with a twinkle in his eye when I was alone.' Needless to say, the affair did not reach the colonel's ear. Hutchison also wrote of Saxons and Buffs sharing hammers during wiring and of a three-week truce at Bois Greniers after the rains of

January 1915. Hitchcock, in his published memoirs, corroborates Herd, since he was at St Éloi just six weeks before the Liverpool Scottish. 'The enemy shouted out "Good morning" to me. When I was in front of the largest crater, I watched six Germans coming out into the open and getting into one of their advanced posts. Six more got out with their rifles slung and with braziers in their hands yelling "Goodbye" to me and went back to their main trench.' Holsteiners were like Saxons in their view of the war. Eyre wrote of them exchanging cigars and schnapps for bully beef and Macconochie before being relieved by the ferocious Bavarians. The 73rd Fusiliers similarly kept their war at a low key. The word 'Gibraltar' was sewn on their tunics to commemorate the victory of 1781 when they had fought with the British army.

British regiments are naturally rather more chary of advertising their lukewarm attitude to war but it seems that county regiments from the south of England were notably less enthusiastic than men from the north. The approach of the Somersets, wrote Captain Jones, was that their job was just to hold the line. Why draw fire? With the right officers, the right front and the right enemy, such an attitude was common.

A temporary ending of hostilities was almost always the result of direct communication. But there was one factor which imposed itself with such force upon men in the trenches on both sides and could cause such complete misery that it made hostility impossible. This was the weather. During the fearfully cold winter of 1917 Bert Chaney saw men walking about in open ground and lighting braziers till the brigadier came round and ordered them 'to make a bloody war of it'. Bescn at Marcoing on the Cambrai front at the same time noted some of the enemy walking about with their hands in their pockets, to his surprise. Since revolver bullets were ignored, the commanding officer ordered a five-day truce. Torrential rain could have a similar effect. Gibbs reported trenches collapsing at Hooge in the winter of 1915 as a result of prolonged rain. Both sides ignored each other. In the same winter Hutchison at Armentières wrote of his men abandoning their trenches and building breastworks, the Germans doing the same. Fires were lit everywhere for warmth. As a result HQ stopped the letters on that section of front for three weeks. Feilding at Lempire in early 1918 described both sides walking about in no-man's-land without shooting when a sudden thaw produced two feet of mud in minutes. After a few days a machine-gun was turned on an enemy officer as a hint and the 'highly irregular practice' came to an end.

This uneasy oscillation between aggression and wary passivity is well illustrated by the events of Christmas 1914.

The *Sphere* in January 1915 had broken the story of the first Christmas, but the censor had intervened so that it only really came out when Captain Chudleigh in the *Telegraph* wrote after the war.

Christmas morning had broken fine and clear and though we had stood to arms as usual, there had been no bombardment on either side. Between 10 and 11 am a subaltern said, 'Have you seen what's going on outside?' Looking through my loophole I saw two of our men and three Germans standing boldly together in the middle of no-man's-land while, on the German parapet 150 yards away, our enemies could be seen sitting or moving freely about. One of our sentries was standing on his platform, hands in pockets with a smile on his face. He shrugged his shoulders and continued to peer through the loophole and said that, about twenty minutes earlier on the right, men had begun to walk out of their trenches in ones and twos and had met and shaken hands in no-man's-land. No Germans had come into our trenches but many of our men were in the German trenches. Little doubt the truce originated among private soldiers and the reactions of officers and NCOs were mixed. In our case, we made a kind of compromise. When our midday meal was over, we stepped out of the back of our trenches, walked over four or five fields, threw off our coats and at high speed dug a trench into which to lay our field telephone. It then got dark and the trenches were filled with lively gossip of the day's doings. Watches, cigarette cases, rings and tubes of ointment were being shown round. They had been received in exchange for goods from the Germans all of whom were Saxons. Then the C SM reported stiffly that an abnormal number of men had been 'absent without leave' during the lunch-time roll-call. I said I would interview some of them before deciding what action to take. He returned with two of the most exemplary and reliable old soldiers in the company. They said they had been sitting on the edge of the parapet. Near by, under a long, covered part of the German trench, a Christmas dinner had been laid out. The Germans repeatedly pressed them to stay and eat it with them and, when they declined, dragged them bodily into the

trench by their legs. They had had an excellent dinner during
which an officer's servant who had been a waiter at Leicester had
arrived with a bottle of French wine 'from the German officers
to the English captain'. They begged pardon since they had not
understood and had drunk it themselves. They returned sober
and, as they departed along the trench, we all tried to satisfy ourselves that the ends of discipline had been served. About 6 pm an
orderly hurried through the trench with the following orders:
'All fraternization with the enemy is to cease immediately. Any
further action of this sort will be dealt with severely.' I went into
my funk hole, lit the stump of a candle and wrote a letter home
from which these notes are taken. Next morning the guns spoke
as usual.

Contrary to general belief, this Christmas truce continued
throughout the war in places. Griffith saw a meeting in no-man's-
land during 1915, with a soccer match, though some with bitter
memories refused to take part. Ewart was in a similar truce the same
year. Graham at Fromelles witnessed chaplains from both sides
leading prayers in no-man's-land. In 1916 MacDougall at Loos
took part in a truce – 'how extraordinary,' he wrote. Bradley at
Hamel in 1916 saw both sides waving to each other. A meeting in
the middle featured at Oppy at Christmas 1917.

In part, tradition was responsible. The exchange of courtesies
by officers at Christmas was customary in European wars and anyway in those days Christmas was the greatest feastday of the year,
the day of families and children and giving. It was hardly surprising
that men of similar culture, so close together and with thoughts so
often on home, should meet on that one special day which only in
the last decade, with longer holidays and grosser commercialization,
has lost its special significance. In another sense the Christmas truce
represented only one more of those curious not peace, not war
situations which broke out so often during trench warfare.

The crucial thing to note, however, is that distrust and scarcely
veiled hostility were a feature of these truces. Chudleigh had used
the Christmas 1914 truce as a suitable time to bury his phone wires.
Further down the line Ewart and his men sang 'Auld Lang Syne'
with the Germans while the leading German left a card, which he
wanted posted to his motorcycling girl friend in Suffolk. At the
same time both sides were bringing up wire and timber. Brian

with the Argyll and Sutherlanders exchanged lager and cigars then played a violent football match with no holds barred and ending with a boxing match between the two champions on each side, which the two men wanted to finish off with rifles at a hundred paces. Bodger described the exchange of smokes and the Germans stroking the English-issue goatskin overcoats but when a German urinated on British barbed wire he was shot. The English respected a brave and resourceful enemy but there was no love or liking. The German remained a legitimate rifle target when he appeared hostile and, if there was any doubt, he was deemed hostile. If there was no hatred, neither was there a relaxation of the will to win; if not that, then at least there was no relaxation of suspicion.

14

ATTITUDES TO THE WAR AS A WHOLE

It is surprisingly difficult today to form an estimate of the way soldiers regarded the war as a whole. Non-combatant spokesmen at home wrote nonsense each and every one. Ian Hay, an old soldier and one of the first best-selling 'authorities' on the war, wrote for them all:

'What kind of battle will it be this time, sir?' inquired Bogle respectfully. 'Oh, our artillery will pound the German trenches for a week or two and then we shall go over the parapet and drive them back for miles,' said Angus simply. 'And what then, sir?' 'What then? We shall go on pushing them until another division relieves us.' Bogle nodded comprehendingly. He now had firmly fixed in his mind the essential details of the projected offensive of 1916. He was not interested to go further into the matter and it is this very faculty of philosophic trust coupled with absolute lack of imagination which makes the British soldier the most invincible in the war. The Frenchman is inspired to glorious deeds by his great spirit and passionate love of his native soil; the German fights as he thinks – like a machine. But the British Tommy wins through owing to his entire indifference to the pros and cons of the tactical situation. He settles down to war as down to any other trade and is chiefly concerned, as in peacetime, with his holidays and creature comforts. A battle is a mere incident between one set of billets and another. Consequently he does not allow the grim realities of war to obsess his mind when off duty.

When one turns from these astonishing pronouncements to the memoirs of the combatants themselves, one finds very few observations beyond the everyday detail or the concrete experience. So too it seemed at the time to an acute observer like Aldington. 'I had been waiting eagerly for the men to get away from their time-honoured jests and speak of their experiences. I was disappointed that they talked in such a trivial way. But part of their impressiveness was their very triviality, their complete unconsciousness that there was anything extraordinary or striking about themselves. They hadn't tried to think it out. They went on with the business of war, hating it, because they had been told that it had to be done and believing what they were told.' Soldiers at the time spoke little and later wrote little on what they thought either of war or about their own role in the war.

One can nevertheless state with certainty that some soldiers undoubtedly did enjoy the war. The last letter written by Gillespie of the Argyll and Sutherlanders was dated 24 September 1915. 'My dear Daddy, this is your birthday . . . it will be a great fight and, even when I think of you, I would not wish to be out of it. I am very happy and, whatever happens, you will remember that.' The next day he led his company into battle and was later found dead on the field holding a copy of Bunyan in his hand. Lieutenant Garnett remarked that 'This is all a great game. So very childish, but I am such a child as to love it. And you poor people at home pay for us to play bears as we used to do when I was four – only now the game is very greatly glorified. I am enjoying it immensely.' Subaltern Grenfell commented: 'I adore war. It is like a picnic without that objectlessness of a picnic. I have never been so well or so happy. Nobody grumbles at one being dirty.' Greenwell's letters are interspersed with such comments as 'this ridiculous war', 'a most ripping day', 'rather amusing country on the whole', 'how much I enjoy the war'. The extreme youth of all these writers, their recent emergence from the structured cocoon of the boarding school and their early deaths before the cumulative strain of war embittered their judgement may account for much of the exuberance.

Youth and a public-school, protective background do not explain the response of so sensible and long-serving a soldier as De Lisle: 'I disliked war in principle but the war years were the best of my life. No sport can equal the excitement of war; no other occupation can be half as interesting.' Lower down the ranks of the army among officers were men like dour Scot Hutchison who spoke of 'the happiest days of my life', while my uncle as a gunner ranker, talking to me of his memories, concluded with the remark: 'Wasn't it fun?' For all these men and men like them, compensations outweighed the mind-bending fear and the smell of the dead.

It is hard to pin these men down. With some, the chief compensation seems to have been what Macmillan grudgingly called 'the undoubted charms' of soldiering. At their simplest these were the drill, the high standard of discipline, the absence of worry about food, shelter, lodging, health. Rather higher in the scale came the comradeship. Looking back just after the war, military surgeon Dearden wrote: 'So ended an unforgettable experience and it is curious in retrospect to find out how much one had enjoyed it. One had shared common tasks with men of every type and station and been admitted to a fellowship and intimacy so rare as to outweigh the beastliness which made it possible.' Beyond the social dimension was the physical rhythm of the war. Quiet periods were for all men, as for Greenwell, 'very pleasant at the front. It was a boy's dream of an endless picnic on an unprecedented scale.' More surprisingly, many found the violent periods as rewarding. Grenfell wrote a poem on the morning of the day on which he died, which Casson thought a perfect expression for such a time:

> And when the burning moment breaks
> and all things else are out of mind
> and only joy of battle takes him by the throat
> makes him blind
> the thundering line of battle stands
> and in the air death moans and sings
> but day shall also clasp him with strong hands
> and night shall fold him in soft wings

Then would come the immediate prospect as men waited for the whistle to blow. Fresh from Dulwich College, Jones found 'the last half-hour or so like nothing on earth. The only thing that compares with it are the last few minutes before a big school rugby match.' When the battle started, even Brenan, who hated the war and looked forward achingly to its end, found it a great challenge. In this he was like Chapman's colonel who 'the worse the trial, the more perfect the balance of his nervous system. This quiet, level-headed man was lifted to a higher plane. He seemed to be nourished by the most terrifying aspects of the war while to me it brought only shrivelling fear.'

In short, as Chapman noted, 'a man might rave against war but from its myriad faces it could always turn towards him one which was his own'. 'It is a mode of life, a society, a custom, an inter-course, a conviviality, a business, an idleness, a madness, a mono-tony, a game, a penal servitude, a rebirth, a second nature – all these.'

Reading through the unpublished memoirs of private soldiers in the Imperial War Museum together with the published memoirs, mostly from the pens of former lieutenants, the dominating impression, however, is that many more men actively hated the war throughout than found pleasure in it. At the top of the army were men like Monash, commander of the Australian corps. 'I hate the business of war – the horror, the waste, the destruction, the inefficiency.' As an officer, Bowra found he could never harden himself to it. He came to dislike it more and more so that 'the memory of the carnage and filth has never left me'. Among the Other Ranks, Frank Richards served with only one front-line man during the whole war who owned to enjoying the life. For every man who, in writing expressed approval of his war, ten can be found in writing to damn it in every aspect.

Even if lovers of war and haters of war are added together, however, their combined numbers fall far short of that majority who were never able to reach a final judgement.

Perhaps age had something to do with this bewilderment. An analysis of one million casualties after the war discovered 80 per cent to be under thirty. Even in time of peace few men in their twenties have sufficient feeling of time contrast to communicate an unusual experience with detachment. Few of them, too, read sufficient to stimulate searching observation or develop those word combinations capable of conveying nuances of emotion. At the time many might have read the novelettes of Florence Warden or Charles Garvice, or such papers as *London Opinion* or *John Bull*. These hardly went beyond the level of vigorous triviality.

Perhaps the simple physical experience of war added to the bewilderment. Looked at overall, there was so little to allow for any awareness of the passing of the year. Mottram observed that 'the barrages became so enormous and mechanical, the succession of persons and places so rapid and their characteristics so obliterated that I doubt if anything was ever so clear as it had once been'. Further, without maps or information, a soldier stood even less chance of separating experiences from each other in a significant way.

Even if a man could compartmentalize and digest what was going on, bewildering contrasts assaulted him daily. Surgeon Hayward wrote: 'entering a building, I found it strewn with corpses. In another hut was a pile of amputated arms and legs. Then we had some rest. I went butterfly hunting. It was these violent contrasts that to me make up the vivid memories of my days in France. Outside, the sun and larks, birds and butterflies; inside, nature violated and out-raged. Alternating with the dread and anxiety and physical exhaus-tion was the happy mess, bridge, picnics and concerts. It seemed hardly real at the time. It is fast becoming a dream.' Even in battle there could be sudden mood changes. Wrote Dearden:

> Last night the sky was the most wonderfully beautiful thing I have ever conceived. There was an enormous amount of gunning going on all round us and the sky was heavy with black and very low-lying clouds. There was no moon and every gun flash was thrown onto the clouds like limelight in a theatre. The whole vault of the sky was ablaze with transient waves of fire following so close after each other as to be almost continuous – orange, red, yellow, violet. All along the front the Verey lights danced, some white, some red, some blue while from time to time a golden rain would bathe the whole area near it in a perfect rose-pink colour. The trees stood out jet black against the flaming sky and the whole scene was one of simply appalling beauty.

This kaleidoscope of impressions and emotions could always disrupt any temporary judgement.

But perhaps the most powerful single factor preventing reflection on the war while it was going on was a psychological one. The easiest response to a bewildering, confusing and constantly changing en-vironment, tinged with constant danger, was to blunt the emotions and perceptions. What was not registered on the conscious mind could not disturb it. Those two most perceptive observers of the war, Moran and Manning, both agreed on this. 'Apathy, an almost universal torpor, was a wall of defence set up by nature to meet the violence of the hour. It kept at arms length the habit of introspec-tion.' 'The strange thing was that the greater the hardships they had to endure, for wet and cold could bring all sorts of attendant miseries in their train, the less they grumbled. They became a lot quieter and more reserved in themselves.'

As danger increased, so did the withdrawal.

> It may have been merely a subjective impression, but it seemed that, when they were in the front line, men lost a good deal of their individuality. Their characters, even their faces seemed to become more uniform. They worked better. The work seemed to take the strain off their minds, the strain of waiting. It was per-haps because they withdrew into themselves and became a little

more diffident in showing their feelings. In himself, each man became conscious of his own personality though the pressure of external circumstances seemed to wipe out individuality. The problem which confronted them all equally did not concern death so much as the affirmation of their own will in the face of death.

In place of curiosity there was therefore egocentricity, a concern only with the most immediate matters. Burrage observed that hearts would break if every death were the occasion of mourning. Instead survivors went through the pack and pockets of the dead, hunting for cigarettes and that most precious of possessions – the safety razor. Looking back on the war, Bescn remembered biting the finger off a dead body to get the signet ring. 'I often wondered later did I really do these things. If so, I could not have been in a normal state of mind.' MacGill conjures up the image of the fighting soldier, prisoner of present time, in a vignette from Loos: ' "Hae ye lost many men" "A good number." "I suppose ye did," said the man but I knew that he was not in the least interested in our losses nor even in the issue of the battle. In fact few of us knew the importance of the events in which we took part and cared as little. If I asked one of our men at the moment what his thoughts were, he would answer, "I wonder when we're going to get relieved," or "I hope we're going to get a month's rest when we get out".'

The end product of all this was a mood of passive acceptance. In the absence of any other course, best to carry on. The only hope was for an end. 'You cannot imagine the longing of every man in this army for the end of the war,' wrote Brenan.

To the outsider there were two surprising facets of this stoic endurance. The first was obedience. This did not mean that individuals did not try to escape. Richards saw men pumping water with their arms above the trench parapet to invite a sniper's bullet. Some men fired their rifles into feet or hands with sandbag muffling to keep scorch marks from the skin. Others put faeces under the eyelid, alcohol in the ears, tobacco in the gut to induce inflammation. Paraffin in the scrotum might be taken for hernia, while cordite chewing would put up temperature, and tightened puttees would produce circulation irregularities. But on the whole the men withstood the pressure for early doors. Standing firm while their comrades did the same, observed Gibbs, 'never once did they revolt from the orders that came to them. Never a battalion broke in mutiny against inevitable martyrdoms. Their discipline did not break. However profound was the despair of the individual, the mass moved as it was directed from one shambles to another with the same valour that uplifted on the first of July.' Complaints might be systematic and frequent but with a tendency to be in inverse proportion to the danger facing the complaining men. 'Over and over again it is the duty of the men to charge against barbed wire into almost certain death. Often no one comes back. Yet there is never any hesitation or questioning,' Feilding noted.

The other point which amazed men not inured to the front line was the outward cheerfulness of men clearly tired, hungry and depressed. Looking back, Dearden was amazed at the untroubled spirit of 1914–18. Cushing 'found Tommy an amazing fellow who grouses only over trifles and found things "tray bong" '. Even so critical an observer as trade unionist Ben Tillett 'was never able to understand the spirit of the men, having almost a cheeriness in it'. In a beautiful aside, Agate highlighted the mode. He greeted a sentry who was soaked to the skin and inquired fatuously if he was wet. 'Not by any means, sir. Quite dry underneath, sir. Mustn't grumble at nuffink, sir. Army discipline, sir.' One can almost feel that sturdy and cheerful deference which nowadays survives only in milk-roundsmen, elderly bus conductors and old British Railmen – the enduring acceptances of Edwardian England.

One of the most perceptive veterans, Hubert Essame, recaptures well the two qualities of the front line.

Fifty years later, the impression which remained of them was above all one of immense mutual loyalty and good nature. Order them to go forward and they would stolidly advance, however intense the fire. Order them to stand fast and they would stay till told to go on or to the end. For the most part they were sociable and kind-hearted men who sang sentimental songs when on the march out of the line. They went to sleep on the slightest provocation. They were unselfish and generous, as quick to go to the aid of a wounded enemy as a wounded friend. They had one supreme quality – a capacity to endure without flinching prolonged bombardment and exposure greater than that of many soldiers of the second war.

Why were these men so obedient, so cheerful, when there was every possibility if past experience was a guide that the orders to which they were obedient were misconceived and the world which they faced with such cheerfulness was squalid and dangerous beyond comprehension?

The best answer I have been able to find is in the nature of Edwardian society – in that degree of poverty which produced a vast number of men with a stunted response to novelty; in the relatively static class divisions which put a premium on social deference and correctness; in the low level of cultural interchange through passive schools and stunted media.

With a wealth of documentation, Rowntree just before the war showed that 30 per cent of the town population (3 per cent using the same criteria in 1961) and 40 per cent of the country population were living in poverty. Moreover it was not simply that poverty included a much larger section of the community than today; the poverty was relatively much greater. Recent studies show that Rowntree's case number 133 was not an isolated case in 1913. Paid 12s. a week, of which 1s. 7½d. went in rent for a tied cottage, the family could not afford eggs, bacon or cheese. 'We don't live, we linger,' said case number 133. He was speaking at a time when one person in four in London was buried on the parish and one in five ended life in the workhouse; when the Hoxton death rate was eight times that of Hampstead and public baths were advertised at 1d. cold and 2d. hot or 3d. and 6d. for 'higher classes'. He was speaking at a time when men raced for spades at building sites or fought for work discs thrown from a cage outside dock gates.

It must be remembered too that many came not just from sections of society poorer than one finds today, and presumably with that suspicious passivity which all social studies have found to be the outlook of the poor; they came also from profoundly conservative and substantial occupational categories now almost forgotten. In 1911 there were one and a half million servants, or one in seven of employed persons. There were in fact twice as many servants as coalminers. Private Harrison in his war memoirs recaptured the experience of these men (and women). Serving Sir Robert Dundas in Midlothian, he had cleaned fifty paraffin lamps before break-fast, sung hymns with the assembled servants at the end of the day and brought tureens of soup to the houses of the poor. For morning prayers prompt at 9 am all servants had been in line according to rank, and visiting valets in the evening sat in order of precedence of their masters round the servants' kitchen table, with the housekeeper checking Debrett to make certain of status.

In 1911 one in four of the population were farm labourers. Since four million had left country for town between 1851 and 1901, many townsmen during the Great War were only one-generation townsmen and must have brought with them the values and outlook of the country. These values, as Evans and Blythe have shown us, were those of a changeless society. Simple men held their tongues, accepting it as the duty of the squire to be rich and mean and odd. Servants turned their faces to the wall when gentlefolk passed, while in their homes were long silences and traditional values. In peasants' slop, trousers held by buskins and with schummachers clumps on their feet, the countrymen seemed to have something of the eighteenth century about them, the more so when at hiring fairs they accepted a farmer's shilling for twelve months' service as finally as any soldier. Their poverty was so grinding that, when they did escape from the soil in 1914, many were said to put on an inch in height and a stone in weight within a month.

If a man did manage to rise from this great stratum of poverty with its narrow horizons and spirit of hopelessness, then his conservatism was highly likely to be enhanced, for, with much less social mobility, hard-won respectability was jealously guarded. In the previous generation Burnett found acceptance of the social system and a great desire to stand well and be respected. Curtains, underclothing, a five-shilling Lewis watch and a billycock hat in Edwardian England were still status symbols to be prized, for the difference between a manual worker on £75 per annum and a policeman on £100 was a difference of separate constellations. Herbert Morrison's father, as a policeman in that war generation, never felt himself able to go to a music hall or drink beer. The dignity of his position demanded attendance at church rather than at chapel, the wearing of stiff shoes out of doors, despite copious bunions, together with a collar and tie in the parlour. Such men knew how easy it was to slide back into the abyss and how much faith should be put in the values of a society which allowed themselves to escape.

Surrounded by physical hardship and condemned to a life of monotonous work with few possibilities of escape, schooling was almost the only area where new ideas might have filtered through. Exposure, however, was brief. In 1902 only 9 per cent of boys were still at school at fourteen. In a town three-decker school there would be fifty to a class, with one boy in 200 going on to university. The running of the school would be severely traditional. Poor children wore black woollen stockings, cobbled boots and heavy clothes. Like soldiers, they responded to words of command, such as 'hands out' or 'books pass'. Capes and bays, mathematical tables and spelling were turned to rote. Their textbooks with prize labels for good attendance or good conduct (did no one ever get a prize for good work?) inside the front covers lie today dead and damned on the fivepenny tray outside secondhand bookshops. With them lie the memories of poverty of spirit – four-handers for blots, four-handers for failing to understand questions. For those whose interest did survive, there was little else to grasp. Beyond the culture of the music hall, yellow-page press and pulp novelette there were no paperbacks, no radio or television and very few cinemas. The multiple images of society, the awareness that political action might change society (there were only 3·1 million union men when the war broke out), belonged to the interwar years, which blurred life roles and spread the dissent of the individual. Before that most men in Edwardian society seem to have been more static-minded than we can imagine. With so little to stimulate them and with so few social hopes, with four and a half million communicants and six and a half million Sunday School attenders on the eve of the war, little wonder that American surgeon Dearden remarked 'these Britishers of the lower classes make extraordinarily good servants'.

That the deferential Other Ranks were drawn almost exclusively from lower- and lower-middle-class regions cannot be proved conclusively but seems highly likely. In an army rapidly expanding and with such a high wastage rate, officers were always in short supply, so that any man with dignity and education above the norm would almost certainly be drawn from the ranks. Those who remained were the poor. When Nevinson drew their faces, censorship rejected all those troop drawings which hinted at the fact. The War Office preferred to retail the 'Old Bill' image which died with the Old Contemptibles. The unpublished memoirs in the War Museum are overwhelmingly those of semi-skilled and unskilled men. Only two writers I have come across checked the social background of their mates, for home life was seldom spoken of in the front line. Plowman listed his platoon: wheelwrights, a farmer, a rail storekeeper, a cabinet maker, a rag conditioner, an oil presser, a shoe salesman, a grinder, driller, wool sorter and many miners.

During March 1918 Cushing questioned his amputees, and found a groom, the Duke of Athol's footman, a silver polisher, joiner, manager, coalminer, postman, grease extractor, handkerchief packer, bassoon player and two Jamaican mule drivers. These two lists produce an assortment as unexpectedly diverse as any random collection of men below white-collar level.

In conclusion it can be suggested that the majority of the front-line soldiers were humble men, further simplified by having been fitted into an army and subjected to constant danger and hardship. At home many had distrusted 'talk', ridiculed men who 'talked posh' and wanted only to 'get on with the job'. Theirs was a simple vocabulary centred on the personal pronoun with a dialogue showing descriptive rather than analytical, interpretative awareness. There was little vocabulary for the unexpected or speculative; instead, a fatalistic, helpless orientation in a world whose causes could not be grasped. Barbusse thought the same of the ordinary poilus. 'They were men rudely torn away from the joys of life. Like any other men whom you take in the mass, they were ignorant and of narrow outlook, full of sound commonsense, disposed to be led and do as they were bid, enduring under hardships, long suffering . . . but at intervals there were cries and dark shudders of humanity that issued from the silence and the shadows of their great human hearts.'

The positive, supportive side of a static society, whose roles were simple, was a particular type of humour. With divisions of regions and class taken as given, men seem to have joined more easily together in a common culture and outlook at that superficial social level which soldiers assumed in France. In this way, a naïve type of patriotism was commonplace. Sergeant Gardner of the 10th Londons sang to the end of the war:

> Bravo Territorials,
> Territorials bravo.
> Boys of the north, south, east and west,
> boys who will always do their best.
> You know, Territorials,
> what a happy band you'll be
> guarding the shores of old England
> While Jack is busy on the sea.
> (On the sea, on the sea, where d'yer kip? on the floor.)

My father recalls a Lancastrian major whose concert piece was inevitably:

Remember where you come from
when you are in the charge tonight.
Remember what you're here for
to do or die for right
so remember where you come from – good old Lancashire.

Though there was an absolute taboo on the instant patriotism of the wartime press and music hall, a large number of men throughout the war were conscious of common membership, a particular way of life, a common landscape, which was in some deep, if barely understood, way threatened by the enemy. Burrage thought that only one man in a hundred would have stayed if he could have gone home with dignity, but the question was: 'Would you let Germany win?' Thus men stood by their country as they might have stood by a pal whose luck was out. In this, most men could agree. One thing they had all learnt at school was to love their country fiercely. Another thing was imperturbability set off by understatement and deprecating jest. When Germans sang the 'Hymn of Hate', English would reply with 'Gott strafe Tickler'. Tolerance was part of this common culture as well as humour. 'For many months men watched the heart-breaking muddle with its waste of life,' wrote Moran. 'They could not help noticing it and talking about it a good deal. But in the end they always found the word of extenuation. They argued that this man meant well or, in the final resort, he was a trier. Men were taken onto the staff because they were liked and, if a general were relieved of his command, another post was immediately found for him. Too often I saw the results on stretchers. Now I have come to find that this immense toleration is just English – not Scottish, Irish or Dominion. It is not part of the creed of men for whom success in life is everything.' Thus the social façade which a common culture dictated was fit to be presented to the bewildering war, was a source of strength, a diffuser of anxiety. Cheerful acceptance of fate came from a relatively static, tradition-oriented people.

15

AFTER THE WAR

The war ended as abruptly as it had begun. The Imperial War Museum have a field message written on the squared notepaper of a field service notebook. It is marked 'Urgent' and timed at 9.30 am on 11 November 1918. It announced that 'hostilities will cease at 11 am today. Form up and march independently to the Château Harveng AT ONCE. Do not forget to bring your cookers with you.' Just as the emphasis on exact time reflects the punctiliousness of the industrialized combatants involved, so the somewhat breathless announcement just an hour and a half before the momentous fact suggests how unexpectedly events had turned out.

Exactness was extended to its limit. Rollfilm records of artillery sound ranging show much firing up to 10.59 am then total silence. Harrison recorded a trench raid on the morning of the eleventh in his diary. At Le Cateau, Nicholson remembered vigorous skirmishing to the end, particularly from one enemy machine-gun nest. On the stroke of the hour, Harrison wrote, the Germans threw their helmets and rifles into the air and came over to shake hands, while Nicholson recorded a 1,000-round burst from the troublesome machine-gun, the gunners then standing up and taking off their forage caps to the English and walking away without looking back.

In some places there was celebration. In Noakes's rest camp other ranks linked arms and raided the guardhouse, pouring a firebucket over the RSM, and marched out of camp without permission, so as to enjoy forty-eight hours of drinking at nearby Cayeux. Keynes remembered a night of train whistle blowing and Verey light discharging. Closer to the front the news was received with indifference or stupefaction. Cushing noted specifically that he saw no throwing of hats or shouting. Feilding reported 'no visible change in demeanour', so that, while the Germans cheered and rang church bells behind their line at Le Cateau, there were few English counter-cheers. Hawkings was 'astounded' by the news of the ceasefire. Bradley wrote of 'my worst ever depression'. Bowra feared that the Germans would resume hostilities. 'The match was over and it had been a damned bad game,' reflected Nicholson sourly.

This lack of celebration is not difficult to grasp in retrospect.

Since the start of that August offensive in 1918 which had seen the relentless pushing back of the Germans, British casualties had been over a third of a million. The war memorial of Watford Grammar School shows more dead for 1918 than for any other year of the war as do the memorials for many other schools. Our advance had been all the time against machine-guns and artillery pieces carefully placed to do execution and bravely handled to the end, while by November our men were between twenty and fifty miles from rail-heads, so that shells and fodder were brought up with increasing difficulty. The new drafts moreover were men who had seen the casualty lists of the great battles of 1916 and 1917. A nation addicted to gambling had no need to teach its citizen soldiers the concept of odds. All these things conspired to give not the slightest indication before Armistice Day that the end was in sight. In this the Great War differed from the Second World War, since during the last three years of the latter it was pretty clear that the Germans could not win.

Even at the top of the army the war in 1918 appeared to have much life in it. Haig admitted in his diary that the Germans were nowhere beaten and, if he expressed optimism at the war ending in 1918, it must be remembered that many times each year since 1915 he had given specific dates within each year after which the German army would be too exhausted to continue fighting. Such well-informed men as Churchill and Fuller were drawing up detailed plans for 1919. Rothermere of the *Sunday Pictorial* coined the phrase 'the seven years' war' on 4 August 1918.

A deeper reason for the apathy of Armistice Day is reflected in Hawkings's statement that it was impossible to consider life without war. When a soldier came from England, he was slotted into a vast organization. In his diary Drinkwater noted dryly: 'Now it looks as if the actual firing line is of little consequence compared with the immense organization at the rear keeping it going.' He guessed that the ratio of support to fighting troops was fourteen to one. The Army Council insisted on three to one, but most men felt with Drinkwater a growing sense of insignificance in the vastness of the military establishment. Surely so much would not have been invested in destruction unless the outcome were anticipated only in the distant future? A random selection of statistics shows 6,879 miles of railway to have been specially built in France just for our army; 51,107 rubber stamps to have been issued; 137,224,141 pairs of socks to have been given out; 5,649,797 rabbit skins to have been cleaned and disposed of by the BEF; 30,009 miles of flannelette consumed in the cleaning of rifles. Noakes remarked: 'I tried to visualize the end of the war and my return home but there my imagination failed me. It seemed almost impossible that the war would ever end. It seemed as if only a miracle could make the military machine loose its hold on me. My mind refused to envisage any more permanent release other than a wonderful vision of leave.'

The omnipresence of death and injury added a psychological dimension to the soldier's complete involvement in war. Just as a man with a terminal illness or family grief is able to concentrate his mind on only one problem, so the soldier's chief adjustment had to be towards the most dreadful possibilities. 'Apathy, an almost universal torpor, was a wall of defence set up by nature to meet the violence of the hour. It kept at arm's length the habit of introspection. We lived in the past. Humour helped. It made a mock of life and scoffed at our own frailty. It touched everything with ridicule and had taken the bite out of the last thing – death.' The need for this was suddenly and without warning removed. A new outlook had to be constructed without leaving the old environment and with the doubt in many minds that, until the peace treaty was signed, war might at any time be resumed.

Thus men were tired and sceptical. The war had gone on too long. In remoter parts of the front, where there were no direct radio or telephone links, a soldier like Abraham reflected that distrust of all army news which marked the veteran. The sergeant of his guard simply announced: 'I'm going to bugger off until 10 pm. I shall expect to find you all here then.' Abraham's platoon wandered about suspiciously and aimlessly in country desolate as only northern France can be, expecting the guns to open fire again at any moment. Abraham's lack of enthusiasm was typical of the front-line soldier on Armistice Day.

If there was little excitement, there was no mutiny. Discipline relaxed on the stroke of 11 and left men nothing to mutiny over. When Noakes and his mates came back from their forty-eight-hour spree, no mention was made of the sacked guardhouse or of the fire-bucket emptied over the R S M. Instead the colonel requested that all ranks join in the national anthem, and this act showed that a larger loyalty was capable of restraining men when battle discipline lapsed. Similarly discreet were the officers of the 10th Londons at Peruwelz in Belgium. The men, including my father, had not needed to be billeted: 'Townspeople just came out and took soldiers along with them to give them a good time. Next morning I woke in alarm to hear the bugles sounding the "half-hour to dress". When the quarter sounded, I was shaving. When at last I went out onto the square, there were so few fallen in that the morning parade had to be cancelled immediately. This was the first sign for commanders that they would have to tread warily. This lesson they learnt quickly.'

Until demobilization men waited in France and Belgium. The more enterprising went off for garrison duty in the Rhineland – one battalion per division. For the rest, concerts and games multiplied and schools were set up to give some semblance of preparation for civilian life. Training there still was, but it was done in attenuated form. Major Chappell of the Somersets, for example,

> decided on training in a most original manner. The battalion went on route march for one mile and proceeded to surround a wood in a most military manner at one-pace intervals, then sent a raiding party to dislodge the enemy. Scores of hares came pelting out to meet certain death when the circle of attackers was reached. There followed a triumphant march home with the spoils of war, some of which were sent to brigade HQ to demonstrate the particular value of this type of training. It was most popular for a week until the divisional commander arrived and suggested that a more martial type of training would not be out of place. NB through bad staff work at battalion HQ no hares had been sent to divisional HQ.

Demobilization had long been worked out, even before the battle of Loos in September 1915. A paper of January 1915 finalized most of the practical arrangements, with a report late in 1917 establishing the order of release. With the knowledge of the disturbances at the termination of the Napoleonic wars and the evidence of what soldiers could do from Leningrad just the year before, the B E F was to be broken up by individuals rather than by units, the priority for long service going to only 10 per cent of early releases. The rest were to be released if they came from particularly indispensable civilian employment or could show a signed slip from an employer proving that they had a job to go to. In preparation for the flood, twenty-six dispersal stations were to be set up, one in each regimental district. Demobbed men were to be given pay in advance for kit and weapons, free travel home and free unemployment insurance. With remarkable *sang froid* the whole apparatus was tested out during February 1918 on the eve of the greatest German attack of the war. Five hundred guinea pigs were passed through Purfleet dispersal station successfully to check the arrangements.

After November the real thing started. For three weeks after 11 November the clerical side was set up, with 20,000 soldiers earmarked for this side. All stocks of grade three standard cloth were requisitioned for demob suits. Then came the flood. Miners, transport men, agricultural labourers came first, with men over forty-one, the hospitalized and the convalescent enjoying the advantage of contiguity and slipping through with the chosen. Each man could keep his uniform and helmet. He got a suit or 52s. 6d. in lieu. If unemployed, he received 24s. a week for the first year and a supplement of 6s. for one child and 3s. for others. Civil service positions were reserved for officers, and help was promised to meet education fees, bring families back home from overseas and stock shops or small businesses.

So much for theory; in practice demobilization worked with all that minute and unreasonable precision which men associated with the army. Smith was fined 4d. for a missing mess-tin lid then given his £20 gratuity. Studying his demob certificate, Noakes was surprised to find his status officially defined as 'transferred to the reserve'. Before leaving Crystal Palace he was subjected to a close body search, a kiss of departure from the army as it were. Sergeant Winter, on the other hand, on entering Dover Castle 'cast my eye along the row of customs officers and who should I see standing there but King who had sat next to me at Owens School. He had not been bright and I had often helped him along with a whispered answer in class. I pounced like a shot. A long, nostalgic chat, a perfunctory examination, so I got away with my service revolver down one trouser leg, prismatic binoculars down the other, with a load of maps, documents, movement orders intended for a possible war record. To these I added a free rail warrant home and £2 in pocket money.' Bodger, after being demobbed at Crystal Palace, did not get home so easily. Despite his protests, he was marched down to the station and escorted to London Bridge thus having to take the train all the way back to Herne Hill. Nevertheless all who have written about demobilization were prepared to put up with such pinpricks for the sake of freedom.

The size of the gratuity surprised all pleasantly. Haig got £100,000; Lieutenant Carrington £226 with £250 added shortly afterwards when he took up his place at Oxford University – more than he got after the Second World War after serving as a lieutenant-general; Corporal Coppard received £28 in four instalments. As a final bonus, £1 was paid for greatcoats when handed in at any railway station booking office. At a time when a working family stored a silver five-shilling piece carefully against the next time of hardship, this shower of gold softened a difficult transition. Thus it was not from men already demobilized that trouble came.

With great precision and customary division, the War Office announced on 1 August 1919 that 106,294 officers and 2,625,811 Other Ranks had been processed. Nevertheless one million men still remained in uniform. Not until 1922 could the final reckoning be made. This process was simply not fast enough for waiting men. In November 1918 men at Addington rest camp telegraphed the king and informed him that they intended to burn down Buckingham Palace. They had had no leave for two years served in Mesopotamia, no pay for nine months and no bath for three months. In this instance Christmas leave saved Buckingham Palace. On 3 January came the next trouble. Ten thousand men marched to the centre of Folkestone, to return immediately they were promised seven days' leave. When next day they were ordered to France, they marched to the town again, now with their rifles, to go back to camp immediately the War Office re-promised the leave. A day later 2,000 men went to see the mayor of Dover. While a deputation was in the Guildhall, the rest sang popular songs to a ragtime piano accompaniment in the open square. Childs at the War Office noted darkly: 'It was pretty obvious that communist influences were at work at the time.' On 6 January three A S C lorries filled with men blowing whistles drew attention to the unfair advantages enjoyed by men with employers' slips. Haig's comment on this sinister whistle blowing was to cast aspersions on 'the dangerous pacifist types who were tampering with the unity of the army'. One must say that, for dangerous men, they had displayed rather less than Leninist foresight. Officers at Osterley, pre-warned, had removed sparking plugs from lorries earmarked for the revolution, and the 'dangerous men' could get no spares. On 8 February 3,000 men with weapons marched on Horse Guards Parade. Their one grievance was lack of food at Victoria station. In all these demonstrations which so worried authority the *status quo* was not threatened. There was little that could not be cured by leave. Coming, however, after the class bitterness of Edwardian times and after the Russian revolution of 1917, the government was careful. Churchill took charge of the demobilization so that pay was increased and greater notice taken of age, length of service and whether men were married. There were no further demonstrations after that – within the army.

The demonstrations of 1919 were from men already demobbed, but again these had a remarkably specific nature. During May 1919 the National Association of Discharged Soldiers and Sailors met at Hyde Park then marched on Parliament, throwing wood blocks and crutches at female bus conductors. On Victory Day, 19 July 1919, there were riots in Glasgow, Epsom, Coventry and Luton. Two days later there was trouble in Swindon, so that the mayor had to impose a (voluntary) curfew. In all these protests the men showed their concern over jobs. The Hyde Park demonstrators had demanded employment at trade union rates or an increase in unemployment pay from 29s. to 40s. weekly. The later protests had focused especially on police stations and labour exchanges. There was no mention of ideology; no hint of organization sufficient to carry the disturbance further. Had there been, the government might well have run into trouble if Noakes's experience is typical. He was with the Guards still through 1919. Only a quarter had been allowed leave during the rail strike of September, while the rest practised street fighting with Lewis guns and bayonets. Noakes wrote of the general dissatisfaction amongst the Guards and doubted whether the use of the army against working men came into the category of 'war service'.

This problem of unemployment proved an intractable one. Most jobs had been picked up early by young men demobilized before the others, munitions workers on the spot or men too young to have been mobilized. By January 1922 there were two million unemployed, and the British Legion reckoned that half a million of these were ex-servicemen. Graves remembered 'ex-servicemen continually coming to the door selling bootlaces and asking for cast-off shoes and shirts'. Many of these were the unskilled with no trade; men like my uncle Joe Winter who remembers hundreds of applications and being turned down even as liftboy at Gamages. Some were men previously well-to-do. Middle-aged medical officers returned with four blue service chevrons, out-of-date equipment and a lost practice. There were others. In 1920 Haig's Officers Association appealed for £5 million to assist 25,000 unemployed officers as well as 33,000 disabled, 10,000 widows and 8,000 orphans. The personal column of *The Times* throughout 1919 reflected the hard times. 'Will patriot give wounded officer £50 to enable him to start civilian life unencumbered.' 'Old Etonian (twenty-seven) married and suffering from neurasthenia but in no way really incapacitated in urgent need of outdoor work. Would be glad to accept post of head gamekeeper at nominal salary.' 'Will any mason help brother mason to obtain an engagement? Major. Served in France. Public-school man aged thirty. Married. Has handled Chinese labour in British Columbia. Do anything. Go anywhere.' 'Will lady or gentleman finance subaltern £100. Five children. Wife seriously ill. No means. Urgent.' 'Will anyone advance £150 to re-open estate agency closed in 1914?' 'Linguist with French, Russian, German. Used to managing foreigners. Not afraid of hard work. Russia preferred. Waiting demobilization.'

Once a soldier had passed the obstacles of demobilization and getting a job of some sort, his problems were by no means over. 'I find it hardest to reproduce the year 1919,' wrote Carrington. 'This was the moment of disenchantment. Millions keyed up to a pitch of unnatural determination found the tension relaxed so suddenly as to throw them off balance. It was long before they resumed a civilian sense of time. To a soldier in the war, it had become second nature to live for the present. When pleasures were few, they were snatched and enjoyed with an intensity such as no civilian knew. The future had so long meant just a series of trips up the line. After the war anything might happen. Friends were parted. Life seemed large and empty. You had to earn a living. It was not easy to start again.' This was probably the greatest problem. Faced with this radical restructuring of a whole social personality, the need to make new friends, the need to go back to the beginning again, some took refuge in despair. Reid wrote of his longing for faces and sounds past; of his intense regret that things would not be the same again; of a vague feeling of hopelessness in facing the future. He was a typical veteran, a man depleted physically and mentally, about to withdraw from relationships and demanding to be treated for the time as an invalid. Cloete went back to an old haunt in the depths of the French countryside and took up the life of a peasant. 'I realized that this was what I needed. Silence. Isolation. Now that I could let go, I broke down, avoided strangers, cried easily and had terrible nightmares.'

Other men might become angry at this need for dependence and turn against authority in any form. Instead of withdrawing into solitude or nomadism, these men might turn to petty crime or angrily demand recompense from a society whose will that they fight had been their breaking point. Even Priestley felt angrily that 'giant locusts had eaten my four and a half years'.

The majority avoided these extremes. They oscillated between them. Gibbs remarked that 'they had not come back the same men. They were subject to queer moods and tempers. Fits of depression alternated with a restless desire for pleasure. Many of them were easily moved to passion when they lost control of themselves. Many were bitter of speech. For some time while they drew unemployment pensions they did not make an effort to get work for the future. They said, "That can wait. I've done my bit. The country can keep me for a while. I helped to save it." Something seemed to have snapped in them. A quiet day at home did not appeal to them.'

My father's experience fitted this picture perfectly. He went back to his old office job initially. His pay had gone up to 25s. a week, and an extra chair was fitted between the new girl who did his old job and the office junior at the bottom of the table.

I decided I wouldn't go back to the office. I would become a taxi driver – out and about all day, to which I was now long accustomed. A special labour exchange for ex-servicemen opened at Morley Hall in Mare St, Hackney. For the present, men didn't want jobs. They were numbed by the changeover. Servicemen felt resignation rather than disaffection. They wanted to be left alone. You signed on daily and asked as a formality if there were a job for you. You were paid out every Friday at 3s. a day. As the queues lengthened, you were told to sign on every second day, then twice weekly. Eventually you came along on Friday just to draw your pay. I was on the dole right through the summer, revelling in the open-air swimming pool of Victoria Park, reading in Hackney Library, rowing on the Lea, assiduously practising the violin. The springs were unwinding.

Then came a two-year course sponsored by the Board of Education to train as a teacher with £102 *per annum* and thus a lifetime's career.

This seems to have been the position for the majority. Men became neither hermits nor criminals but required a period of quietness, a second adolescence as it were, to shed the past and get back into life at a lower key than they were used to. When the vicar of Eye appealed for combat records from his parishioners, he ran into delays of twelve months and was then only given photographs with no particulars. While doing his course at the London Institute of Education, my father noted that nobody ever talked about the past and only by chance did he learn that So-and-so had been a major or staff captain.

The curious fact about this difficult period of readjustment, which might take just a couple of years for my father or ten years for Carrington, was that the soldier was likely to face hostility from civilians. Initially there had been no sign of it. The Aberdeen *Journal* wrote about the return of 'Taggart's Own' during April 1919 followed by the 51st in May. The town was packed tight as a trawler deck with herrings. Cheering civilians broke the ranks to welcome their men back. At Watford a feast was laid down. The veterans originally had been expected to bring their own crockery and there was to have been no beer or fireworks though a bonfire was planned, not to cost too much, however. A letter in the West Herts. and Watford *Observer* revealed the official parsimony in good time, so that finally a worthy celebration took place.

The mood of celebration was transient. The historian of wartime Leeds noted 'a general desire to forget this horrid war'. Sunderland well reflected the temper of the time. Only 2,000 of the 16,000 serving soldiers attended a reception on Victory Day, while a bakers' strike timed for the day effectively undermined the digestion of those who tackled the set menu of pork pies followed by trifles and jellies.

In part this mood of sourness must have been due to the hardships which immediately followed war's disruption. Two hundred thousand people died of Spanish influenza in that first winter of the peace, while there were shortages of basic commodities as in 1945. Eggs stood at 9d. each and most towns were down to their last few days of coal on Armistice Day.

Nevertheless there is evidence that the war had bitten deeper than a casual observer might think; that war had in fact become hateful to many people, the soldier too, since his khaki was the most obvious visible sign of that war. The *Morning Post* in March 1918 had ordered its upper-class readers: 'Be cheerful; face facts and work; attend volunteer drills regularly; cultivate your allotment; don't exceed your rations; don't repeat foolish gossip; don't listen to idle rumours and don't think you know better than Haig.' This list would scarcely have been as precisely itemized if the highest in the land were not offending in these particulars. At the other end of the society as well there was evidence of strain. 1917 had produced a bumper crop of strikes, with 588 affecting nearly a million workers.

Linking the social classes was a common over-reaction to stress. Air raids in 1918 produced spectacular rushes for the safety of London tube stations. Just as the Royal Society expelled aliens from its ranks, so the popular press hounded London Jews, since they were safe from air raids on London. The fact that it had been hysteria in the first place which had driven Jews and aliens out of London was conveniently forgotten. Whenever the news of a battle came through, there was a rush for the hospital trains at the main-line stations. When Abraham marched through the streets of Sheffield with a draft during March 1918, Union Jacks were torn off the rifles by onlookers. Later, even troops had to be moved by night, such was the feeling against the continuing slaughter.

Even after the war the mutterings continued, so that local papers were filled with frustration. The Liskeard rural district council in late November demanded that 'in view of the diabolical murders and barbarities perpetrated on women and children, soldiers and sailors (including the Prince of Wales), for which the Kaiser and his confederates are responsible, the council appeals to the government to secure extradition'. The local Board of Guardians suggested that they should be sent to a convent (*sic*) 'and if they would not work, let them die'. On Victory Day itself the citizens of Besford and Wadborough conducted a mock trial and burned an effigy of the Kaiser on a hilltop. At Keiss Public School near Aberdeen Mr Clements, the headmaster, had registered as a conscientious objector. He narrowly survived a motion to remove him from his post though eleven voted for it, two opposed and five abstained. Though a two-thirds majority had not been reached and Mr Clements survived, the vindictive mood was ominous.

The basis of this militant civilian mood seems to have rested on two factors. The first was a resentment at the social changes the war had brought with such speed. The general cost of living had risen by about 75 per cent during the war while relative wage levels had fluctuated. Shellworkers did well; workers whose production was disrupted by U-boats did badly. All workers were hit by the Conscription Act, the Munitions Acts, housing shortages and the dilution of union labour. All men were shocked by the induction of women into jobs considered previously as necessarily male. Even the rich were hit by change. Wilton Estate is an example. In 1914 income tax took 4 per cent of gross rents; by 1918 it was taking 25 per cent. Direct tax, which had taken a further 9 per cent in 1914, by the end of the war was taking 30 per cent. Rents in the period remained static while the price of wheat doubled and trebled. Gentry unable to balance the two trends went bust, so that between 1918 and 1921 a quarter of the acreage of England changed hands, assisted no doubt by the hard blows suffered by the officer class at the front line. Thus the jostling at bus queues and shop queues reflected the fact that there had been too many social novelties too fast.

The other source of anger was the blood cost of the war. Censorship had deprived people at home of almost all knowledge of what was going on. Increasingly they thought of days less in terms of ground gained and more in terms of lives lost. The impact came through those pages in local newspapers which daily or weekly gave the full list of dead or missing. Each page had photos of the faces ringed in black, beardless, adolescent faces unmarked by the bolder features of adulthood. The sheer quantity still has power to numb the mind as one goes through the files of yellowing papers from every part of the country. Macmillan wrote at the time: 'one was haunted by the memories and fears on sick leave or light duty. By that time the list of dead piled up month by month and year by year to a frightful sum. One scarcely dared to read the newspapers if a new battle had begun.' Even the possibility of death was sufficient to unbalance men left at home. Thus during July 1916 Oswestry farmer Thomas Giltens blew his head off with a shotgun in a local wood. His son had just joined the army. For his family he left a handwritten letter: 'Dear family, forgive me. I cannot live. I have not slept for some time and I am very tired. Heaven and earth forgive me.' Most took no such easy escape; they just worried unceasingly. Feilding was reported four times as killed in action during the war. As late as January 1919 some 15,000 prisoners were still unaccounted for.

The demobilized soldier was therefore likely to find many uncomfortable feelings directed towards himself. In December 1918 there were already letters in the press complaining of 'non-workers'. No one wanted to hear or see anything to do with the war. Khaki disappeared from the streets as soon as the twenty-eight-day period after demobilization came to an end. Only the failures of the war published their memoirs in self-justification; men like French, Fisher, Jellicoe, Tirpitz, Ludendorff and Hindenburg. For the rest, as veteran Professor Woodward noted, the soldiers counted for less than any generation for 300 years. Like Xenophon after his heroic 1,000-mile march through Asia, the English soldier was likewise banished. Lloyd George, that latter-day Cleon, was soon to follow. Perhaps guilt had something to do with it as well. Some felt the blood guilt lying on the men they had commissioned to kill by proxy. They felt too that they owed the veterans recompense for their hardships. Clemenceau had said in France 'they have claims upon us all'. Beggars make everyone feel uneasy.

Vera Brittain wrote bitterly of the result of it all:

> Four years. Some say consolingly, 'Oh well,
> what's that? You're young and then it must have been
> a very fine experience for you.'
> And they forget
> how others just stayed behind and got on –
> got on the better since we were away.
> And when we came home and found they had achieved
> and men revered their names but never mentioned ours
> and no one talked of our heroics now
> and we must just go back and start once more again.
> 'You threw four years into the melting pot' –
> 'Did you indeed' these others cry. 'Oh well.
> The more fool you.'
> And we're beginning to agree with them.

The returned soldier therefore had difficult problems in settling back into civilian life; but how did he look back on his experience of the war meanwhile? Did it leave any permanent marks on his awareness? What sort of experiences did he remember? Did he continue to feel in attenuated form comradeship with those who had shared similar experiences?

In the few years immediately after 1918 most men seem to have retained a vivid pictorial recall. 'When I was demobbed,' wrote Drinkwater, 'I used to have bad nightmares. I used to wake up in the middle of the night bathed in perspiration. It was an incident when we were caught in no-man's-land. Bullets were striking the ground all round us.' For Andrews the nightmares were more varied. Buried by shells, surprised by gas, a solo bayonet duel – all the great fears in fact of the front-line man. Despite the fact that he had burned all his letters, the faces of dead comrades still came to him in these dreams. Abraham was troubled into the 1930s by one recurrent nightmare. He saw himself alone in a sunny, silent trench surrounded by a stealthy enemy. He had been forgotten in his company's withdrawal and left with orders not to move. This dream had no connection with his actual war experience. Hyder's single recurrent dream was firmly connected to his past. Having raided and taken a pillbox in Ploegstraat Wood, he had heard with growing intensity and for some time the sound of a wounded man dragging himself down the tunnel entrance of the pillbox. Not knowing what was making the sound, he had shot the man dead before finding him to have been a harmless and wounded German. 'This was twelve years ago and still at night comes a sweat that wakes me by its deadly chill to hear again that creeping, creeping.'

After these vivid visual memories faded, some men were left with the recollections of vast tracts of their war. Harris and Green had found the same thing after the Napoleonic wars – 'I shall remember those words of the captain [making him regimental shoemaker] as if they had been spoken but yesterday, for that which was spoken in former years in the field has made a singular impression on my mind.' Many memoirs of the Great War mirror rifleman Harris. 'The memories will live with me to the end.' 'Many years have passed and have softened the memories but they have not faded nor do I think they ever will.' In a haunting phrase Nurse Millard talked of 'the dark caravan that winds endlessly through the memory of my youth'. Of the 250 or so memoirs I have read, the dominant impression I retain is of the unexpected detail of the memories and their veracity whenever I could check them. Though the memoir writers represent the tiniest fraction of the men who fought, the great majority of survivors still read all the books on 'their war' and show in their talk how much they too remember, and how much therefore will die with them.

The majority of old soldiers, however, lived more fleetingly with the past as newer experiences overlay their war. Looking back over his diary in 1928, Dearden could recall nothing of the early days and could only recapture his presence in the events outlined for the later years 'as in a previous incarnation'. When Cloete came to write his superbly vivid memoirs recently, he found his diary gone and surviving documents or field messages devoid of meaning. The days and nights of terror which they recorded had gone completely. Photos of himself forty years before as a Kitchener soldier seemed to Brophy like ancestral figures, while Mottram felt only a tenuous link with his own name inscribed on the butt end of a service revolver. Even where there was some point of contact, there seemed often to have been a pervasive sense of unreality. 'To most men looking back, it seemed like a dream.' Dr Hayward, recalling the violent contrast of hot sunshine, larks singing, the violently bright cornflowers and the broken bodies of the suffering men with their red blood against the blue cornflowers found it hardly real at the time. Even a detailed diary might not be proof against all this. Captain Sparks of the 7th Somersets thought he had shackled himself to his memories beyond the power of dreams, for he had written of his experiences in the Cambrai attack just two years afterwards when the war ended for him, not wishing the memory to fade. Re-reading this document in 1931, he found it impossible to regain the point of view. The emotions and opinions seemed those of another man.

Nevertheless such powerful events could not be exorcized. Periodically memories would surface to take a man unawares and leave him uneasy. Elshaw ducked for years at the sound of thunder or of a car accelerating. Reid wrote that the smell of summer woodland always triggered memories of Delville Wood and became more vivid with the years. Cut green timber took Griffiths back to Mametz Wood and conjured up one particular memory – that of a suspended leg high in a tree, torn from a corpse. In the same way a harvest field always took Lucy back to Mons, and the sound of a boot on wood took Taylor to the duckboard trenches of Hamel. For Captain Worsley the trigger was an event on which most veterans turned their backs, the Cenotaph on Remembrance Sunday: 'It is now difficult and even a week later it was difficult to recall my three hours in Delville Wood. It is only on Armistice Day that I can live them again but I don't want to tell anyone about it. There was hand-to-hand fighting with knives and bayonets, cursing and brutality on both sides, mud and stench, dysentery and untended wounds . . .'

There is something infinitely moving about these unexpected and personal memories. Griffith remembered the first two movements of Bach's concerto for two violins, which had been playing in an empty house in Bailleul in June 1917: 'As I listen to the concerto nowadays, I am back in the small town in 1917 with lorries and guns thundering over the pavé towards the opening stages of the battle of Messines.' Another old soldier, Griffith, was startled by his first route march of the Local Defence Volunteers in 1940, another war later. 'A quarter of a century slipped away in a flash. There came the memories of the Menin road, of the loose, shifting, exasperating cobbles, of the smell of cordite and the scream of shrapnel, of the mud and stench and misery of Flanders, of hopes and fears in battles long ago. There were few youngsters in that platoon of ours.' With Carrington it was the Berlin Wall that brought it back, the obsession with no-man's-land. 'This side of the wire everything is familiar and a friend; over there, beyond the wire, is the unknown, the uncanny. Over there are people about whom you can accumulate scraps of irrelevant information but whose real life you can never penetrate. The people will shoot you dead if they catch a glimpse of you, even miles behind the line.'

Now and again comes the suggestion that more survives than veterans believe. Holdsworth of the Royal Field Artillery never joined reunions after the war. He had faced it, then thought it over and done with. But, when he fell seriously ill, in his delirium all the old memories surfaced and were written down for the benefit of the family, then deposited in the War Museum. Griffith had a similar experience:

The cares and pleasures of living in 1919 drove away all thoughts of war. I did not dream about it. It was something that had happened to someone else. The business of life was to grow children and to succeed in work. I rarely met any old soldiers. Some two or three years later I made a brief record of my share in the war, a mere account of events, some fifteen hundred words in all. I thought it might interest my sons when they grew up. I put it in a drawer and forgot about it. I had kept no diary. It was a mere chronology. Then, three years later in spring cleaning, it came out of a pile of papers and I sat down to read it. I can still remember the shock I received, saying, 'Well, if this is all you can say about the biggest experience of your life, of years of hazardous living, it would be better to say nothing than to be proved incapable of writing an account of it.' So I tore it up. But inside me there seemed to be an upsurge of remembering that brought back the war that I thought I had overlaid with the day-to-day business of living. I began to relive the days and nights. There was a kind of emotional explosion within me. I saw Mametz Wood, where my own brother was killed. I stopped and went back from Winchester to Givenchy. I found that I had given some kind of picture of the war as I had seen it and in doing so had become accustomed to and even reconciled with remembering. I found there was no peace in me until I had faced and recorded the high point of the war. Then came afterwards a kind of peace within me. I had spent my emotional capital in this detailed recovery and had been purged of the pain of war.

Looking back over the records of men's recollections, one has the distinct impression that most men remembered much, in whatever form. One has the impression too that there was always something secretive about their remembering. Chapman recently highlighted this impression with his marvellous autobiography, itself called *The Survivor* since for the remainder of his life after 1918 he was haunted by the feeling of being one of a generation specifically marked out and separated from other generations. How many men, now old, are there who carefully keep letters, trench maps, photos signed on the back 'Yours till hell freezes', those embroidered cards sold as souvenirs in Flanders? 'How many keep a special file, taken out when no one is present, from which lost youth and lost friends may be remembered with tears? Last year the Bradford Pals made their last trip to their old battlefields. Survivors are too frail but, said George Morgan on television, 'When our generation goes, it'll all drop off. But we can't forget, you see. We'll never forget.'

The problems associated with the wounded after the war were even more severe than those of the uninjured. Quite simply their numbers were so vast. The first great war of high explosive reaped a fearful harvest of mutilated bodies. By 1920 there were 113 special hospitals, with 18,603 beds, dealing with the most severely disabled and supplemented by 319 separate surgical clinics, thirty-six ear clinics, twenty-four eye clinics, nineteen heart centres and forty-eight special mental hospitals. Even this number was strained to the limit. One hospital specializing in the removal of steel between April 1919 and March 1925 treated 771 officers and 22,641 men surgically. Queen Mary's hospital, Sidcup, which touched only facial injuries, in the same period operated on 2,944 men.

Even these figures underestimate the toll of the injured, for this particular harvest was long in the maturation. In the year 1928 new issues included 5,205 artificial legs for the first time, 1,106 artificial arms and 4,574 artificial eyes, for, as wounds worsened or failed to heal, so men came forward each year. In 1933 the *Yorkshire Post* informed its readers that as a result of war-gas keritis or eye ulceration thirty-three men had newly lost their sight during the previous year.

What was the final total? In 1929 final pension settlements were made, for times were bad and memories had faded along with gratitude. Ten years after the war therefore injury was stabilized and the final figure came out at 2,414,000 men in receipt of a pension of some sort – 40 per cent of all serving soldiers. These ranged from 26,416 rheumatics and 1,907 flat feet through to 65,000 in mental hospitals for 'shellshock', the 9,074 men who had lost an arm, and the 40,000 partially blinded.

All these figures were, of course, conservative. Many with war injuries received less than they should have done or even nothing. Read's friend, Taylor, was hit in the lower arm at Mametz Wood in 1916 and laughed aloud at the time at the prospect of Blighty. Despite several operations, he was still feeling the pain recently in his old age but without a pension to sweeten it. Old Contemptible Frank Richards received his final award of 5s. for a dose of gas. Later he wrote in bitterness: 'I have never been the same man as what I was before. Indeed, no man has been treated with greater contempt than what I was.' Many injured men were at the time grateful to escape from the clutches of the army even if they had to sign themselves A1 in health to do so.

After a slow realization of their problems during the war, some basic provision had been made early on. The body concerned was the War Injury Pensions Committee, convened in May 1916, which first issued little silver lapel badges (often sold later in the war for 2s. ready cash), to protect men from military police and patriotic women, then looked at compensation. The final scale was laid down with military precision. A full disablement pension at 25s. with 2s. 6d. per child extra made clear the status of the soldier, for this was about the equal of an unskilled labourer's wage at the time. If just an arm were missing, the man would get 16s. weekly if it were missing at the shoulder, 14s. if below that but above the elbow and 11s. 6d. if below the elbow. At each point, the left arm was valued at just 1s. less. Legs received similar treatment geographically. Further adjustments had to be made for rank. A corporal thus received an extra 2s., a sergeant 4s., and so on. The absurdity of it all passes belief. A soldier with ten lost fingertips would be as effectively maladaptive as a man with no arms at all, while a disabled man had to pay the same price for his food whether he had once been a simple private or a sergeant.

Using studies of the injured today, it seems probable that financial hardship in the twenties and thirties was only the most tangible of the readjustment problems for the wounded. Initially they had been almost over-cheerful. As good soldiers they had accepted their wounds defiantly, and official war photographers had capitalized on this period. This would change abruptly when the need was realized to build up a new life in the new capacity. Then the soldier's view of himself would freeze as if he were 'dying' as a fit person and in a mood of deep depression, mourning for his former self. If the veteran was a mature person with good intelligence, wide interests, a loving family and high aspirations, he might come through. More often, men seem to have grieved over their losses and would become dependent with the frustrations of dependence, would minimize their own capacities and project their resentment of an unjust fate upon the world. Sulkiness, irritability, unpredictability mark the cripple of war as often as the peace crippled.

If modern studies give a fair indication, then much of the irritability is understandable. Nearly all would try to use their lost limbs in moments of forgetfulness, while half of the artificial limbs issued would be rejected by the body. Stump relapses would mean frequent returns to hospital, with arm healing generally worse than leg. Those partially blinded would become afraid of the night and of bright sunshine; would dramatize headaches, eyestrain and blurring in moments of stress.

Irritation would be increased by tactless friends. The disabled wanted simple acceptance and affection. They might receive awe or horror – 'At one of our patriotic teas,' wrote Miles, 'a young soldier beckoned me with his head and eyes to come to him. I went to speak to him and he whispered to me, "Would one of your young ladies feed me please? I have no arms." I went up to one of our young waitresses and asked her if she would. But we both cried so we had to hide ourselves for a few minutes. The soldier who sat next to him was so tender and held up the cup for him to drink from and put bits of cake into his mouth.' The wounded would usually be misunderstood. During 1917 Frank Chester lost an arm. He had played cricket for Worcester at the age of fourteen, and at sixteen was considered for a Test cap. Forced to stop playing cricket, his captain, 'Plum' Warner, said of him: 'He has played for his country in the greater game and that is a splendid thing, greater than any mere England and Australia at cricket.' This can have been little comfort to him at the time though later he became one of the greatest umpires in the game. Once such cheap praise had been dispensed, with gifts and medals, admiration became charity and the wounded were generally offered the role of helplessness and dependence, which made them the more anxious and insecure. It is notable how very few crippled men could bear to look at the past to write their memoirs. Men machine-gunned through the hand like Macmillan feel their pain today and write, but Carton de Wiart is the only blinded or limbless man I can recall who has left a memoir of his war.

What of the dead? As a result of the war, about 9 per cent of males under forty-five years of age in Britain had been killed. Men talked of the loss of 'the flower of the country' or of 'the lost generation'. Priestley, with many, believed that the lack of talent in the direction of our affairs during the 1930s was due to the slaughter of the Great War – 'and nobody, nothing will shift me from the belief which I shall take to the grave that the generation to which I belonged, destroyed between 1914 and 1918, was a great generation, marvellous in its promise.'

The distinguished historian Lewis Namier was asked to write on the same theme in 1941. Then too we were faced with a similar possibility. Namier argued that the Napoleonic wars had had no such demonstrable effect and that, if anything, more opportunities had been created for young men. There might have been a fading of collective aims or a dwindling of common hopes but not a 'lost generation'. Indeed, he pointed out, ex-officers ranked second only

to lawyers as an occupational category in the Commons during the
1920s.

A statistical analysis of birth-rate figures suggests a criticism of
Priestley's pessimism from another angle. Leeds is a typical example. Birth figures in 1914 had been 23·6 per 1,000. During the
1916–18 period they dropped to 17 then leapt to 25 in 1920, down
to 22 in 1921. It would appear therefore that Leeds's loss had been
made good in just over one year. Hertfordshire figures look at another aspect. One can compare the numbers within various age
groups at 1911 and 1921. There is a deficit at the later date in the
2–9 and 20–39 age groups as one might expect, but there is a substantial compensating bulge in the 0–1 group. It is a bulge destined
to travel up the age table like the Severn Bore with replenishment
behind it. In the 1921 national census therefore the age distribution
curve compared with 1901 and 1966 reveals hardly the slightest
difference. It is as if death and suffering in war are statistically insig-
nificant. American mathematicians today calculate that a nuclear
strike killing two million Americans would be made good in a year,
that five million would be replaced in two years, ten million in eight
years and eighty million in fifty. For the Great War, a similar result
is suggested. The carnage of the Somme, Ypres, Arras and all the
set battles of the west front was of little long-term consequence,
provided that one can ignore the grief associated with loss.

To make death meaningful, one must go to the villages and into
the homes. Bowne End in Hertfordshire is a village of eighty houses.
Sixty-eight of its men fought and twelve died. This fits the national
average, but settlements would be hit harder in those regions from
which crack regiments took their men. In a twelve-mile ring around
Turiff in Scotland one in four of the 1,081 serving soldiers died.
This unequal sharing of the burden stood out again with regard to
individuals. In my father's family four brothers fought and all came
back to live into old age. The *Kentish Mercury* on 2 May 1919
featured Mr Thomas Shaw of New Cross. He had sent five sons to
the war. All had died. The first had died in September 1916; the
last in August 1918. Mrs Coster of Garston Cottage near Watford
lost four of her five sons, the last with just one week of fighting left.
She followed them shortly. Such blows do not feature in the debate
over the 'lost generation'.

The impact of death on relatives also eludes quantification. First
would come the War Office telegram – '. . . greatly regret to report

the death of Private . . . occurred at . . . on . . . inst.' Then would
follow the commanding officer's note – 'It is with deep regret . . .
sad news . . . your gallant son was one of my best soldiers . . .
mourned by the entire regiment . . . met death in the most intrepid
spirit . . . effects will be despatched to you in due course.' Last and
most valued would be the more personal notes from comrades or a
single message from the platoon scribe speaking on behalf of
simpler men.

The news might come very fast. Etonian Christopher Tennant
went to France on 10 August 1917. On 29 August he wrote home:
'This is a great adventure and I am enjoying it.' On 1 September he
went up the line for the first time; on 3 September he was killed,
and just three days later his parents received notification. His C O
wrote that he had been hit by shrapnel on the duckboards just 200
yards from company H Q on his way out of the line for Paris leave
and that he had died within half an hour. 'The men are so fond of
young officers and it is very nice to see the way they looked after
your boy.' One of those who helped was Tennant's batman, Hobbes.
In his letter were the young officer's last words, 'Oh, Hobbes, I'm
hit in the eye,' and Hobbes's own judgement, 'I lost a good master
in Mr Tennant and I shall never have another like him.'

The news of death, on the other hand, might not be certain for
some time. Lieutenant William Campbell died during 1st Ypres
on 18 October 1914. His father read of the death in the local
paper of 12 November and received final confirmation only in April
1915. Among many similar advertisements, *The Times* of 4 January
1919 carried one from Guy Davey of Aldborough near Norwich;
'Any information concerning Major S. Davey, 40th Battalion
Machine-Gun Corps, who was reported missing at Ervillers on
25 March 1918 will be gratefully received.'

When the news came, it hit people with almost inconceivable
force. In his memoirs Asquith wrote: 'Whatever pride I had in the
past and whatever hope I had for the future, by much the largest
part was vested in Raymond. Now all that is gone.' Kipling's poetry
changed instantly on receiving news of his son's death. His poems
became short of length and line with the parsimony of grief
while their tone became remote and the magical inner ear for
dialogue was lost. The most moving account I know from the
great public figures of the time was from music-hall comedian
Harry Lauder.

1 January 1917. News after four days. Realization came to me slowly. I sat and stared at that slip of paper. I had looked on my boy for the last time and it was for this moment that we had all been waiting ever since we had sent John away. We had all known that it was too much to hope that he should be one of those spared. For a time I was quite numb. Then came a great pain and I whispered to myself over and over again the one terrible word 'dead'. It seemed that for me the board of life was blank and black. For me there was no past and there would be no future. Everything had been swept away by one sweep of the hand of fate. My friends came to me. They came rushing to me. Never did a man have better friends. But I was beyond the power of human words to comfort. That New Year night that I shall never forget no matter how long God may let me live, God came to me. And we shall come some day, his mother and I, to the place where he is waiting. He will spy me. 'Hello, Dad,' he will call. I will feel the grip of his young, strong arms about me just as in the happy days before that day which is of all the days of my life the most terrible and hateful in my memory.

The hammer blow came just the same to people simple and unknown. Cook told us of 'Pozzie' Gibson. One night there had been a *strafe*, so men waited for the anticipated German raid. 'We were scared. Our teeth chattered.' To this point, Gibson had been a figure of fun because of his passion for jam and his generally unsoldierly bearing. Now Sergeant Newsome pointed out that Gibson had his head over the parapet. 'It's quite alright, Sergeant,' he said. 'I'll keep a good lookout. There's no sign of anyone yet and, if they do come, I'll let them have it.' Cook wrote that Gibson never lacked friends after that and that, when he died, Cook himself went to see Gibson's mother. She lived in the poorest quarter of Hunslet. 'I've lost my only boy,' was all she said, then became mute with grief.

This grief did not last merely for a moment. Modern analysts of death and bereavement have made us more aware of the long-term effects. One sample found that 12 per cent of widows died within a year; another reported that for a year 14 per cent still saw the ghost of the deceased, 39 per cent sometimes still felt the presence. Presumably even more in the postwar generation would be affected, since the deaths of young people are usually more stressful than those of the old because they seem violations of the natural order. Relatives, in fact, would not accept death. Kaethe Kollwitz drew a hundred likenesses of her dead son as part of her search. The Aberdeen *Journal* of October 1919 wrote of other searches for lost men. The organist of Gilcomston Church went to a spiritualist after seeing the graves of his two dead sons. Another Aberdeen man spoke of 'the beautiful messages of courage and hope' he had received through spiritualism.

In the archives of the Imperial War Museum is a slim, beautifully produced book. It tells the story of William Percy Campbell. An Open Scholar of Hertford College, Oxford, he had gone with his family on holiday to Weymouth during the August Bank Holiday of 1914. William never went down to the beach until the post arrived but was his old self for the rest of the day if no official envelope arrived. One night he said to his brother, 'I may be killed, you know,' then to his father next morning, 'that when he awoke the horror of what might be coming was vivid but it passed away in the day's work'. On the last night at home he had told his brother: 'We shan't see each other again. This is the last time.' Then came the departure at the railway station. 'Even now, sixty years later, I do not like to watch a train moving out of a station and disappearing into the darkness.' After the war his brother spent months around Ypres, helped by soldiers who had fought with William, and pieced together in minute detail the last hours of William's life. Here again was the search. 'Percy was in my father's thoughts day and night but he could not talk about him to the men who had been with him when he was killed. During the rest of my father's life there was probably not a single day on which he was unaware of Percy. His grief was all the greater because he believed that he had not appreciated him in his lifetime and had not always been fair to him. We know so little about death except in the physical sense – why some should die with their task hardly begun.'

For some there was no hope, no point in further looking after a written record had marked some sort of coming to terms. Seabrook wrote recently of his childhood memories in Leicester. In his street lived a woman who had lost all her three sons on the Somme. Each night she would call them from their uncomprehending play on an empty road. From her neighbours there was no comfort – nor was there real comfort for any of those who had lost part of themselves.

A modern sociologist tells us that the Beveridge Report changed society more than the Great War. If change is what is quantifiable, he must be right. Hirst in 1927 placed a precise, actuarial value on a dead soldier. He was worth £828 as against £676 for a German, £580 for a Frenchman and just £404 for the Russian. With this calculation in mind, one thinks of a cemetery on the road to Villers Bretonneux which holds the grave of Captain Cormack, aged thirty-eight. His inscription reads, 'The Lord God hath taken away our hero Daddy'. The visitors' book of another cemetery, Bailleul Road East, has an entry in a fine, clear hand by a lady who had visited the graves of her three brothers and was on the way to Soissons to see her husband's grave. In the first case, the loss was one of £828; in the second £3,312. Perhaps there is a dimension missing here. Perhaps the ease with which these dead men were replaced by the birth-rate bulge in the 1919–20 period misses something too.

In so far as the dead were a health hazard or a morale-sapping inconvenience, they were dealt with early. Kitchener in September 1914 had already established a mobile unit. Late in 1915 the French government gave the land on which the unit buried English soldiers to England in perpetuity. During 1916 they had been buried where they fell, just like those small, frail poppies scattered broadside over the broadbacked hills of northern France. Raemakers's vision of the skeleton death stalking the fields to sow his harvest had been realized at this time of harvesting. But in 1917 policy changed. Trenches were pre-dug before battles to concentrate and make easier the marking up of the wooden crosses with slot-machined metal strips. This policy was continued as the number of bodies grew. A Graves Registration Committee pamphlet in summer 1919 announced that half a million bodies could not all be brought back and the principle of equality demanded that, if all could not be brought to England, none should be. The reason presumably was the expense. They little realized the vastly greater expenses that would be incurred ultimately as a result. Instead, and in contrast with American soldiers who were all shipped home for private burial, the pamphlet announced 'a strong sentiment' in all ranks that isolated graves looked lonely and that the instinct of the service demanded that 'the dead rest with the main body of their comrades'. The result was what we have today – a vast number of cemeteries, strung like beads on a rosary the length of our part of the west front. At the time it must have seemed to relatives another example of the involuntary inhumanity of the army. It was as if the heavenly RSM were bawling out the dead for a final inspection in grave units. Though relatives could choose their own inscriptions, it was at their own expense. When the Rosenbergs wished their son to be commemorated as an artist and poet, this was at their cost of 3s. 3d.

Once the initial hectoring was over, the work was done with great beauty. A cynic might perhaps remark that the turning point was when the War Office handed over to the Imperial War Graves Commission late in 1921. Then 533 gardeners, mostly veterans, tended the 500 cemeteries and first laid those 300 miles of flower beds which press upon the gravestones. The search for a suitable motto for these stones had begun already in 1917 with the bereaved Kipling chosen to find a legend. Starting with 'Who stands if England fall, who dies if England live', he worked through to an abstraction from Ecclesiastes, 'Their name liveth for evermore'. Regimental badge, name, rank, date of death were then added above the cross, parents' inscription beneath. Today they stand rank on rank, silent and compelling silence. A great weight of grief rests on these stones found elsewhere in Europe only on the sites of Hitler's death camps. For those whose bodies could not be found, there are memorials. They total 462,877 on fifty-eight separate plaques. Today's traveller can only be numbed for, though the dead could not be more clearly quantified or visualized or individualized, the overwhelming sadness for these young men deprives all who see of numerical sense.

The cemeteries are not closed. Newly found corpses are still placed in them. By 1920 nearly 4,000 men were engaged full-time to comb the battle areas. The front was divided into squared areas, each searched six times, but ten years after the war forty bodies were still being handed over weekly by the French for reasons of both piety and reward since a ten-franc bounty went with each corpse. Between 1921 and 1928 nearly 30,000 corpses were interred, of which only about a quarter could be identified since fibre identity-discs issued before 1916 had rotted. Some could be named from engraved watches, some by dentures after a mate had located the area in which the men may have fallen. One cavalry NCO, buried shortly after Mons, had been named, though his grave had been unmarked, from the regimental badge on his pipe stem and after the exchange of a hundred letters. It seemed that no effort was too much to care for the bodies of men who had been handled with so little regard while they had been alive. Still these corpses come to

the surface, brought up by the winter rains and the spring plough-
ings. Just twenty years after the end of the war close to a thousand
were first buried. In 1974 Jock Bright at Thiepval told me of a body
identified as one of the Buffs brought up near by by the plough that
year. As with shells, so with bodies: time draws them to the surface
in some vast, slow current after death has hurled them into the
ocean depths of the earth and the mud. The standing total is today
at 1,104,890 dead and 517,773 missing.

Interest in the cemeteries was immediate. Already in 1920 the
YMCA was running an inclusive £6 tour of the Somme field. The
Church Army, British Legion and Red Cross followed suit, financed
by public subscriptions and flag days. A visitor – or 'Pilgrim', as he
was termed – would leave Victoria at 8.45 am and be at Ypres by
8.17 pm that day at a cost of £1 2s. 11d. single. There, he would put
on his golfing suit, stout boots and a pair of leggings as advised by
the Legion brochure and hire a car. Half a mile down the Dickebush
road, a former British officer ran a recommended garage and hired
out cars at two francs the kilometre. The high point of these great
pilgrimages came in July 1927, just ten years after the opening of
3rd Ypres, when Plumer opened at the Menin Gate of Ypres a
memorial to those whose bodies had not been found. 'He is not
missing; he is here' was Plumer's message, transmitted by radio
back to England. The yellowing newspaper photographs of the
event show a disproportionate number of women in black. Their
leanness and stooped shoulders are visible. By the end of 1928 the
whole thing was over. Eight thousand men and 3,000 women made
the last journey. The women wore on their coats the medals of their
dead husbands and they brought with them small wreaths (5s.) or
large (£3). There was a brief stirring in 1932, when an arch at
Thiepval did for the Somme what the Menin Gate did for Ypres
field, then silence. Set in the heart of the Somme battle area, it
looks over those bloody ridges now empty, ridges which rise and
fall like the sound of a dark and swelling Bach prelude.

Visitors still come in small groups. At Delville Wood cemetery
170 visitors signed the visitors' book in the year 1973. Among them
was Private 30017 Walker on 4 August 1973 – 'a lot better than
when I was first here in 1916'. Below him his brother signed – 'on
this spot'. On 19 April three Chelsea Pensioners arrived, one aged
eighty-four. Private Steele in June wrote 'rest with God, Ernie, till
we meet again'. On any day in the year men and women can be

seen, a few old but most the sons and daughters of the war generation. They are always silent and go first to one particular graveyard. Then they like to walk over those broad chalk downlands,
where space seems as long drawn out as on the steppes and where
skylarks and poppies unnerve still as they did sixty years ago. Frail
and tiny, these poppies seem to wither almost as soon as they are
picked. Even pressing cannot preserve them. So it is with the
memories of those who come to this countryside.

We seem now in a crucial decade. The youngest veterans have
passed their threescore years and ten. Their ranks are thinning fast.
On 15 July 1975 the Old Contemptibles marched together for the
last time. 'We soldiered through the rain and the mud, so why
should we worry about a few hailstones,' commented their chair-
man when Flemish weather hit their parade. But of the 170,000
originally qualified, only 300 managed the last march, with the
youngest over eighty. In the final roll-call time had taken more than
the Germans ever could.

On Shooter's Hill, overlooking London, just as Mount Kemmel
overlooks the Ypres salient, there is a milestone. Years of London
grime have made it almost indecipherable. The local guide book
does not mention it. The inscription reads '8 miles to London
Bridge. 130 miles to Ypres in defence of which Salient our losses
were 90,000 killed, 70,500 missing and 410,000 wounded'. War
veterans survive almost as isolated – silent witnesses of a massive
event, of which few today know much. This is the sadness of old
age at any time but particularly of those who have seen the importance of the chief happening of their youth, thought at first by everyone to have been 'the Great War', become the First War and then
just another war in the Ordinary Level history syllabus.

But human witnesses still stand firm. Ask any old Fleming in
Poperinghe the way to Talbot House of Toc H fame and, if he is
over seventy, he will direct you with a few words of broken English,
darkly remembered from long ago. Not far away, on the French
frontier close to Armentières, lives Captain Frederick Osborne of
the Royal Fusiliers. He joined up in 1914 with five of his mates from
Folkestone. The only souvenir they all wanted was to get back
home safely. At the end of the war, he was the only survivor and
stayed on to tend the cemeteries of the Ploegstraat area, marrying a
Flemish wife. In 1962 he retired after a lifetime of looking after the
dead of his youth and of all his memories. He speaks Flemish like a

native and is respected in the village. Café owners send any touring Briton to his little house. There his great pride is his vegetable garden, and his great pleasure is to talk of his sons to any visitor. The accent remains stubbornly Kentish and the little radio set on the front-room table is tuned always to the BBC. Captain Osborne is typical of the many who felt a compelling duty to stay where so many of their comrades had died and to come to terms with grief where grief had been born. All the time their numbers dwindle.

As with the witnesses so with the land. Time has apparently eroded continuously the physical impressions of the war. In 1918 a war zone of 250 miles in length and thirty miles in breadth had consumed 1,659 townships and over half a million houses. Gillespie thought that a fine, broad road should have been built along no-man's-land with seats and shady trees for pilgrims. This Via Sacra might have become the saddest and most beautiful evocation in the world. Eleven days after writing down his idea, Gillespie was killed and his idea with him. The French had known too many wars on their northern frontier to remain fixated upon their loss in such a concrete way. They had fought and won; that was the end of it. The war zone thus filled again immediately after the armistice, peasants lured back by the offer of three years' rent-free tenancy. With dogs and pistols they defended their corrugated-iron huts, each hut numbered to give the claim for reparations legal footing. The French government levelled the ground, with German prisoners picking out the war debris. Putting in for double his losses, the French peasant triumphed in this zone of endemic war as he had always done – provided that he stayed alive and survived the fighting.

Perks continued long afterwards for the farmers. Copper wire could be sold for scrap with the drive bands of shells. Barbed wire could keep animals in check as effectively as it had done soldiers. Dugout iron would shelter penned animals. Odd windfalls might end in the cooking pot, like the horses of the British army or the 10,000 pigeons sold at Lille and Courtrai in 1919. Souvenirs in battle areas sustained a constant cash flow. At Hill 60 near Ypres army buttons sold for sixty centimes ($\frac{3}{4}d.$), or a Smith and Wesson revolver brought in twenty francs (2s. 6d.). But the peasant thought little of this, for in France alone there were 600,000 widows and nearly a million fatherless children. Men so involved wished to forget and to remove the physical signs of a war that had taken their sons and violated their family soil. When Williamson went back to Bullecourt, he approached an old labourer. 'Pretending ignorance I asked an old man working in a field of corn what all the successive lines of old, squat concrete buildings might mean. Slowly he drew himself upright, flung an arm in a gesture that included all the earth and the sky and cried out in a great, gruff, slow voice that must have emptied his lungs, "*La ligne Indenboo-oor-r-k-k finie*", and bent again to the tilling of his field.'

Thus the footprints of war, hateful to the natives, were smoothed out with time. In 1928 Williamson found the tree trunks on the Ypres–Vlamertinghe road scarred at waggon axle height. Lorries remained by the roadside where they had fallen ten years before and waggons still filled in surface shellholes. In 1938 Swinton found the vehicles and shellholes gone, but the small change of war remained – an SRD rum jar at Fricourt; the smell of gas at Flat Iron Copse; machine-gun-pitted tree trunks in High Wood. In the same year, 1938, Thomas went back to Cambrai and located his former brigade HQ in the corner of a corn field, with tin helmets and rifles still in the entrance. These are all gone and still the erosion goes on. In a mine crater at La Boiselle in 1973 I found two steel helmets gashed with shrapnel together with an old machine-gun ammunition box. A year later the crater had been filled in and a crop of wheat was growing where it had been. Of the three crosses visited by George V on the Butte de Warlencourt, point of our furthest advance on the Somme, two have been stolen and the third is about to collapse with dry rot.

Some things will endure for centuries. Though razed to ground level, the Hindenburg line at Bullecourt runs like a seam of karst limestone, defying the tenacity and patience of the peasant. The concrete *Stollen* and watchtowers on Aubers Ridge ignore the most powerful explosive charges. The mine crater at La Boiselle, a hundred yards across and twenty-three yards deep, has so far defied the most enterprising building contractors. Every year too the spring ploughing brings up a vast harvest of shells and grenades, which by law must be piled by the roadside at selected places ready for collection by itinerant army bomb squads, while the unemployed wander the fields and collect shrapnel balls by the kilo for sale as scrap. But, for the most part, the surface scars of the Great War are a secret language requiring knowledgeable translation. Inevitably men with this linguistic knowledge are dwindling. As Guy Chapman sadly put it a short time before his death: 'One wonders how much longer such a book as *Vain Glory* will have meaning and what it will mean to a generation which never heard of Hannescamps, Tower Hamlets, Vimy Ridge, Happy Valley, the Brickstacks and the rest.'

NOTES

1. The 1870 Education Act made primary schooling compulsory, while the follow-up in 1902 gave LEAs power to award scholarships to promising pupils.

2. Whitman wrote after the US civil war: 'Such was the war. It was not a quadrille in a ballroom. Its interior history will not only never be written. Its practicality, minutiae of deeds and passions will never be even suggested. The active soldier with all his ways – his incredible dauntlessness, habits, practices, tastes, language, his appetite, rankness, his superb strength and animality and lawless gait and a hundred un-named lights and shades of the camp – will never be written.'

3. 'Tubby' Clayton founded Talbot House in Poperinghe, a place of rest for all ranks, where religion was unobtrusively served in the surviving chapel in the attic while easy chairs, books (forage caps taken as security for their return) and free writing paper were offered below.

4. Flanders is the name of that Belgian province in which Ypres lay, physically a very small part of the British line but a section which saw almost unbroken activity.

5. Horatio Kitchener, professional soldier, was a popular hero even before the war. As the man who beat the Mahdi in Sudan and later the Boers, his face was a national institution. One day after our declaration of war, he was made Minister of War by Asquith, not without hesitation. He thus became the first serving officer to hold that post.

6. All recruitment figures are taken from those published by HMSO.

7. See *The American Soldier*, S. Stouffer, 1949; *Men under Stress*, R. Grinker and J. Spiegel, 1945; *The Warriors*, J. Glenn Gray, 1959.

8. The size of army units can be only approximate. Casualties led to few units during the war ever being up to establishment.

REFERENCES

(Works cited are only those mentioned specifically in the text or secondary works from which particular examples were taken.)

Published memoirs cited in the text

J. Agate, *Lines of Communication*, Constable, 1917
R. Aldington, *Death of a Hero*, Chatto & Windus, 1929
H. Allen, *Toward the Flame*, Harper, 1934
W. Andrews, *Haunting Years*, Hutchinson, 1929
E. Ashmead Bartlett, *From the Somme to the Rhine*, Newnes, 1921
B. Bairnsfather, *Bullets and Billets*, Bystander, 1916
H. Barbusse, *Under Fire*, Dent, 1926
C. Barnes, *From Workshop to War Cabinet*, Jenkins, 1924
C. Bean, *Letters from France*, Cassell, 1917
L. Birdwood, *Khaki and Gown*, Ward Lock, 1941
W. Bishop, *Winged Warfare*, Hodder & Stoughton, 1918
E. Blunden, *Undertones of War*, Cobden Sanderson, 1935
C. M. Bowra, *Memories*, Harrap, 1966
G. Brenan, *A Life of One's Own*, Cape, 1962
T. Bridges, *Alarms and Excursions*, Longmans, 1938
C. Brooke, *Brotherhood of Arms*, Clowes, 1941
A. Burrage, *War is War*, Gollancz, 1930
A. Buxton, *Sport in Peace and War*, Dent, 1926
E. Callwell, *Experiences of a Dugout*, Constable, 1920
C. Carrington, *Soldier from the Wars Returning*, Cambridge, 1965;
    Somme Memories, Stockwell, 1928;
    A Subaltern's War, Davies, 1929
S. Casson, *Steady Drummer*, Bell, 1935
E. Cawston, *Kaiser's War*, Kent & Sussex, 1970
L. Chandos, *From Peace to War*, Bodley Head, 1968
G. Chapman, *A Kind of Survivor*, Cassell, 1975;
    Vain Glory, Cassell, 1968;
    A Passionate Prodigality, Cassell, 1933
M. Clapham, *Mud and Khaki*, Hutchinson, 1930
P. Clayton, *Plain Tales from Flanders*, Centenary, 1930
S. Cloete, *A Victorian Son*, Collins, 1972
G. Coppard, *With a Machine-Gun to Cambrai*, HMSO, 1969
W. Croft, *Three Years with the 9th Division*, Murray, 1919

F. Crozier, *Brass Hat in No-Man's-Land*, Cape, 1930

H. Cushing, *From a Surgeon's Journal*, Constable, 1936

H. Dearden, *Medicine and Duty*, Heinemann, 1928

B. De Lisle, *Reminiscences of Sport and War*, Eyre & Spottiswoode, 1939

C. de Wiart, *Happy Odyssey*, Cape, 1950

G. Dugdale, *From Langemarck to Cambrai*, Wilding, 1932

F. Dunham, *The Long Carry*, Pergamon, 1970

V. Eberle, *My Sapper Venture*, Pitman, 1973

M. Evans, *Going Across*, Constable, 1952

W. Ewart, *When Armageddon Came*, Rich & Cowan, 1933

G. Eyre, *Somme Harvest*, Jarrolds, 1938

R. Feilding, *War Letters to a Wife*, Medici, 1929

Fifty Amazing Stories of the Great War (no editor), Odhams, 1936

N. Fraser-Tytler, *Field Gun in France*, Hutchinson, 1922

J. Fuller, *Memoirs of an Unconventional Soldier*, Nicholson, 1936

J. Gibbons, *Roll on Next War*, Muller, 1935

P. Gibbs, *Realities of War*, Heinemann, 1920;
  The War Despatches, Gibbs & Philips, 1964

A. Gillespie, *Letters from Flanders*, Smith, Elder, 1916

N. Gladden, *Somme*, Kimber, 1974;
  Ypres, Kimber, 1967

S. Graham, *Challenge of the Dead*, Cassell, 1921;
  A Private in the Guards, Macmillan, 1919

A. Grant, *Letters from Armageddon*, Houghton Mifflin, 1930

R. Graves, *Goodbye to All That*, Cassell, 1929

Great War Adventures (no editor credited), Dent, 1934

G. Greenwell, *An Infant in Arms*, Allen Lane, 1972

W. Griffith, *Up to Mametz*, Faber, 1931

R. Hamilton, *War Diary of the Master of Belhaven*, Murray, 1924

D. Hankey, *A Student in Arms*, Melrose, 1916

B. Liddell Hart, *Memoirs*, Cassell, 1965

F. Hawkings, *From Ypres to Cambrai*, Morley, 1974

I. Hay, *Carrying On*, Briggs, 1917

F. Hitchcock, *Stand To*, Hurst & Blackett, 1937

T. Hope, *The Winding Road Unfolds*, Tandem, 1965

L. Housman, *War Letters of Fallen Englishmen*, Gollancz, 1930

J. Hutchison, *Foot Slogger*, Hutchinson, 1931;
  So This is War, Hutchinson, 1930;
  Warrior, Hutchinson, 1932

J. Hyndson, *From Mons to 1st Ypres*, Wyman, 1924

J. Jack, *General Jack's Diary* (ed. J. Terraine), Eyre & Spottiswoode, 1964

D. Jones, *In Parenthesis*, Faber, 1929
P. Jones, *War Letters of a Public Schoolboy*, Cassell, 1918
R. Kipling, *Souvenirs of France*, Methuen, 1933
B. Latham, *A Territorial Soldier's War*, Constable, 1967
H. Lauder, *A Minstrel in France*, Melrose, 1918
J. Lucy, *There's a Devil in the Drum*, Faber, 1938
H. MacBride, *A Rifleman Went to War*, Hobbs Merrall, 1935
P. Macgill, *The Great Push*, Jenkins, 1928
H. Macmillan, *Winds of Change*, Macmillan, 1966
F. Manning, *Her Privates We*, Murray, 1930
P. Maze, *A Frenchman in Khaki*, Heinemann, 1934
H. Miles, *Untold Tales of Wartime London*, Gibbs & Philips, 1930
S. Millard, *I Saw Them Die*, Harrap, 1936
J. Monash, *War Letters*, Angus Robertson, 1935
C. E. Montague, *Disenchantment*, Chatto & Windus, 1922
R. Mottram, *Personal Records of the War*, Scholartis, 1929
M. Moynihan, *People at War*, David and Charles, 1973
C. Nevinson, *Great War*, Grant Richards, 1918
B. Newman, *Anthology of Armageddon*, Archer, 1935
W. Nicholson, *Behind the Lines*, Cape, 1939
F. Noakes, *The Distant Drum*, Tunbridge Wells, 1952
J. Boyd Orr, *As I Recall*, Weidenfeld, 1962
A. Osburn, *Unwilling Passenger*, Faber, 1932
H. Owen, *Journey from Obscurity*, Oxford, 1965
C. Pannichas, *Promise of Greatness*, Cassell, 1968
E. Parker, *Into Battle 1914–1918*, Longmans, 1964
M. Plowman, *A Subaltern on the Somme*, Benn, 1927
J. B. Priestley, *Reminiscences and Reflections*, Heinemann, 1962
H. Pritchard, *A Hunter in Modern War*, Cobden Sanderson, 1919
C. Purdom, *Everyman at War*, Dent, 1930
M. Quigley, *Passchendaele and the Somme*, Methuen, 1928
R. Rees, *A Schoolmaster at War*, Haycock, 1927
J. Reith, *Wearing Spurs*, Hutchinson, 1966
F. Richards, *Old Soldiers Never Die*, Faber, 1933
S. Rogerson, *The Last of the Ebb*, Barker, 1937;
    Twelve Days, Barker, 1933
S. Sassoon, *Memoirs*, Faber, 1930
G. Slater, *My Warrior Sons*, Davies, 1973
L. Smith, *Four Years Out of my Life*, Philip Allan, 1931
Scrapbook of the Somerset Infantry, 1931
E. Swinton, *Twenty Years After*, Newnes, 1938;
    A Year Ago, Newnes, 1916
R. Tawney, *The Attack and Other Essays*, Allen & Unwin, 1953

B. Tillett, *Memories and Reflections*, Long, 1931
J. Tyndale-Biscoe, *Gunner Subaltern 1914–18*, Cooper, 1971
A. Waugh, *Early Years*, Allen, 1962
A. Wavell, *The Good Soldier*, Macmillan, 1948
J. Wedgwood, *Essays and Adventures of an MP*, Allen & Unwin, 1924
A. West, *Diary of a Dead Officer*, Herald, 1918
H. Williamson, *Wet Flanders Plain*, Faber, 1929
W. Wood, *Soldiers' Stories of the War*, Chapman and Hall, 1915
E. Woodward, *Short Journey*, Faber, 1942
A. Worden, *Yes, Daddy*, Macmillan, 1961

Unpublished material cited in the text

Diaries of: E. Beale, W. Bradley, H. Brian, C. Burnley, H. Drinkwater, N. Ellison, E. Herd, H. Ingham (private source), C. Lane, J. Macdougall, W. Pennie, F. Rickson, B. Sanderson (Churchill College, Cambridge), C. Wilson

Memoirs of: A. Abraham, R. Bescn, W. Bland, J. Bodger, C. Cain, E. Chaband, W. Cook, H. Cooper, D. Dennison, J. Drury, A. Elshaw, J. Fleming-Bernard, A. Gawn (private source), J. Gerrard, W. Harrison, L. Hewitt, E. Holdsworth, E. Kingsbury, H. Parker, I. Read, T. Rogers, T. Silver, H. Williams, H. Winter and J. Winter (private source), J. Worthington

Assorted material of: P. Barber, J. Christie (Eton College), G. Ellis

(All the material is from the archives of the Imperial War Museum unless otherwise stated.)

Newspapers and periodicals

Aberdeen *Journal*, Bradford *Daily Argus*, Catford *Advertiser*, Cornwall *County News*, East London *Advertiser*, Hackney *Gazette*, Hertfordshire *Advertiser*, St Albans *Times*, Isle of Wight *Advertiser*, Kentish *Mercury*, The Lincs, Boston and Spalding Free Press, Stroud *News*, West Herts. and Watford *Observer*, Whitby *Gazette*

Sphere, Tatler, John Bull

Local history cited in the text

F. Armitage, *Leicester*, Backus, 1933
R. Brazier, *Birmingham and the Great War*, Cornish, 1921

P. Lawrence, *Eye*, Swinton, 1927
D. McEchern, *The Sword of the North*, Carruthers, 1923
J. Robertson, *Turriff*, Ex-Servicemen's Committee, 1926
W. Robertson, *Middlesbrough's War Effort*, Hills, 1923
J. Rowson, *Bridport at War*, Laurie, 1928
W. Scott, *Leeds in the Great War*, Library & Arts Committee, 1928
W. Vint, *Sunderland*, Hills, 1923

Statistical information

British Dominions Year Book, 1917
F. Hirst, *Consequences of the War to Great Britain*, Oxford, 1929
The Official History of the War, HMSO
Statistics of the Military Effort, HMSO, 1923

Social history

Incorporated material was taken from these sources:
R. Blythe, *Akenfield*, Allen Lane, 1969, Penguin, 1972
P. Laslett, *The World We Have Lost*, Methuen, 1965
C. Peel, *How We Lived Then*, Lane, 1929
C. Petrie, *Scenes of Edwardian Life*, Eyre & Spottiswoode, 1965
D. Read, *Edwardian England*, Harrap, 1972
R. Roberts, *Classic Slum*, Penguin, 1973
J. Seabrook, *The Underprivileged*, Longmans, 1967
F. Thompson, *English Landed Society in the Nineteenth Century*, Routledge, 1963

The British army

J. Baynes, *Morale*, Eyre & Spottiswoode, 1967
A. Brett James, *Life in Wellington's Army*, Allen & Unwin, 1972
J. Fuller, *The Army in my Time*, Rich & Cowan, 1935
V. Germains, *Kitchener's Armies*, Davies, 1930
L. Gordon, *Military Origins*, Kaye, 1969
J. Hall, *Kitchener's Mob*, Clowes, 1916
E. Hardy, *Mr Thomas Atkins*, Newnes, 1900
King's Regulations, 1912
R. Kipling, *Barrack Room Ballads*, Methuen, 1972;
   The New Armies in Training, Methuen, 1915
The Manual of Military Law, 1914
F. Richards, *Old Soldier Sahib*, Faber, 1936
Standing Orders of Queen's Own Cameron Highlanders, 1909

Battles and battlefields

British Legion, *Pilgrimage*, BL, 1928
H. Essame, *Battle for Europe 1918*, Batsford, 1972
T. Lowe, *The Western Battlefields*, Lowe, 1920
M. Middlebrook, *The First Day on the Somme*, Allen Lane, 1971
E. Swinton, *Twenty Years After*, Newnes, 1938
H. Taylor, *Goodbye to the Battlefields*, Souvenir, 1928

Weapons and tactics

C. Broad, in the *Journal of the Royal Artillery*, 1922
C. Foulkes, *Gas*, Blackwood, 1934
General Staff 'Instructions for platoons in the offensive', 1917
C. Hutchison, *Machine-Guns*, Hutchinson, 1938
The Official History of the War, HMSO
E. Solano, *Drill and Fixed Training*, Gale and Polden, 1914
Tactician, *Tactics for Field Officers*, Gale and Polden, 1916
War Office, 'Organisation of the infantry battalion for the attack', 1917

Psychology of war

R. Ahrenfeld, *Psychiatry in the British Army*, Rees, 1958
B. Bettelheim, *The Informed Heart*, Free Press, 1960
A. Du Picq, *Battle Studies*, Gale and Polden, 1870
E. Ginzberg, *The Lost Divisions*, New York, 1959
J. Glenn Gray, *The Warriors*, New York, 1959
R. Grinker, *Men Under Stress*, New York, 1945
L. Moran, *Anatomy of Courage*, Constable, 1945
C. Myers, *Shellshock in France*, Cambridge, 1940
I. Oswald, *Sleep*, Penguin, 1966
C. Parkes, *Bereavement*, Penguin, 1975
S. Stouffer, *The American Soldier*, New York, 1949

INDEX

Abbeville, 149
Aberdeen, 166
Aberdeen *Journal*, 244
Abraham, A., 96, 143, 237, 245, 248
Addington, 240
Aeroplane, 127-9
Aisne, River, 19
'Akenfield', 96
Albert, 149
Aldington, R., 47, 71, 73, 133, 223
Alexandra Field Force Fund, 165
Allardyce, J., 61
Allen, H., 118, 121, 132, 189, 211, 214
Allenby, General E., 94
'Amateur officer', 194
Amiens, 149
Anderson-Morshead, Lt-Col., 182
Andrews, W., 32, 38, 167, 189
Andruicq, 144
Anglo-Persian Petroleum Company, 168
'Arf a Mo' cigarettes, 149
Argyll and Sutherland Highlanders, 222
Armentières, 135, 153, 219
Army: traditions, 51-2; unit structure, 53-7
Arras, 18, 46, 145, 149, 159, 185, 203
Artillery: types, 115-16; use of, 116, 175-176; sounds of, 116; effects of, 116-19; counterfire problems, 119; infantry's suspicions of own artillery, 119-21
Ashanti, 108
Ashmead-Bartlett, E., 122
Asquith, prime minister H., 256
Atkins, E., 190, 210
Atkins, T., 47, 51, 213
Aubers Ridge, 90, 264

Badajoz, 155
Badische Anilin Fabrik, 121
Bagnold, E., 135
Bailey, Pte, 206
Bailleul, 250, 259
Bairnsfather, B., 19, 67
Baker-Carr, C., 113
Ball, F., 173
Balliol College, 18

Banbury, 25
Bantam regiments 85
Bapaume, 82
Barber, P., 93, 95, 101
Barbusse, H., 233
Barnes, C., 35
Barnett, Pte, 218
Baths, 146-7
Bathy, Sgt-Maj., 182
Batoville, 209
Battle: news of, 171; the last night, 171-3; to the front, 173-5; barrage, 175-6; over the top, 177-8; advance, 179-81; hand-to-hand, 182; chaos, 183-5; feelings afterwards, 186-9
Bayonet, 39-40, 109, 110
Bazentin, 183
Beale, E., 17, 167
Bean, C., 118, 186, 210
Beaumont Hamel, 218
Belhaven, Master of (Hamilton, R.), 88, 91, 122, 129, 189, 213
Bell, J., 194, 197
Berlin, 116, 127
Berthelot, General, 182
Bescn, R., 219, 228
Besford, 245
Béthune, 149, 182
Beveridge Report, 258
Beyer chemicals, 121
Billets, 142-3, 146
Billingsgate, 35
Birdwood, General L., 47, 54, 196
Birmingham, 34
Bishop, W., 80, 185
Black Watch, the, 81, 83, 209
Blackmore Vale, 168
Blakeman, Pte, 26
Bland, W., 98
Blangy, 157, 213
Bleriot, L., 127
Bluff, the, 103
Blunden, E., 217
Blythe, R., 168, 231
Bodger, J., 156, 222, 239
Boer war, 20, 39, 47, 107, 139, 203, 204, 217

Bolt, E., 24
Bombers, 110–11
Bottomley, H., 30, 167
Boulogne, 68, 72, 143, 166
Bourne End, 255
Bow Bells concert party, 153
Bowra, C. M., 17, 41, 48, 180, 226, 235
Boyd Orr, J., 62, 65, 96, 187, 192
Boy's Own Paper, 31
Bradford Pals regiment, 251
Bradley, W., 87, 143, 221, 235
Brecht, B., 70
Brenan, G., 225, 228
Brett-James, A., 149
Brian, H., 19, 145, 221
Bridges, T., 69, 215
Bright, J., 261
British Legion, Royal, 241
British Medical Journal, 97, 109, 127
Brittain, V., 247
Brooke, R., 31, 32
Brophy, J., 249
Brussels, 33
Buchan, J., 26
Buckingham Palace, 240
Buffs regiment, 261
Bull-ring, 72–4
Bullecourt, 184, 264
Bultitude, Pte, 178
Burnett, J., 231
Burnley, C., 19
Burrage, A., 73, 74, 134, 144, 145, 157, 167, 228, 234
Butler, S., 99
Buxton, A., 156

Cain, Pte, 37
Cambrai, 213
Cameronians, 42, 179
Campbell, H., 58
Campbell, I., 61
Campbell, W., 256, 258
Cannock, F., 21
Canterbury festival, 23
Caporetto, 20
Carnoy, 17
Carrington, C., 24, 62, 81, 88, 109, 137, 166, 176, 203, 240, 242, 250
Carver, Lt, 32, 175
Casson, S., 120, 225
Casualty clearing station, 197–8
Casualty figures, 192–3
Catford *Journal*, 23, 24, 177

Cawston, E., 212
Cayeux, 235
Cemeteries, 259–62
Chaband, E., 179, 194
Chandos, Lord, 68, 98, 117, 122, 179
Chaney, H., 48, 219
Chantilly, 17
Chapman, G., 50, 58, 225, 251, 265
Chappell, Major, 238
Charing Cross Hospital, 202
Charley's Bar, Amiens, 67
Charterhouse School, 63
Charteris, J., 202
Chelsea Hospital, 21
Cheshire regiment, 52
Chester, F., 254
Chlorine gas, 121–2
Christie, J., 68, 118, 134
Christmas celebrations, 220–22
Chudleigh, Capt., 220
Churchill, W., 23, 236
Clapham, M., 19, 205
Clapham Junction, 86
Clayton, P., 18
Clemenceau, G., 247
Clements, F., 245
Cloete, S., 76, 93, 108, 127, 151, 152, 164, 177, 182, 184, 195, 207, 242, 249
Cocks, Pte, 169
Collicot, Pte, 210
Collins, Pte, 138
Cologne, 211
'Comic Cuts', 209
Concerts, 157
Connaught regiment, 93
Conscientious objectors, 31
Conscription, 29
Cook, W., 18, 33, 58, 92, 103, 121, 256
Cooper, H., 114, 182
Coppard, G., 43, 44, 56, 148, 171, 202, 209, 240
Cormack, Capt., 259
Cornwall, 30
Cornwall *County News*, 36, 169
Costello, Sgt, 30
Coster, Mrs, 255
Court martial, 43
Courtrai, 263
Coventry, 241
Cox's agency, 69
Crécy, 109, 144
Crimean war, 25, 77
Croft, W., 109

Crozier, F., 181, 205
Curlu, 82
Cushing, H., 27, 68, 98, 193, 233, 235

Dacres Park, 23
Daily Argus, 23
Daily Express, 105
Daily Mail, 27, 33, 66, 170
Daily Mirror, 25
Daily Telegraph, 220
Dardanelles, 17
Davie, Pte, 96
Davies, Capt., 78
Dawson, C., 33
De Gaulle, C., 144
De Lisle, B., 129, 212, 215, 224
De Wiart, C., 47, 91, 254
Dead: statistics of, 203; sensations of, 204–6; burial of, 207–8, 259–61; attitude of living towards, 208; impact of, 254–9
Dearden, H., 131, 205, 225, 227, 229, 232, 249
Death penalty, 43, 140
Debrett, 231
Delville Wood, 183, 249, 261
Demobilization, 238–40
Department of Information, 26
Deptford, 35
Dettingen, 52
Donaldson, F., 64
Dorsetshire Yeomanry, 37
Douro, 217
Dover, 239, 240
Downes, Pte, 160
Drake, Pte, 145
Dresden Conservatoire, 24
Drill, 39
Drinkwater, H., 58, 78, 81, 89, 96, 105, 146, 159, 161, 236, 248
Drury, J., 117
Du Picq, A., 44, 182
Duchess of Westminster's Hospital, 68
Dugdale, G., 65, 82, 213
Dulwich College, 18
Dundas, R., 230
Dunham, F., 211
Durham regiment, 131

Eagle, F., 35
East Africa, 193
East London Advertiser, 26
East Surrey regiment, 209

Eberle, V., 81
Economist, the, 168
Eden, A., 20
Edinburgh, 61
Education Acts, 16
Edward VII, 25
Ellis, B., 165
Ellison, N., 28, 34, 60, 82, 83, 95, 143, 165
Elshaw, A., 249
Elwin, Sgt, 93
Epsom, 241
Étaples, 72
Eton College, 63, 134
Evans, M., 44, 69, 86, 87, 140, 183, 209, 211, 231
Evesham Journal, 26
Ewart, W., 133, 221
Eye, 244
Eyre, G., 90, 217

Falls, C., 15
Fanshaw, C., 187
Fatigues, 158–9
Faucon d'Or, 67
Faulkener's Hotel, 148
Feilding, R., 53, 55, 61, 92, 120, 166, 189, 191, 192, 215, 247
Fenton, Lt, 90
Festubert, 82
Feversham, Earl of, 156
Field punishments, 43
Fisher, Capt., 30
Fisher, J., 247
Fitzclarence, C., 167
Flamethrower, 126
Flanders, 20
Flannery, Pte, 181
Fleming-Bernard, J., 61, 116, 122
Folkestone, 39, 71, 166, 240
Food, 102–3, 147–8
Footslogger's nodule, 79
Foulkes, C., 126
Fowey, 36
Fraser-Tytler, N., 120, 184
French, Field-Marshal, 127, 168
Fricourt, 155
Fromelles, 221
Frost, R., 35

Gale, Maj., 38
Gallipoli, 118, 193
Gambling, 153–5
Garden Fields School, St Albans, 165

Gardner, Sgt, 233
Garnett, Lt, 224
Garvice, C., 101, 266
Gas: fear of, 121; types, 121; chlorine, 121-2; phosgene, 122; mustard, 122-4; countermeasures, 124-5; British gas, 213-19
Gawn, A., 72
George V, 127, 264
Germans: hostility towards, 209-11; admiration for, 211-13; factors limiting hostility towards, 213-19
Gerrard, J., 90
Gheluvelt, 19, 167
Gibbons, J., 66, 96, 144, 150
Gibbs, P., 212, 215, 219, 228, 243
Gibson, P., 256
Gilcomston, 258
Gillespie, A., 83, 143, 164, 224, 228, 263
Giltens, T., 246
Gitana, G., 160
Givenchy, 217
Gladden, N., 83, 133, 148, 159, 179, 188, 212
Glasgow, 202, 241
Gloucestershire regiment, 52, 179
Glyde, J., 180, 211
Glyn, E., 101
'Goodbyeee', 163
Gort, General, 45
Graham, S., 40, 41, 44, 154, 206, 207, 221
Grant, A., 94, 118, 172, 176
Graves, R., 35, 63, 88, 133, 241
Graves Registration Committee, 259
Green, Rifleman, 248
Greenwell, G., 81, 88, 111, 225
Greenwich, 23
Grenade: early types, 110; specialists, 110-11; power of, 111
Grenfell, J., 224, 225
Grey, Pte, 23, 58
Grierson, General, 127
Griffiths, W., 34, 85, 100, 118, 175, 187, 249, 250
Grundy, Pte, 205
Guards regiments, 43, 209
Guillemont, 211
Gunners, 119-21

Hackney, 31
Hadfield helmet, 116
Haig, Field-Marshal, 54, 62, 127, 130, 156, 170, 236, 240

Haldane, R., 63
Hall, Capt., 60
Hamburg, 23
Hamel, 87, 95, 249
Hampstead, 230
Hanbury-Sparrow, A., 124
Hangard Wood, 60
Hankey, Lord, 38
Hann, Pte, 131
Hardy, Rev., 60
Harley Street, 68
Harris, Rifleman, 57, 248
Harrison, W., 102, 230, 235
Harrison's Pomade, 97
Harrods, 67, 81
Hatfield house, 50
Hawkings, F., 19, 235, 236
Hay, I., 223
Hayward, Dr, 198, 226, 249
Hazlitt, W., 157
Heath, A., 35, 38, 176
Hedauville, 184
Herd, E., 94, 102, 218
Herne Hill, 239
Hesdin, 156
Hewitt, L., 122
Hicks, R., 36
Hill 60, 263
Hindenburg, P., 247
Hindenburg line, 264
Hipe, 51
Hirst, F., 259
Hitchcock, F., 100, 219
Hitler, A., 20
Hoare, Pte, 111
Holdsworth, E., 250
Holroyd, Corp., 59
Holstein regiment, 219
Hooge, 58, 94, 219
Hope, T., 54, 132
Horse Guards Parade, 241
Hoxton, 230
'Hullo my dearie', 163
Humour, 233-4
Hutchison, J., 64, 92, 167, 218, 219, 224
Hyde Park, 241
Hyder, Pte, 248
'Hymn of Hate', 234
Hyndson, J., 19, 211

Iddy umpties, 53
'If you were the only girl', 163
Imperial Hotel, 28

Imperial War Graves Commission, 260
Indian Mutiny, 51
Ingham, H., 55, 162

Jack, J., 68, 90, 92, 188, 212
Jackson, Corp., 160
Jackson's Dump, 149
Jellicoe, J., 247
Jenkins, Pte, 35
John Bull magazine, 130, 167, 226
Johnson, Lt, 168
Jones, Capt., 219
Jones, D., 56
Jones, P., 18, 32, 215, 225
Josephs, A., 30

Kafka, F., 51
Keating's powder, 97
Keiss, 245
Kelly's College, 192
Kemp, PC, 168
Kentish Mercury, 25, 255
Kettle, T., 56
Keynes, G., 35, 67, 203, 235
King's Own Yorkshire Light Infantry, 52, 83
King's Regulations, 48, 69
Kingsbury, E., 33, 37, 39, 69, 163, 189, 195, 204, 256, 260
Kipling, R., 31, 37, 39, 69, 163, 189, 195, 204, 256, 260
Kirchner, 81
Kitchener, H., 23, 29, 37
Kollowitz, K., 258

La Bassée, 213
La Boiselle, 264
La Gorgue, 153
Lancet, 130
Lane, C., 43, 94, 177
Langemark, 86
Latham, B., 68
Lauder, H., 256
Laverty, K., 168
Lawrence, R., 138
Le Cateau, 235
Le Creusot, 30
Le Touquet, 68
Leave: system, 165–6; soldiers' response, 166–8; civilians' response, 168–9; termination of, 169
Leavesden Mental Hospital, 140
Lee, L., 167

Lee Enfield rifle, 107–9
Leeds, 29, 30, 244, 255
Leicester, 34, 148, 258
Leicester Square Empire, 33, 219
Leicestershire regiment, 171
Lewis, Pte, 194
Lewis gun, 112–13
Liddell Hart, B., 45, 55, 112, 158
Lille, 263
Lillers, 149
Liskeard, 245
Livering, Pte, 176
Lloyd George, D., 113
London Opinion magazine, 226
London regiment, 238
Loos, 27, 60, 70, 133, 181, 184, 196, 221, 238
Lost generation, 254
Lucy, J., 43, 64, 91, 104, 138, 167, 212, 249
Lysol, 97

MacBride, H., 83, 91, 101, 103
MacDonald, R., 63
Macdougall, E., 68, 98, 221
Macdowell, J., 168
McGill, P., 179, 180, 228
McGrath, Maj., 69
Machine-gun : Lewis gun, 112–13 ; Vickers gun, 112; drawbacks, 112–13
McKee, A., 182
Macmillan, H., 32, 89, 138, 164, 194, 196, 224
Maconochie, 102, 147, 159
Macpherson, Dr, 140
Mametz Wood, 183, 184, 249
Manchester *Guardian*, 105
Manning, F., 55, 132, 150, 171, 177, 186, 188, 227
Marching: order of, 75; pleasures of, 76–77; pains of, 77–9
'Marching through Georgia', 162
Marcoing, 219
Marryatt, F., 31
Maude, General, 89
Maxse, I., 158
Mayne, Pte, 191
Maze, P., 59, 131, 175, 178, 199, 205, 217
Meaulte, 143
Medals, 189–92
Medicine: aid post, 196–7; casualty clearing station, 197–8; base hospital, 198; medical knowledge, 202–3

Menin Gate, 204, 261
Menin road, 250
Mesopotamia, 193, 240
Messines, 19, 203, 212, 215
Middlesex regiment, 186
Middleton, Pte, 58
Miles, H., 169
Millard, S., 123, 201
Milner, F., 28
Minden, 52
Mining, 126-7
Monash, General, 28, 47, 226
Mons, 33, 216, 249
Montague, C., 141
Moore, J., 46
Moran, Lord, 62, 101, 129, 131, 134, 135, 137, 138, 173, 205, 227, 234
Morgan, G., 251
Morning Post, 245
Morrison, H., 231
Mortars: types, 113; specialists, 113-14; German mortars, 114; fear of, 114
Morval, 133
Mottram, R., 60, 82, 105, 143, 155, 226, 249
Mud, 96
Muller's Nutrient, 130
Mustard gas, 122-4
Myers, C., 130, 136, 137

Namier, L., 254
National Roll of Honour, 33
Neutrality League, 24
Neuve Chapelle, 20, 27, 70, 189
Neville, Capt., 176
Nevinson, C., 233
New Society magazine, 35
New Statesman magazine, 24
Newquay, 169
News of the World, 25
Nicholson, W., 63, 96, 117, 235
Nissen hut, 146
'Noah's Ark trains', 166
Noakes, F., 39, 81, 83, 85, 86, 149, 157, 165, 180, 188, 235, 237, 238, 239, 241
Norfolk regiment, 52
Northumberland Fusiliers, 83
Nottingham, 34

Obedience, 229-33
Officers: old army, 63; new sources of, 63-4; problems with 64-5; training of,

65-6; role props, 67-9; leadership in battle, 59-62
Old Contemptibles, 262
'Old Officer', 46, 65
Oppy, 221
Oros cigarettes, 149
Osburn, A., 203, 262
Osterley, 240
Oswestry, 246
Owen, W., 72, 129, 164
Owens School, 239
Oxford, 31

Pack, 77
'Pack up your troubles', 163
Pals regiments, 38
Pamplona, 217
Parker, H., 37, 111
Parkes, Pte, 110
Parkin, Pte, 35
Parr, J., 77
Partridge, E., 137
Pay, 148-9
Peard, Capt., 95
Pennie, W., 17
Penrose, W., 169
Pensions, 251-3
Penzance, 34
Peruwelz, 238
Phosgene gas, 122
Piccadilly, 151
Pike, Maj., 28
Pilgrims, 261-2
Ploegstraat, 118, 213, 262
Plowman, M., 54, 261
Plumer, General, 54, 261
Police News, 25
Pope and Bradley, 67
Poperinghe, 131, 153
Porton, 125
Post, 164-5
Post-war: demobilization, 238-40; discontent, 240-42; adjustment, 242-4; civilian attitudes, 244-8; soldiers' memories, 248-51; the injured, 251-3; the dead, 254-62; today, 262-5
Potsdam Farm, 190
Pound, R., 60
Powell, Pte, 38
Pozières, 118, 184, 210
Pratt, Pte, 109
Pressey, Pte, 148
Price, B., 62

Priestley, J. B., 38, 55, 90, 134, 163, 243, 254
Prince of Wales Hospital, 68
Prince of Wales Relief Fund, 25
Princeton County School, 192
Prisoners of war, 213-16
Pritchard, H., 65
Punishments: type, 42-3; effect, 43-4
Purfleet, 239
Putney Mental Hospital, 18
Puttees, 51

Quéant, 206
Queen Mary Hospital, Sidcup, 252
Queensland regiment, 81
Quigley, M., 180

Raemakers, P., 206, 259
Raglan, Lord, 25
Raid, trench, 91-5
Rawlinson, H., 19
Read, I., 78, 141, 187, 214, 252
Recruitment: rate of, 27, 29; motives for, 31-5
Red Hussar cigarettes, 149
Rees, R., 95, 124, 201
Regimental aid post, 196-7
Reid, J., 133, 242, 249
Reith, Lord, 194
Reserved occupations, 30
Rest: billets, 142-3, 146; French civilians, 142-6; baths, 146-7; food, 147-8; pay, 148-9; spending, 149-53; gambling, 153-5; sports, 155-7; concerts, 157; fatigues, 158-9
Rhineland, 238
Rhondda, 33
Richards, F., 142, 226, 228, 252
Richardson, Pte, 184
Rickson, F., 96
Rifle: mechanism, 107; firing problems, 108-9; sound of 109; wounds from, 109
Robey, G., 163
Rogers, T., 68
Rogerson, S., 17, 55
Rosenberg, I., 260
'Roses of Picardy', 163
'Roses round the Door', 163
Rothermere, Lord, 236
Rouen, 72, 149, 152
Rowley, Col, 131

Rowntree, B., 32, 230
Royal Lancaster regiment, 182
Royal Scots Fusiliers, 38
Royal Society, 245
Royal Sussex regiment, 82
Royal Welch regiment, 82, 209
Royal West Kent regiment, 52
Ruby Queen cigarettes, 149
Rum, 103
Russell, B., 18
Russo-Japanese war, 113

Sadleir-Jackson, Brig., 210
Sailly Laurette, 212
St Albans, 25
St Eloi, 218-19
St Omer, 149
Sandhurst, 63, 65
Sassoon, S., 15, 88, 129, 133, 141, 198
Saunders, Pte, 100
Saxon regiment, 218
Scott, F., 218
Seaman, J., 31
Seeley, General, 139, 206, 212
Serre, 207
Servants, 67
Shaw, G. B., 24
Shaw, T., 255
Shells, 20
Shellshock: statistics, 129-30; sources of, 130-33; wearing-down process, 133-5; breakdown, 135-6; treatment of, 136-137; supports against, 137-40
Sheridan, M., 163
Sherwood Foresters, 62, 187
Shooters Hill, 262
Sibford, 25
Signallers, 53
Sikhs, 108
Silver, T., 35
Simplicissimus, 96
Smith, L., 96, 143
Soissons, 206, 259
Somersetshire regiment, 37, 219, 238
Somme, 40, 56, 77, 82, 96, 103, 184, 187, 203, 212, 218
Songs, 162, 164
Souchez, 90
South Staffordshire regiment, 87, 187
Spanish influenza, 244
Sparks, Capt., 249
Sphere magazine, 23, 220
Sport, 155-7

Steele, Pte, 261
Stirling, Capt., 62
Stokes mortar, 20
Strathcona, regiment, 212
Stream, Pte, 131
Strombus gas alarm, 124
Suffolk regiment, 38
Sunday Advertiser, 24
Sunday Pictorial, 236
Sunderland, 244
'Sweetest Blossom', 163
Swindon, 25
Swinton, E., 159, 184, 264
Symonds, Col, 60
Symons, F., 127

Talavera, 156
Talbot House, 262
Tatler magazine, 31
Tawney, R., 180, 203
Taylor, C., 70, 249
Tel el Kebir, 83
Tennant, C., 256
Terraine, J., 49
Thiepval, 205, 261
Thomas, P., 35
'Tickler's jam', 110
Tillett, B. 229
Times, The, 25, 48, 105, 242
Ting, Pte, 58
Tintagel, 28
Tipperary, 162
Titbits magazine, 25
Toc H, 18
Tolstoy, L., 204
Topsham, 37
Train journeys, 73–4
Training: length of, 39; drill, 39; tactical
  concepts, 39; purpose of, 40; harshness
  of, 40–42; justification, 44–5; con-
  demnation of, 45–9; bull-ring, 73
Trench life: trench system, 80–81;
  length of trench duty, 81–2; induction,
  82–3; takeover, 83–5; timetable, 85–6;
  night, 86–8; enemy action, 88–91;
  raids, 91–5; cold, 95–6; mud, 96;
  vermin, 96–8; disease, 98–9; sleep, 99–
  101; information, 101–2; food, 102–3;
  minor comforts, 103–5
Tribunals, 29, 30, 34
Trotsky, L., 44
Trumpeter cigarettes, 149
Turner, Pte, 90

Turriff, 255
Tyne Cot, 204

U-boats, 24, 27
Unruh, General, 217

Van Diemen's 'farm', 183
Vaux, 82
Verdun, 115
Vermin, 96–8
Vickers machine-gun, 112–13
Victoria Station, 166, 169, 241, 261
Villers Bretonneux, 20, 81, 259
Villers Plouich, 65, 82, 213
Voigt, F., 152

Walker, Pte, 261
War Injuries Pensions Committee, 252
Warden, F., 226
Warlencourt, 264
Warner, P., 254
Warrant, H., 35
Watford Boys' Grammar School, 31, 38,
  52, 236
Watford *Observer*, 26
Watson, J., 90
Waugh, A., 60, 82, 166, 183
Wavell, A., 46
Wear, Pte, 134
Webb, S., 152
Wedgwood, J., 178
Welch, Corp., 109
Weller, Corp., 176
Wellington, Duke of, 100
West, A., 18, 202
West Briton, 28
West Hertfordshire and Watford *Observer*,
  244
Wheeler, Rifleman, 77, 162
Whitby *Gazette*, 26, 28, 216
Whitman, W., 17
Whyatt, R., 167
Wigan, 37
Willcox, Pte, 57
Willey, B., 17
William II, Kaiser, 113
Williams, H., 17, 168
Williamson, H., 115, 264
Willingness Forms, 34
Wilson, A., 129
Wilson, C., 202
Wilton, 246
Winchester, 31

Winter, H., 34, 47, 60, 70, 83, 131, 176, 190, 239
Winter, J., 47, 69, 75, 206, 241
Woodbine cigarettes, 149
Woodward, E., 25, 184, 247
Worcestershire regiment, 19, 167
Worden, A., 161
Worsley, Capt., 249

'X', John, 35

Yorkshire Post, 252
Ypres: the Salient, 82, 144, 149, 191, 261, 264; 1st Ypres, 19, 108, 194, 216; 2nd Ypres, 68, 121; 3rd Ypres, 96, 158, 180, 183, 205

Zeppelin, 24
Zweig, A., 194